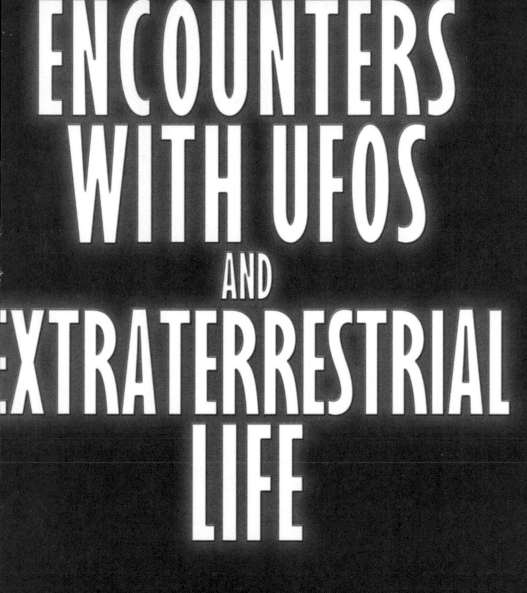

ENCOUNTERS
WITH UFOS
AND
EXTRATERRESTRIAL
LIFE

ENCOUNTERS WITH UFOS

AND

EXTRATERRESTRIAL LIFE

MICHAEL PYE AND KIRSTEN DALLEY, EDITORS

Rosen
PUBLISHING®

New York

This edition published in 2013 by:

The Rosen Publishing Group, Inc.
29 East 21st Street
New York, NY 10010

Additional end matter copyright © 2013 by The Rosen Publishing
Group, Inc.

Library of Congress Cataloging-in-Publication Data

Encounters with UFOs and extraterrestrial life/Michael Pye,
Kirsten Dalley, editors.
    pages cm.—(Mysteries uncovered, secrets declassified)
Includes bibliographical references and index.
ISBN 978-1-4488-9252-5 (library binding)
1. Unidentified flying objects—Sightings and encounters.
2. Extraterrestrial beings. I. Pye, Michael, editor of compilation.
II. Dalley, Kirsten, editor of compilation.
TL789.E48 2013
001.942—dc23

2012032645

Manufactured in the United States of America

CPSIA Compliance Information: Batch #W13YA: For further information, contact Rosen Publishing, New York, New York, at 1-800-237-9932.

Published by arrangement with New Page Books, a division of Career Press, Inc.© Michael Pye and Kirsten Dalley

Contents

Preface

From ancient times up until today, mysterious objects in the sky and reports of visitors from the stars have captured our attention. Brief mentions of such otherworldly events appear in texts as old as the Bible, in ancient drawings and architecture, and even in famous paintings depicting scenes that most would consider straight out of science fiction. The number of modern sightings has continued to grow exponentially. Even if there is only a whisper of truth to these accounts, they are worth our scrutiny and investigation. Some cases have mountains of evidence that cannot easily be dismissed.

Our main reason for compiling this volume was to further ignite discussion—even disagreement—so that everyone—believers and skeptics alike—can get the answers they've been looking for. UFO researchers can hardly be considered "fringe" nowadays, although some would insist on using that term. Many of the contributors to this volume are "hard" scientists who have braved the censure and rejection of their peers to boldly go where no-one else has gone (no-one else in their field, at least). The fact is that ufology has now entered the mainstream, and the people who are currently investigating UFOs and accounts of alien visitation bring a healthy dose of much-needed skepticism to their inquiry. For these researchers, the need for truth overrides the desire to believe.

Governments all over the world have admitted that they've held back information pertaining to these matters. Some of this information has slowly made its way out into the world. The British government recently released more than 8,000 documents that had previously been classified and sequestered far from the public eye. And a 1950 memo addressed to J. Edgar Hoover was recently released by the FBI, which seems to provide irrefutable proof that aliens crash landed in Roswell. The question still remains, however, of how many of these important documents were destroyed, and what, if anything, is still being held back.

Gathered here are completely original essays that run the gamut of the UFO phenomenon—everything from the familiar (Roswell and Kingman) to the—dare we say it?—more alien (the ancient aliens theory and parallel universes). Whether you agree with any of the findings or not, these contributions are sure to pique your curiosity and challenge your credulity. It is our belief that there is more to the world than what has already been given the stamp of approval by academia and orthodox science.

The truth is out there. Whether or not you are willing to find it, is up to you.

Michael Pye and Kirsten Dalley

A Cosmic Watergate: UFO Secrecy

By Stanton T. Friedman

I learned long ago, as a young nuclear physicist working on classified advanced nuclear systems in industry, that a key step in determining the truth about any situation is asking the right question(s). With regard to the question of whether important information about flying saucers is currently being withheld from the public, the question is definitely *not* "Can governments, such as that of the United States, keep secrets for many decades?" Governments don't keep secrets. Individuals and the organizations they work for keep secrets. The question then becomes "Can government-funded organizations and the people who work for them keep secrets?" The answer is a very definitive yes. That said, there are three major factors that must be present in order for these individuals and organizations to keep secrets:

1. **The need to know** is crucial. To gain access to classified documents, e-mails, reports, equipment, and/or facilities, one must have a need to know. Mere curiosity, scientific or otherwise, is not enough.

2. **Security clearances** are needed, which are only awarded after detailed background investigations. Depending on the level of clearance involved, this can include an investigation of relatives and friends, as well. What's more, having a Secret clearance at a particular facility

that gives you access to particular documents or equipment does not necessarily provide you access to other similarly classified documents that are not covered by the need to know.

3. There must be an **infrastructure** that supports and enables this secret-keeping. There have to be facility clearances and approved storage facilities (usually with fireproof combination safes) for the storage of classified documents. Fences, guards, identification for all employees, recognition devices, and so on are also required. Again, having access to one part of a facility doesn't necessarily mean access to all parts. There will also be paper trails consisting of signed security documents, security briefings, and so on. Reinvestigations are often required periodically, such as every five years, which will also be documented. Classified documents are typically inventoried every year, as well.

There are many examples of large-scale classified projects involving thousands of people, all of which were able to be kept secret from the general populace—and often even from the very people working on these projects. The classic example is the Manhattan Engineering District, established early on during WWII to develop nuclear weapons. At one time as many as 60,000 people were involved at many different locations. The K-25 Gaseous Diffusion Facility at Oak Ridge National Laboratory in Tennessee, for example, was a mile (1.6 kilometers) long and was using 5 percent of all the electricity produced in the United States to pump gaseous uranium hexafluoride through tiny holes in metal barriers (this was to gradually enrich the gas in the lighter uranium isotope, U-235, a necessary component of nuclear weapons). Workers were instructed to turn a handle when the dial showed a certain value. Due to the security measures that had been put into place, many workers had no idea what it was they were working on.

A number of other similar large and expensive facilities were built, including the Los Alamos National Laboratory (LANL) in New Mexico, Sandia Laboratories in Albuquerque, New Mexico, Lawrence Livermore Labs in Northern California, and Hanford Works in eastern Washington State. Less than 10 years ago, each facility employed more than 8,000 people and had an annual budget of more than a billion dollars. The total annual budget for the first three facilities combined was more than $3 billion, which exceeded the total budget of the National Science Foundation for all its research projects put together. During the war these were the so-called black programs. Their very existence was classified. The LANL employed outstanding scientists, including Nobel Prize winners; all received their mail at a post office box in Santa Fe. Vice-President Harry Truman was completely unaware of the project until 13 days after the death of President Roosevelt on April 12, 1945. Once he was sworn in as president, he had to be briefed about the program in order to make crucial decisions regarding its use.

Even Congress was often unaware of these programs. Consider the U-2 spy plane. The Central Intelligence Agency (not the USAF) awarded the contract to design and build it to the Lockheed Skunk Works (officially the Lockheed Advanced Development Programs facility) in Burbank, California, in 1954. The plane had to be able to fly for long distances at extremely high altitudes (which the Soviet ground-to-air rockets could not reach), and had to be able to carry newly developed spy cameras, also developed in secret. An important aspect of the U-2 program was that each flight was personally approved by the President of the United States. Neither the American public nor Congress was told about the program, primarily because we were violating the air space of the Soviet Union. The Soviet people were not told, either. Although the Soviet government was well aware of the flights, they could not admit they could do nothing about them. A U-2 piloted by Gary Powers was shot down over Soviet airspace on May 1, 1960. In order to avoid the release of classified data, the United States government issued the standard response—in other words, it lied. The plane was "blown off course by bad weather"—at least, that was the story until Soviet Premier Nikita Khrushchev televised pictures of the pilot and the camera. (Powers was supposed to have taken a cyanide pill in order to prevent what he knew from falling into Soviet hands.) President Eisenhower finally bit the bullet and admitted that it was a spy plane.

The problem of how to continue to obtain up-to-date information about the Soviet Union was filled by another super-secret system called the Corona Spy Satellite. At satellite altitudes, it (unlike the U-2) was not violating Soviet air space, which was certainly a major advantage from a political viewpoint, and unlike the U-2 could not be shot down. A unique approach was used to retrieve the information it collected. The de-orbited film containers were snatched out of the sky and captured by airplanes, usually away from populated areas (over the Pacific Ocean or the deserts in Australia, for example). The first 12 launches were unsuccessful, but the 13th, in 1960, proved luckier. The United States obtained more data about Soviet military facilities from this one launch than it had from all the U-2 flights that preceded it put together. Incredibly, however, the first public announcement about the Corona Satellite was not made until 1995, 35 years after the fact. As this basic rule of secret-keeping shows, you can't tell your friends without also telling your enemies. After all, they listen to the radio, read the newspapers, and watch TV, too.

In order to keep these kinds of secrets, code words are often used to describe a new invention or specialized material. For example, at one point during the General Electric Aircraft Nuclear Propulsion program, employees could not say a word about the lithium hydride they were working with. This is because its low density and high hydrogen content makes it suitable for use in hydrogen bombs. After a while it was okay to say "lithium hydride shielding material" instead of, for example, "green salt," but no one could say anything about what it was really being used for. That came later. (As a side note, it's been suggested that only top-level people have clear-ances. This could not be further from the truth. Secretaries that pro-cess classified documents must have appropriate clearances. Even people who sweep the floors must have clearances and be appro-priately instructed regarding the need to protect information about anything they see, including visitors and equipment.)

Now that we know more about how individuals and organiza-tions within the government are able to keep secrets, I am going to discuss the many different kinds of secrets that have been kept regarding UFOs. Some secrets have concerned actual details of the materials these UFOs are made of, including materials recovered from a crash site[1] (such as the desert north of Roswell in July, 1947) or from a UFO that was downed by the military. Assuming that there are such secrets (and I believe that there are), of course we would want to determine how the components and materials were manufactured, and what special treatments, if any, were required (such as rolling, forging, and molding under high or low pressure or in special atmospheres). Such work would have to be done by tal-ented professionals with top-notch equipment and high-level secu-rity clearances. However, they wouldn't necessarily need to have any knowledge of the source(s) of the materials being evaluated. (It would be easy to create the pretext that they were from a downed enemy spy satellite, for example.) One objection to the Roswell story from a British debunker was that if a saucer *had* crashed, numer-ous professional scientists would have been summoned from their respective academic institutions to deal with the materials. This is frankly absurd. By July of 1947, there were literally thousands of engineers and scientists employed both in industry (on classified development programs) and at the national laboratories, as noted previously. They had the finest equipment. The point is that any materials recovered would have been sent to them via classified couriers. Their focus would be on making the appropriate measure-ments and not on publishing in the "scientific" literature. Unlike their colleagues in academia, they are not driven by the "publish or perish" philosophy. There are literally millions of classified advanced technology research reports generated each year, and they are distributed under proper security regulations and at conferences where classified papers are presented.

Other secrets would likely have to do with the flight characteristics of UFOs. For example, what is its acceleration and electromagnetic signature? Does the color of the gas around its surface change as the UFO changes velocity, and if so, how? Three different means of obtaining this kind of information would, by necessity, be under government control. They are:

1. Observations made by cameras, radar, and sophisticated sensors on board military aircraft chasing UFOs or being chased by them.
2. Measurements made by ground-based sensors and radar (for example, how did the surface temperature of the craft change with time, altitude, velocity, and/or maneuvers?).
3. Measurements made by spy satellites of these same characteristics.

It must be noted that the sophisticated equipment required to make such measurements is under the direct control of the government. Simply put, the data are born classified.

The same UK researcher who raised the objection to the Roswell story also stated that "one can't keep secret what one cannot control." While it may be true that we can't control the behavior of UFOs, we *can* control the information obtained about them by the classified systems mentioned here. Sightings by members of the public rarely, if ever, provide any scientific or engineering data. Thus public sightings are of almost no utility in that sense. An important aspect of these data collection systems is the compartmentalization involved in their implementation. Think of a wagon wheel with many spokes, a hub, and no rim. The data gatherers send their data to the hub, but not to the other spoke installations. Some central group must then be responsible for evaluating the information that is coming in from all directions, and farm it out as appropriate.

Another way of gathering data is to reverse-engineer something. Back-engineering groups certainly existed prior to Roswell. For example, both sides during WWII made every effort to analyze the other side's recovered munitions, tanks, aircraft, and so on. The goal was to determine the capabilities of the other side's technology and to try to duplicate it if it proved to be superior to its own. Clearly, flying saucers have flight capabilities that are well beyond anything that has ever been achieved on this planet. They would make wonderful devices for high- and low-altitude reconnaissance flights, and excellent weapons delivery and defense systems. As well, duplicating saucer radar profiles could enable enemy targets to disguise themselves and sneak by unnoticed, or perhaps just dismissed as just another "harmless" flying saucer. For these reasons, every military community would very much like to duplicate the technological capabilities of flying saucers. Reverse-engineering efforts in the United States would likely be focused on enhancing current technology, and determining the best methods of combating the saucers, should that become necessary. Recovered wreckage of an alien vehicle would certainly be of use in such a quest, and this kind of technology would perforce be a closely guarded secret. The enemies of the United States would love to get their hands on what we know, perhaps in order to combine it with what they have already learned from their own observations of saucers. (After all, UAF crashes have not been confined to North America.)

Another little-discussed aspect of the business of secret-keeping is the use of recovery teams. What happens when classified documents or materials are shipped on a vehicle that is then involved in an accident? The U.S. government keeps very close track of classified shipments. In the event of an accident, a perimeter is established around the component or wreckage. People are kept away, and cover stories are made ready to be put in place. By way of an example, when the

Cosmos 954 Soviet spy satellite (which had a compact nuclear reactor on board) came down near Great Slave Lake in Northern Canada on January 24, 1978, a recovery team was quickly dispatched to find it and recover as much of the radioactive wreckage as possible. The goal was not so much to protect the few people in the remote area from radioactivity, but to evaluate the technology. A total of 48,000 square miles (124,000 square kilometers) was searched, and many pieces of wreckage were found. In the case of the American satellite USA 193, also known as NROL-21, a different approach was used to prevent its highly classified technology from being recovered by other nations. When the satellite failed shortly after launch in December of 2006, it was destroyed in space by a Navy SM-3 missile in February of 2008. It had been built at a cost of $10 billion by Lockheed Martin and Boeing for the National Reconnaissance Office. The annual "black budget" of the very secretive NRO has been estimated to be anywhere from $15 to $30 billion. The point here is that secrets can be kept, for years if necessary.

A particularly sensitive aspect of recovery operations would involve an aircraft destroyed by a UFO while the aircraft was trying to shoot it down. This kind of wreckage would need to be recovered as quickly and carefully as possible, and families would not be able to be told about the real reason behind their loved ones' deaths. This same situation applied to crews of the many special high-tech reconnaissance airplanes shot down during the early days of the Cold War while "tickling" Russian, North Korean, and Chinese coastal radar installations.[2] Families were not told what happened to the crew member relatives until 2001. *Shoot Them Down* by Frank Feschino Jr. discusses these situations in great detail, including the fact that orders were issued to military pilots in 1952 to shoot UFOs down if they didn't land when instructed to do so.[3] Mr. Feschino also notes that the *New York Times* listed 200 fatal military plane crashes between 1951 and 1956. Generally speaking, records of these events were unavailable at the time; however, we now know that words such as "disappeared" and "disintegrated" were sometimes used to describe the pilots' plights.

Another oft-neglected aspect of the secrecy discussion is the simple fact that Top Secret information cannot be included in a memo that is classified only as Secret. A particularly important example is in a now well-known memo written by U.S. Air Force Lieutenant General Nathan F. Twining, dated September 23, 1947. It was addressed to the Commanding General Army Air Forces and titled "AMC Opinion Concerning Flying Discs." Twining was the commander of the Air Materiel Command at Wright Patterson Air Force Base, near Dayton, Ohio. Comments by him on July 8, 1947, clearly indicated he had already been looking into the question of flying saucers. Pilot Kenneth Arnold's highly publicized sighting of nine objects flying at more than 1,200 miles (1,931 kilometers) per hour near Mt. Rainier on June 24 had definitely stirred things up. Twining certainly took the subject seriously. The two-page memo had only been classified as Secret and had first been made public in the final report of the University of Colorado UFO study in 1969.[4] One comment therein has been used in attempts to demonstrate that the military had not recovered a flying saucer at Roswell or any other place—namely, "the lack of physical evidence in the shape of crash recovered exhibits which would undeniably prove the existence of these objects." Cynics maintain that the comment proves that there was no crash wreckage. However, the fact is that such information would certainly have been classified as "Top Secret Code Word" and thus could not have been included in a merely Secret document, which had very wide distribution. As a matter of fact, the Truman to Forrestal Memo, which authorized the establishment of Operation Majestic 12, was dated one day later, September 24, 1947. It was classified Top Secret-Eyes Only. Twining was listed in the Top Secret/MAJIC Eisenhower Briefing Document of November 18, 1952, as a member of the Majestic 12. The proof that such matters would have been classified Top Secret Code Word is the simple fact that the National Security Agency UFO documents, which were released in 1980 under the Freedom of Information Act, were all classified Top Secret UMBRA, as were a host of CIA UFO documents also not "released" until after 1980. I put "released" in quotes because it's a deceptive word, here. The justification for withholding the NSA UFO documents from the NSA to Federal Court Judge Gerhard Gesell, dated 1980, was itself 80-percent blacked out. In 1997, because of the new Executive Order 12958, the justification was only 20-percent expurgated and 156 NSA UFO documents (all predating 1980) were "released"; all but about one sentence per page was whited out, supposedly because everything else related to very sensitive "sources and methods" information. It seems improbable that more than 95 percent of the text could be related to sources and methods and that only the remaining line dealt with UFOs. The CIA Top Secret UMBRA UFO documents were, in a number of instances, *all* blacked out except for perhaps eight innocent words per page. One page just had "Deny in Toto" written across the top. Apparently they couldn't even find eight words that could be declassified. It took me five years to get copies of some of these.

Many people are under the impression that everything is automatically declassified after a certain amount of time. This is false. Some few documents do have such limits and are declassified after, say, 25 years. The very great majority are not, however. The Eisenhower Library in Abilene, Kansas, admits to having more than 250,000 pages of classified National Security Council files. The National Archives in College Park, Maryland, has Record Group 341(USAF HQ files 1948-1956). The Finding Aid (itself 52 pages long) notes that the RG occupies more than 9,000 feet (2,743 meters) of shelf space occupied by acid-free, archive boxes. This is roughly the amount of material that would be held by 1,000 four-drawer filing cabinets. Visitors cannot go through the material at will. They can request that up to 12 boxes be brought to them at one time, but they can open only one file folder at a time. If the material is still classified, it is replaced by a withdrawal sheet. At the presidential archives, one can then request a mandatory classification review of that item. This means it must be sent to the originating agency for review. They may then send it to one or more other agencies for *their* review. Response time can run anywhere from one to five years. Some material is eventually declassified this way, but it is a painstaking process. Most of the materials in such files have not been scanned or computerized. Visitors to presidential libraries often ask to have computer searches done for materials about a certain topic, such as Operation Majestic 12. "Can't be done" is the typical response.

It must be noted that in addition to the standard security classifications, such as Restricted, Confidential, Secret, and Top Secret, there are other specialized categories. For example, there is Top Secret Code Word, which covers Special Classified categories and is often designated by a code word such as UMBRA, ULTRA, MAJIC, and so on. Normally, a much smaller subset of people on a particular project would have access to Top Secret Umbra work than just Top Secret material. There is no one system that covers all organizations and is able to classify, store, and distribute all classified material. It has been suggested that if the Army does things a certain way, other government entities and agencies must also do things the same way. Definitely not so.

Those who have heard the phrase "loose lips sink ships," a WWII legacy, may not be aware that President Franklin Roosevelt appointed Byron Price, then the executive news editor of the Associated Press, as Director of Censorship on December 16, 1941, only nine days after Pearl Harbor. His focus was on getting the press and radio stations not to discuss certain things, such as troop and ship movements, the flow of war materials, and even data about the weather. He somehow convinced media figures such as columnist Drew Pearson and writer William L. Lawrence not to discuss the development of nuclear weapons, even though they had somehow discovered the secret. The word was out to not use the word "uranium," and there was to be no reporting of the damage caused by the Japanese FUGO balloon bombs. There wasn't much in the way of actual laws to legislate this stuff, but the power of persuasion did its work. In an important example, General George C. Marshall, Chief of Staff during WWII, made a major and eventually successful effort to quietly convince New York State Governor and republican presidential candidate Thomas Dewey not to mention anything about the fact that the United States had broken the Japanese military codes. By breaking the Japanese codes, the United States had been able to glean some extraordinarily useful tactical information about Japanese manpower, ship movements, and so on. Even a hint that the code had been broken (during Operation Purple) would have caused it to be changed and undoubtedly would have cost many allied military deaths. Naturally, Dewey agreed.

The leaders of the SETI (Search for Extraterrestrial Intelligence) Institute have insisted that there is no evidence that aliens are visiting planet Earth, and if they were (and if such events as the crash and recovery of an alien spacecraft near Roswell had actually transpired), it would be impossible to keep it a secret. Dr. Seth Shostak of the SETI Institute has, in common with other leaders, such as Dr. Jill Tartar and Dr. Frank Drake, ignored the large-scale scientific studies such as "Blue Book Special Report 14,"[5] but has noted that SETI would go public almost immediately with the news if they ever received a radio or laser signal from extraterrestrials. He has also pointed out that, after all, this is the same fumbling government that fouled up (with FEMA) in the aftermath of Hurricane Katrina and that runs the post office (badly). You would think that if someone were serious about the question of the government's ability to keep secrets, he would focus on actual intelligence agencies—the CIA, the DIA, the NSA—and not on FEMA or the post office. Not surprisingly, the SETI community has made a habit of ignoring the rather obvious national security aspects of flying saucers. Additionally, the impact of hearing about a radio signal from hundreds of light years away would be considerably less than the impact of news that aliens are here now.

If the U.S. government were ever to actually reveal the truth, there would be several obvious attendant concerns, one being the political risk involved in admitting its lack of prowess against alien intruders. Another cause for concern would be the inevitable protests from certain fundamentalist religious groups that there is no intelligent life besides that on earth, and/or that the so-called aliens are actually the minions of Satan come to take over the planet. Then there is the larger political question of who speaks for the planet. Reaction to the September, 2010, false claims that the head of the United Stations Outer Space Affairs Committees has been designated a point of contact for alien intruders was not all favorable. No government or military group would willingly be subservient to a single planetary leader.

And now for the actual untruths. There are a number of cases *on record* of the U.S. Air Force flat-out lying about flying saucers. A particularly egregious example was the press release that was given national distribution on October 25, 1955, which announced the completion of a large-scale investigation on UFOs. The following statement was made by the Secretary of the Air Force, Donald A. Quarles: "On the basis of this study we believe that no objects such as those popularly described as flying saucers have flown over the United States. I feel certain that even the unknown three percent could have been explained as conventional phenomena or illusions if more complete observational data had been available." Strangely enough, the title of the report, "Project Blue Book Special Report 14," wasn't given. Presumably, if it had been given, some reporter would have asked what had happened to reports one through 13. The truth is that they were all classified. Nor was there any information given as to who did the study—an outstanding research and development organization, Battelle Memorial Institute, based in Columbus, Ohio, not far from Project Blue Book, which was based at the Air Technical Intelligence Center at Wright Patterson Air Force base in nearby Dayton. If its name had been given, along with the individuals who worked on the project, reporters probably would have wanted to interview them. I located a copy of the report at the University of California–Berkeley library around 1961, and was shocked to find more than 240 charts, tables, graphs, and maps with data about 3,201 UFO sightings. Every sighting was evaluated as to its quality, and categorized according to the final assessment: Balloon, Aircraft, Astronomical, Insufficient Information, Psychological Manifestation (only 1.5 percent), Miscellaneous, or Unknown. No sighting could be listed as an Unknown unless all four final report evaluators agreed. However, two evaluators would be enough to classify it as a Known. The fact is that the percentage of Unknowns was 21.5 percent, *not* 3 percent. As well, 9.3 percent of the sightings were classified in the Insufficient Information category. Unknowns were not designated as such because they lacked information; in fact, the better the quality of the report, the more likely it was that it would be relegated to Unknown status. Furthermore, the Battelle Memorial Institute did a statistical cross-comparison between the Unknowns and the Knowns. The probability, based on six different observable characteristics, that they were just "missed" Knowns, was less than 1 percent. There is no wiggle room here: Quarles flat-out lied. There were other confabulations, too, such as when annual press releases were issued that conveniently left out sightings that were still under investigation. All of the single-witness sightings, no matter the quality, were automatically shifted to the Insufficient Information category.

But of much greater concern is the statement made when Blue Book was closed at the end of 1969. The conclusions were as follows: "1.) No UFO reported, investigated, and evaluated by the Air Force has ever given any indication of threat to our national security; 2.) there has been no evidence submitted to or discovered by the Air Force that sightings categorized as unidentified represent techno-logical developments or principles beyond the range of present-day scientific knowledge; and 3.) there has been no evidence that sight-ings categorized as 'unidentified' are 'extraterrestrial vehicles.'" If somebody besides the Air Force (the CIA, the NSA, the DIA, the NRO, the ONI, or Majestic 12) had been involved, the statements might be technically true, but they were totally misleading nonetheless. There was certainly an awareness of techniques beyond the sci-entific knowledge of the time, but they had not yet been put into practice. (For interested parties, a detailed critique of these claims is presented in Appendix E of my 2005 book, *TOP SECRET/MAJIC*.)

It was many years later when the actual memo leading to the closure of Blue Book was discovered by the late Robert Todd, in response to a FOIA request. In this memo, we found this statement from the author, USAF Brigadier General Carroll Bolender (October 20, 1969): "[R]eports of UFOs which could affect national security are made in accordance with JANAP 146 or Air Force Manual 55-11, and are not part of the Blue Book system.... Termination of Project Blue Book would leave no official federal office to receive reports of UFOs. However, as already stated, reports of UFOs which could affect national security would continue to be handled through the standard Air Force Procedures designed for this purpose." When I managed to locate General Bolender, he verified that, just as he had said, there were two separate channels: one for run-of-the-mill reports, and the other for the more important sightings that could pose a threat to national security. No media outlet has ever told the American people that the "hot reports" didn't go to Project Blue Book, or that the reports that could affect national security were still being investigated *more than 40 years after the Blue Book closure.*

Perhaps the most disturbing examples of false claims made by the Air Force were the statements made in the two hefty Air Force reports about Roswell, "The Roswell Report: Truth vs. Fiction in the New Mexico Desert" and "The Roswell Report: Case Closed." They would make excellent examples of misleading and flat-out false propaganda for a college course. One of the most outrageous claims stated that reports of bodies associated with the Roswell Incident were caused by the numerous crash-test dummies dropped all over New Mexico. The facts indicate that no dummies were dropped until 1953, six years after the incident, and that the dummies were 6 feet (1.8 meters) tall, weighed 175 pounds (79 kgs), and were dressed in Air Force uniforms. This was confirmed to me in person by the officer in charge of the program, Colonel Madsen. (A picture of him and one of these dummies can be found in the "Case Closed" report.) Even the *New York Times* accepted this silly explanation for what was really found (spindly short bodies with large heads).

In sum, it is very clear that various agencies of the United States government had and continue to have the capability of keeping secrets, and have intentionally and consistently withheld facts and information regarding—and even actual wreckage of—alien space-craft. It is also clear that the journalistic and scientific communities have used less than due diligence in getting to the bottom of the real stories. History tells us that a huge quantity of information has been withheld from the public with regard to many technological research and development programs, and the world of UFOs is no exception. As a scientist who worked on many exciting classified advanced technology programs for 14 years, I am personally not in favor of releasing technical data that could be of use to poten-tial enemies. But the fact that we are not alone has many implica-tions for the future of the human race, and almost certainly for an understanding of the entire history of our planet. Frankly I feel the best way to elicit such a disclosure would be for a major media group (such as the *Washington Post* or the *New York Times*) to put as much effort into blowing the lid off this "Cosmic Watergate" as went into exposing the political Watergate in the 1970s. We need a new Woodward and Bernstein team. If there are any interested parties out there, I would be happy to help.

Notes

1. Berliner, Donald and Stanton T. Friedman. *Crash at Corona.* New York: Cosimo Press, 2004. (A copy autographed by the author is only $16.99 postpaid. Send to: UFORI, PO Box 958, Houlton, ME 04730-0958.)

2. Burrows, William E. *By Any Means Necessary: America's Secret Air War in the Cold War.* New York, NY: Farrar, Straus and Giroux, 2001.

3. Feschino, Frank Jr. *Shoot Them Down.* Lulu Publishing, 2007. (Available through Amazon.com and from UFORI. Send 32.00 to: UFORI, PO Box 958, Houlton, ME 04730-0958.)

4. Condon, Edward U. *Scientific Study of Unidentified Flying Objects.* New York, NY: Bantam Press, 1969.

5. "Project Blue Book Special Report No. 14" for USAF, by Battelle Memorial Institute, 1955. (Available through UFORI. Send $25.00 to: UFORI, POB 958, Houlton, ME 04730.)

The Real X-Files

By Nick Pope

The British government's UFO project had its roots in a 1950 initiative by the chief scientific adviser of the MoD (the UK's Ministry of Defense), the great radar scientist Sir Henry Tizard. Tizard was intrigued by media coverage of UFO sightings and decided that these should not be dismissed without first undertaking some proper, scientific study. Accordingly, he agreed that a small group should be set up to investigate the phenomenon. This was dubbed the Flying Saucer Working Party. In its final report, issued in 1951, the group concluded that all UFO sightings could be explained as misidentifications of ordinary objects or phenomena, optical illusions, psychological delusions, or hoaxes. The main body of the report ended with the following statement:

> We accordingly recommend very strongly that no further investigation of reported mysterious aerial phenomena be undertaken, unless and until some material evidence becomes available.

However, from 1952 to 1957, there were a series of high-profile UFO sightings that included numerous incidents in which UFOs were seen by Royal Air Force (RAF) pilots or tracked on military radar. These forced the MoD to rethink its skepticism and investigate the phenomenon—something it did right up until November 30, 2009.

During the lifetime of the MoD's UFO project, the Department received more than 12,000 sighting reports. In addition to these files, there are policy files, public correspondence files, and files detailing how the MoD handles the subject when it is raised in Parliament and in the media. There are hundreds of files and literally tens of thousands of pages of documentation. Some of the older files were available at the National Archives, and UFO researchers and authors such as Timothy Good and Georgina Bruni used the Freedom of Information Act to obtain a few high-profile documents, such as the file on Britain's best-known UFO case, the Rendlesham Forest incident. But for the most part, very little of this material had ever been made public. Then, in 2007, the MoD dropped a bombshell and announced that it was to release the entire archive of UFO files and transfer them to the National Archives. There were four reasons for this decision:

- The MoD was receiving more Freedom of Information (FOI) requests on UFOs than on any other subject.
- The French government had released their UFO files in 2007, setting a precedent that would have been difficult to ignore.
- MoD believed this would be a good way to demonstrate their commitment to FOI and to open government.
- MoD hoped that releasing the files would defuse the accusation that they were covering up information on UFOs.

The first reason was the key one. Hundreds of people were bombarding the MoD with FOI requests, and the administrative burden of responding to hundreds of requests (some of which were highly complex) was becoming unbearable. In the years before the release, the Directorate Air Staff (DAS)—the MoD division that had the policy and investigative lead in relation to the subject—received UFO-related FOI requests as follows:

♂ 2005: 199 requests

♂ 2006: 140 requests

♂ 2007: 120 requests

The 2007 figure was as of September 18, the date DAS wrote to the Under Secretary of State for Defense, recommending that the files be released.

Other parts of the MoD that were involved in investigating UFO sightings, such as the Defense Intelligence Staff (DIS), were also receiving large numbers of FOI requests on the subject. Following MoD's release of a formerly classified study into UFOs (code-named Project Condign), Under Secretary of State for Defense Tom Watson wrote on the MoD's Website in 2006:

There is a real and enduring interest in Unidentified Flying Objects. By far the most popular topic of FOI requests has been UFOs, followed by recruitment enquiries, enquiries from staff, and historical events such as World War Two, the Falklands conflict and the Balkans. Recent freedom of information releases on UFOs have attracted media interest from as far away as Japan.

The MoD realized that if they released the files proactively, most FOI requests could be dealt with by simply referring people to the National Archives.

The MoD decided not to release the material all in one go, mainly because of the administrative burden of redacting the files. Redaction involves deleting information covered by the various exemptions to the Freedom of Information Act, to ensure that classified information and personal data relating to members of the public or MoD officials isn't released. Names, addresses, and other personal details relating to witnesses and officials have to be removed to comply not only with the Freedom of Information Act, but also with the Data Protection Act. Other exemptions cover categories such as defense and national security. Examples of the sort of information that is still being withheld include details of the capability of military radar systems, information passed to the UK in confidence by allies, commercially sensitive information, and information which, if disclosed, would reveal intelligence sources or methods of gathering intelligence. It's a massive job and a tricky one. Tens of thousands of pages of documentation have to be read word by word, to ensure that the material is properly redacted. To date, batches of files have been released on the following dates:

- ♂ May 14, 2008
- ♂ October 20, 2008
- ♂ March 22, 2009
- ♂ August 17, 2009
- ♂ February 18, 2010
- ♂ August 5, 2010

In all, this has involved the release of 90 out of 160 files. The process is due to be completed in late 2011 or early 2012, depending on other commitments at the MoD and the National Archives. The files are being released in chronological order, starting with the oldest material. This means that while there is still much interesting material to come, many of the files that have yet to be released consist of FOI requests about UFOs from members of the public.

Because I used to work on these files, the National Archives asked me to assist with the release program. Prior to the release of the first batch of material, I selected a range of cases to highlight to the media—some explained, some unexplained, and some merely humorous. I also recorded a short film to promote the release. There was some nervousness prior to all this, however: When the French government released their UFO files in one go in 2007, demand was so high that their dedicated Website crashed. To prevent this, the National Archives brought in extra processing power and back-up systems in advance, but fortunately they were never needed.

Still, their prudence was justified by the statistics: Within two weeks, the Website had been accessed more than two million times. Predictably, the release of each batch of files generated massive coverage in the media.

The Best of the X-Files

Much of the material in the files is mundane (for example, Mr. Smith is out walking his dog late at night and sees a vague light in the sky that could be anything—usually a misidentification of aircraft lights, a bright star or planet, a satellite, or a meteor). However, among the more routine material are some truly amazing incidents: UFOs seen by police officers and pilots, UFOs tracked on radar, craft seen performing speeds and maneuvers far beyond the ability of our most advanced military aircraft or drones, and intriguing photos and videos that even impressed the MoD's technical wizards. What *isn't* in the files, however, is some "spaceship-in-a-hangar" smoking gun. Following are some details on what I consider to be some of the more interesting cases, to put some flesh on the bones and to give readers a more detailed insight into these real-life X-Files.

Despite there being a wealth of more recent material in the MoD's UFO files, it is an allegation regarding something that happened many years ago that has captured much of the recent media and public attention. One of the files contains a letter from a scientist whose grandfather served as one of Winston Churchill's bodyguards. He claimed that during World War II, Prime Minister Winston Churchill conspired with a U.S. general (later to become president) named Dwight D. Eisenhower, to suppress the truth about a spectacular UFO sighting witnessed by the crew of an RAF aircraft returning from a reconnaissance mission. The UFO had apparently been capable of extraordinary speeds and maneuvers and yet showed no hostile intent. It clearly wasn't some new German secret weapon. Churchill feared that the details would cause public panic and shatter people's religious faith. Thus, he ordered that the details should be classified.

Skeptics point out that the Churchill story is hearsay. Sadly, most MoD UFO files dating prior to the 1960s were shredded many years ago, so we may never learn the truth. But there are some intriguing clues—for example, we know from a previously released document that Churchill was intrigued and concerned about UFOs. In a 1952 letter to the Secretary of State for Air, Churchill wrote "What does all this stuff about flying saucers amount to? What can it mean? What is the truth?" Another document from the same batch of MoD files relates to a Joint Intelligence Committee meeting in 1957, at which the subject of UFOs was discussed, with particular reference to some objects that had been tracked on military radar. The events were unexplained and a report was delivered by the RAF's Head of Intelligence. So while we can't verify the story that Churchill ordered a UFO cover-up, we know that he and some senior figures in the military and the intelligence community were actively discussing the mystery.

A poignant case in the files is that of Milton Torres, a United States Air Force (USAF) pilot who stated that on May 20, 1957 (the exact date is actually the subject of some confusion and debate) he was ordered to open fire on a UFO that was being tracked on radar. He was based at RAF Manston in Kent and was scrambled to intercept a UFO that had been tracked over the UK. He claims that he came within seconds of firing off a salvo of 24 air-to-air rockets, before the UFO accelerated away at a speed of what appeared to be around Mach 10. Torres stated that he was subsequently told that his mission had been classified Top Secret and that he was to stay silent about the incident. Torres only spoke about the incident in public (years later, at a reunion) after the MoD had released his account, as he believed that the fact that the government itself had placed this information into the public domain meant that any official restrictions on his discussing the matter had been removed. The poignancy of this case arises because Torres felt he couldn't even tell his father about this incident, despite the fact that he would have loved hearing about it. Sadly, his father died before the matter came to light, and Torres is extremely distressed that he never told him about these events. (It is important to note that the account in the MoD file is not an official USAF or MoD witness statement, but a transcript of an interview with Torres, undertaken many years after the event and lodged with a lawyer, who subsequently forwarded it to the MoD. As with the debate about Winston Churchill, we are unlikely to find contemporary documents, in view of the destruction of older UFO files.)

Torres is not the only military pilot to have been ordered to open fire on UFOs. While such cases are not mentioned in the MoD UFO files and are therefore outside the scope of this essay, it's worth noting that Parviz Jafari (Iran, 1976) and Oscar Santa Maria Huertas (Peru, 1980) were placed in similar positions and either fired at or attempted to fire at UFOs that had strayed into restricted military airspace.

Cases Involving Commercial Aircraft

One of the most interesting and disturbing cases in the MoD UFO files occurred on April 21, 1991. I remember this incident very well, as I was involved in the official investigation. We were informed by the Civil Aviation Authority (CAA)—the UK equivalent of the U.S. Federal Aviation Administration—that there had been a near-miss involving a commercial aircraft. The aircraft was an Al Italia MD-80 with 57 passengers on board. It was flying at about 22,000 feet (6,706 meters) over Kent, near Lydd, when a brown, cigar-shaped object passed so close to the aircraft that the pilot shouted "Look out, look out!" fearing a collision was imminent.

In the normal course of events, any near-miss would be investigated by the CAA. However, most such incidents involve other aircraft, and as the crew were not able to identify the object, it was treated as a UFO incident and passed from the CAA to the MoD. We launched a full investigation and eliminated all the usual possibilities, including weather balloons, military aircraft, and so on. We even checked to see whether we had accidentally fired off a missile of some sort. We drew a complete blank, and the incident remains unexplained to this day.

This incident had a profound effect on me, because I realized that a commercial aircraft came within seconds of being blown out of the sky over the UK. This illustrated that whatever one believes about UFOs, the phenomenon raises important defense and air safety issues. However, some people at the MoD and the CAA did not treat the incident as seriously as I did, simply because of their automatic, defensive reaction upon hearing the word "UFO." This was deeply troubling and convinced me that I should make every effort to ensure that all UFO incidents were investigated thoroughly and in a proper scientific manner. It also convinced me that I should make efforts to ensure the subject was taken more seriously within the military and the aviation community.

Another case involving a near miss between a commercial aircraft and a UFO occurred on January 6, 1995, and involved a Boeing 737 carrying 60 passengers, on approach to Manchester airport. When over the Pennines at a height of 4,000 feet (1,219 meters), both the pilot and the first officer saw an unidentified object pass on the right hand side of the aircraft at high speed. It was described as wedge-shaped and illuminated, and with what looked like a black stripe down the side. Neither man was certain how close the object had come to colliding with the aircraft, but the first officer instinctively ducked as it went by. Nothing unusual was seen on radar. The CAA's report into this incident (titled "Airmiss Report No. 2/95") concluded as follows:

Having debated the various hypotheses at length the Group concluded that, in the absence of any firm evidence which could identify or explain the object, it was not possible to assess either the cause or the risk by any of the normal criteria applicable to airmiss reports. The incident therefore remains unresolved.

The Bentwaters Incident

Bentwaters (or the Rendlesham Forest incident, as it's more commonly known in the UK) is Britain's most interesting and compelling UFO incident. Material on this case has been in the public domain for many years, but some new documents have emerged more recently as part of the UFO files release. Before going into this, it's worth giving a brief overview of the events themselves.

In the early hours of December 26, 1980, military personnel at the twin bases of RAF Bentwaters and RAF Woodbridge (USAF bases in the UK) saw strange lights in the forest. Thinking a light aircraft might have crashed, they went out to investigate. What they found was a small triangular craft that had landed in a clearing in Rendlesham Forest. Nearby farm animals were going into a frenzy. One of the security police officers, Jim Penniston, got close enough to touch the side of the object. He and another of the airmen present, John Burroughs, attached sketches of the craft to their official USAF witness statements. One of these sketches details strange symbols Penniston saw on the craft's hull, which he likened to Egyptian hieroglyphs.

Amazingly, two nights later, the UFO returned. The deputy base commander, Lieutenant Colonel Charles Halt, was informed and, together with a small group of men, went out into the forest to investigate. As they progressed, radio communications were subjected to interference and powerful mobile generators (called "light-alls") that Halt had brought to illuminate the forest began to cut out. Despite his initial plan to "debunk" the UFO sighting, Halt and his team then encountered the UFO, which at one point shone beams of light down at his party and at the Woodbridge facility. "Here I am, a senior official who routinely denies this sort of thing and diligently works to debunk them, and I'm involved in the middle of something I can't explain," he subsequently commented during an interview about the events.

Charles Halt documented his encounter by recording his observations on a hand-held cassette recorder. The 17 minutes of tape are widely available on the Internet. Halt reported the various incidents to the MoD in a memorandum dated January 13, 1981. Despite the innocuous title "Unexplained Lights," the document described the UFO as being "metallic in appearance and triangular in shape... hovering or on legs." In what may have been either a typographical error or a slip of the memory, Halt gave incorrect dates for both sightings, recording each as having taken place a day later than was, in fact, the case.

The MoD's investigation included a search for radar evidence that might have corroborated what was seen, but the error in the dates meant that the wrong tapes were checked. Of far more interest was an assessment of radiation readings that had been taken from the landing site with a Geiger counter. The readings had peaked in three holes in the ground which formed the shape of an equilateral triangle, which had been found at the spot where the craft landed. Staff in MoD's DIS who specialized in scientific and technical intelligence stated that the readings seemed "significantly higher than the average background." Their report suggested that the radiation level was around seven or eight times what would have been expected for the area concerned.

One of the interesting pieces of information to emerge in the newly released files is correspondence between Lord Hill-Norton (a former Chief of the Defense Staff) and Defense ministers. In his retirement, Lord Hill-Norton was passionately interested in the UFO phenomenon, but had become increasingly frustrated that despite having been the UK's senior military officer, he had never been briefed on the subject. Correspondence shows his particular frustration with MoD stating that the Rendlesham Forest incident was of "no defense significance"—MoD's standard line when trying to downplay the subject. In a letter to the MoD's Minister of State, dated October 22, 1997, Lord Hill-Norton clearly disagreed:

My position both privately and publicly expressed over the last dozen years or more, is that there are only two possibilities, either: a. An intrusion into our Air Space and a landing by unidentified craft took place at Rendlesham, as described. Or b. The Deputy Commander of an operational, nuclear armed, US Air Force Base in England, and a large number of his enlisted men, were either hallucinating or lying. Either of these simply must be "of interest to the Ministry of Defense," which has been repeatedly denied, in precisely those terms.

Another interesting document to emerge revealed that shortly after the incident, General Gabriel (the commander in chief of the United States Air Forces in Europe) visited Bentwaters and took possession of the tape recordings of Charles Halt's encounter. But the Americans never told the British at the time, and we only found out many weeks later. An internal MoD document clearly written with a certain degree of frustration finishes by saying, "Perhaps it would be reasonable to ask if we could have [the] tape recordings as well."

The Cosford Incident

As with Bentwaters, some details of this case had been in the public domain for some years. But as with Bentwaters, the release of the MoD's UFO files has allowed the full story of this extraordinary incident to be told. Seeing the file was a fascinating blast from the past for me personally, because I had led the official investigation.

The first sighting took place on March 30, 1993, at around 8:30 p.m. in Somerset. This was followed by a sighting at 9 p.m. in the Quantock Hills. The witness was a police officer who, together with a group of scouts, had seen a craft that he described as looking "like two Concorde aircraft flying side by side and joined together." A further sighting came from a member of the public in Rugely, Staffordshire, who reported a UFO that he estimated as being 200 yards (about 200 meters) in diameter. He and other family members explained that they had chased the object in their car and got extremely close to it, believing it had landed in a nearby field. When they got there a few seconds later, there was nothing to be seen. Many of the witnesses described a triangular craft, or three lights in a triangular shape, which they believed were on the underside of the craft. Indeed, in an apparent coincidence, these sightings occurred three years to the very day after the famous wave of sightings in Belgium that culminated in the scrambling of F-16 fighters in order to intercept a UFO that was being tracked on radar.

One report about this same incident, which sounded as if it really had come straight out of *The X-Files*, involved a sighting of the UFO over a farmer's field. When the witnesses investigated, the UFO had disappeared, but all of the cows were standing in a circle in the middle of the field, facing each other in complete silence.

The UFO was seen later that day by a patrol of RAF Police based at RAF Cosford. Their official police report (classified "Police in Confidence") stated that the UFO passed over the base "at great velocity...at an altitude of approximately 1,000 feet [305 meters]." It described two white lights with a faint red glow at the rear, and a lack of engine noise. The RAF Police report also contained details of a number of civilian UFO sightings that they had been made aware of in the course of making enquiries with other military bases, civil airports, and local police.

Later on that night, the meteorological officer at RAF Shawbury saw the UFO. He described how it had moved slowly across the countryside toward the base, at a speed of no more than 30 or 40 miles (48 or 64 kilometers) per hour. He saw the UFO emit a narrow beam of light (similar to a laser) at the ground and saw the light sweeping back and forth across the field beyond the perimeter fence, as if it were looking for something. He heard an unpleasant low frequency humming sound coming from the craft and said he could feel as well as hear this, as though he was standing in front of a bass speaker. He estimated the size of the craft to be somewhere between a C-130 Hercules transport aircraft and a Boeing 747. Finally, he said that the light beam had retracted in an unnatural way and that the craft had suddenly accelerated away to the horizon, many times faster than a military aircraft.

The radar data was inconclusive and one of the key radar systems was not working on primary radar during the reporting period, so only aircraft working Secondary Surveillance Radar could be seen. But with this and with other checks, it was possible to build up a picture of all aircraft and helicopter activity over the UK, so that we could factor them into the investigation and eliminate them from our enquiries if appropriate.

The Ballistic Missile Early Warning System at RAF Fylingdales, with its powerful space-tracking radars, was an important part of my UFO investigation. They quickly alerted me to the fact that there had been a re-entry into the Earth's atmosphere of a Russian rocket carrying a communications satellite, called Cosmos 2238. We postulated that this was a possible explanation for a cluster of UFO sightings that occurred at around 1:10 a.m. on March 31. My head of division was normally skeptical about the UFO phenomenon, but on this occasion his brief to the assistant chief of the air staff (one of the UK's most senior RAF officers) concluded: "In summary, there would seem to be some evidence on this occasion that an unidentified object (or objects) of unknown origin was operating over the UK."

This is about as close as the MoD will ever get to saying that there's more to UFOs than misidentifications or hoaxes.

Crop Circles and Psychic Predictions

Just as was the case in the fictional TV series, these real-life X-files contain more than just material on UFOs. One of the other subjects covered was crop circles. The military and MoD's first involvement with this mystery occurred in 1985. A farmer had found a spectacular formation on his land and telephoned the Army Air Corps base at Middle Wallop to ask what they were up to. The farmer suggested that the pattern might have been formed by the downdraft from a helicopter's rotor blades. The Army does a great deal of flying training in the area, some of which involves practicing landings. It needs permission from landowners to do this, which makes it important for them to stay on good terms with local farmers. Because noise from military aircraft leads to many complaints each year, it's important for the military to stay on good terms not just with farmers, but with the public more generally. With this in mind, the Army moved quickly to deal with the suggestion that the "damage to the crops" (which is how the farmer termed it) had been formed by a low flying helicopter.

The matter was investigated by a senior officer, Lieutenant Colonel Edgecombe, who flew over the formation and took photographs. He subsequently attended a public meeting and gave a categorical assurance that the downdraft from a helicopter's rotor blades could not create such symmetrical and well-defined formations. He also pointed out that the Army would not in any case damage farmers' crops in this way. Finally, he told the meeting that he had forwarded a report of his investigation, along with the photographs, to the MoD. This report went to the UFO project, but they did little more than acknowledge it and thank Edgecombe for his hard work.

This incident was to have unforeseen consequences for the MoD. The Army's prompt and very public actions had been noted by certain crop circle investigators, who took it as a sign that the military were interested in the phenomenon. It was also discovered that the report had been sent to the UFO project, which confirmed in some researchers' minds a link between the two phenomena, when in fact there were many conflicting theories about crop circles.

Another chapter in the annals of UFOs concerns a bizarre story dating from 1990, when a man presented himself at a military base in Stanmore and said that he'd had a dream about an attack at a military base in London. He felt it was a psychic warning. A few weeks later there was a terrorist bomb attack on the base at Stanmore, in northwest London. The Air Force police launched an investigation, but nothing was ever found. Interestingly, 10 years later, the MoD decided to conduct a study on remote viewing, following earlier U.S. programs such as Star Gate, Grill Flame, and Sun Streak. An inconclusive report was written, which was published on the MoD's Website following an FOI request. The MoD was desperately embarrassed about this and did everything it could to avoid using words such as "psychic" in the cover note, hoping the media wouldn't notice. When MoD published this study on their Website on February 23, 2007, the introductory note simply read:

A study was undertaken in 2001–2002 to investigate theories about capabilities to gather information remotely about what people may be seeing and to determine the potential value, if any, of such theories to Defense.

I mention this because it aptly demonstrates how the MoD consistently tried to downplay these subjects with the public and media, sometimes by using dirty tricks to belittle the subject, and sometimes by deliberately using such archaic terms as "UFO spotters" and "flying saucers." This rhetoric was a way for the MoD to at once distance itself from the subject *and* cast doubt on the motives, skill, and intelligence of both researchers and anyone who could possibly be interested in such subjects.

As a humorous side note to all of this, pre-FOI, officials often used to make indiscreet remarks about witnesses and UFO researchers. If, for example, a particularly bizarre sighting was reported, or if the person making the report was somewhat eccentric, a manager might write a note for a more junior official, which would read something like this: "This person is clearly deranged. Please

send him/her our standard reply and let's hope he/she goes away."
Material that is classified can be blacked out, but material that is
simply embarrassing cannot, so none of these remarks could legiti-
mately be erased. This has led to some interesting cases of UFO witnesses and ufologists finding out what the MoD *really* thought about
them, their sightings, and their theories. Post-FOI, MoD officials are
far more wary about this sort of thing, but it's still possible to find
out what they think if you understand the coded way in which they
now write. For example, some UFO files have the title "Persistent
Correspondent," which roughly translates to "this person is a nui-
sance and is causing a lot of unnecessary work."

The reaction to the release of the files was mixed and, ironically, not as enthusiastic as the reaction from the wider public.
Some criticized the MoD for what they felt was a lack of proper
investigation in many of the cases. But much of this stemmed from
the fact that, in many cases, the most likely explanation was found
straight away and the witness received little more than the standard letter explaining the MoD's policy on UFOs and stating that
most sightings had conventional explanations. Others failed to
appreciate that in the shadowy world of government, the paper
trail hardly ever tells the full story. A number of ufologists thought
that the file release program was part of a coordinated government campaign to acclimatize the public to the idea of an extraterrestrial presence, prior to an official announcement that aliens
were visiting the Earth: "Disclosure," as it has been dubbed by the
UFO community (I describe the MoD's release program as "disclosure with a little D"). Others felt that the absence of a smoking-gun
document meant that the whole program was *dis*information. "All
the really good stuff is being held back" was a phrase that was
often used on various blogs, forums, and e-mail lists within the
community. My involvement in the release program, and the fact
that I was inevitably the person to whom the media turned to for a
quote, added fuel to the fire. Indeed, many in the UFO community

believe that I'm still working for the government and that my 2006 resignation was a ruse.

As I have explained, the key motive for the file release was to ease the administrative burden caused by the hundreds of people who were bombarding MoD with FOI requests. This was partly success-ful, as UFO-related FOI requests certainly declined from the levels seen 2005, 2006, and 2007. However, just as this problem receded, another one emerged. The numbers of UFO sightings reported to MoD began to rise exponentially:

- ♂ In 2006, there were 97 reports
- ♂ In 2007, there were 135 reports
- ♂ In 2008, there were 285 reports
- ♂ In 2009, there were 643 reports

Moreover, a larger and larger proportion of these UFO reports were clearly caused by members of the public misidentifying so-called Chinese lanterns, those ubiquitous fire balloons that are increasingly popular at weddings, barbeques, and other social functions. The MoD's corporate irritation with the UFO phenome-non finally seemed to reach a breaking point. After more than 60 years of official research and investigation into the mystery, the Department decided that enough was enough. Effective December 1, 2009, the MoD terminated its UFO project. In an amendment to an existing document in the Freedom of Information section of the MoD Website, titled "How to report a UFO sighting," the news was disseminated in a way that was clearly designed to not attract atten-tion. The document was clearly edited, and contact details were replaced with a brusque announcement stating that "in over fifty years, no UFO report has revealed any evidence of a potential threat to the United Kingdom" and that the "MoD will no longer respond to reported UFO sightings or investigate them."

This was not the end of the story, however. In response to a query from a journalist, the MoD press office made an interesting comment. The quote was published in the *Sun* on January 22, 2009, in a story that ended thusly: "The MoD defended its decision to shut the UFO division. A spokesman said: 'We do not feel there is any military value in reviewing the public's sightings.' The key point is that the quote didn't say there was no military value in reviewing UFO sightings, only that there was no military value in reviewing the *public's* UFO sightings. Where evidence suggests that UK airspace has been penetrated by an unidentified object, this must automatically be of defense interest and would therefore be investigated properly, if only because of the risk of espionage or terrorism. Indeed, I am sure that sightings from pilots and uncorrelated targets tracked on radar will continue to be looked at, albeit outside of a formally constituted UFO project. That's the implication of the comment from the MoD press office. On the one hand, this is understandable, and it's clear that the vast majority of sightings reported by the public were misidentifications of ordinary phenomena or objects (largely, in recent years, those Chinese lanterns). On the other hand, it's patronizing to assume that no useful information could ever come from the public, and it's just plain unscientific to ignore data.

The relationship between the MoD, the UFO lobby, and the phenomenon itself is full of ironies, a prime example of which is the fact that the release of information was seen as part of a cover-up. And what about the fact that the opening of the UFO files was followed by the closing of the UFO project? Or the fact that the Ufologists who dreamt of a day when they could see the MoD's UFO files were disappointed when their dreams came true? Or the fact that the MoD ceased the investigation into UFOs just as the sightings reached near-record levels? If these ironies seem bizarre, perhaps they are to be expected given the nature of the UFO phenomenon itself.

I'm grateful to have had the opportunity to look at the UFO phenomenon as part of my government work. It gives me a perspective on the subject that few others have had. Though I no longer work for the MoD, I continue to take a close interest in UFOs. Through my media work, I do my best to keep this subject in the public eye. These are exciting times. As of this writing, numerous countries are releasing their UFO files, and we're seeing increased mainstream media coverage of the subject. I don't know what further developments or revelations lie ahead, but I suspect we're in for quite a ride.

Doubt Beyond Reason

By Gordon Chism

My childhood was spent in Reno, Nevada, during the Second World War. I was captivated by the romance of fighter planes and pilots. I could name every plane in the sky and give its type, top speed, and manufacture, boring to tears anyone who would listen. I was, however, completely unaware of the flying saucer sightings in the late 1940s and the early 1950s. The only contact I had with the subject was through the movies. There was a string of scary visitors-from-outer-space films featuring sinister plots to abduct people, vaporize army tanks and infantry, and take over the world. I didn't take any of this seriously. I thought the outer space movies were very similar to the vampire and werewolf movies—anything to provide a little relief from all the westerns. Whenever the subject of UFOs did surface, I had complete contempt for it. Being a teenager, I knew everything. I knew that the nearest star was about four light-years away. I also knew it was impossible to get anywhere close to the speed of light, and a trip to that star in one of our rocket ships would be a journey of thousands of years.

I had two really good friends in high school—Bill Rose and Ken Taber—and together we would often hunt for jackrabbits, go waterskiing, and mess around with cars. Ken's father had a duck-hunting cabin at Stillwater, a tiny community consisting solely of a few cabins and a country store on the edge of the Carson Sink, a couple of miles out of Fallon, Nevada, and about an hour east of Reno. Running out of places to go, the Carson River formed a series of small lakes, cattail channels, and shallow mud flats—a great site for hunting carp with bows and arrows.

In the summer of 1958, we had just graduated from high school and would be heading to college in the fall. We organized a carp-hunting expedition with the three of us and my younger brother, Will. We were including Will because we had commandeered his '36 Plymouth coupe, which he was planning to restore. We strong-armed him into agreeing to make a swamp buggy out of it. We took off the body, fenders, bumpers, headlights, and anything else that wasn't necessary to make the car run, in an effort to get its weight down to where it could drive across the mud flats without getting stuck. The Plymouth became an insect-like concoction of frame, engine, and bare wheels—it was a strange sight flying down the highway. Bill took the wheel of the Plymouth, and the rest of us followed in Bill's station wagon. Our expedition to Stillwater was underway. The next day we were off to the mud flats. We were anxious to see if the old Plymouth could get us to virgin carp-hunting ponds. The Carson Sink is half nature preserve, half duck-hunting area. Division Road is a raised, straight gravel road that delineates the two halves—hunting to the west, nature preserve to the east. We drove out Division Road to about the middle of the sink and turned off onto the mud flats. The old Plymouth did better than we expected. It went anywhere we wanted to go, with no complaints.

We spent the rest of the day bow-hunting carp. We would sneak up on a pond, looking for the fish sunning themselves in the shallows. The humps of their backs stuck out of the brownish, opaque water as much as two inches (51 mm). The carp would sense our approach and start into deeper water. We waded out into the pond about knee-deep, paying attention to the water's surface. If we looked closely we could see small ripples on the surface as the fish moved off. If we got close enough to panic them, they would thrash away at great speed. We had to aim about six inches (152 mm) ahead of the wake and let our arrows fly. At times the fish would try to sneak past us, going the other way. We could feel them brush against our bare legs as they tried to escape. It was challenging, primal, and utterly absorbing.

When the spell of the hunt was broken, we realized that the sun had set. Our swamp buggy had no lights so we decided to head back to the cabin. As we were driving along Division Road in the gathering dusk, Bill called from the back of the buggy that we should speed up a bit. There was a car behind us with its high beams on and it was gaining on us. There was a pause, then Bill shouted, "Never mind, the car just took off!" We stopped the buggy and looked back up the road. There was a bright light about 200 yards (183 meters) back and 50 feet (15 meters) above the road. It looked to be about 20 feet (6 meters) in diameter and slightly oblong on the horizontal plane. It would slowly gain in brightness until it illuminated the road beneath it, and then slowly dim again to a soft glow. We stared in dumb disbelief. What was it? It made no noise. It certainly wasn't any kind of aircraft that we were familiar with (we all considered ourselves to be aircraft aficionados). It definitely had mass, but it didn't seem to have a hard surface; the plasma-like glow was fuzzy at the edges. As we tried to regain our composure, the thing started to move.

It moved slowly and precisely in spite of a slight evening breeze. It stayed about 200 yards (183 meters) away in a parallel path alongside of us. This situation was quickly developing a major "creep factor." It seemed to be aware of us—we were certainly aware of it! It was moving in the direction of the cabin. We decided to return to the cabin, get the station wagon, and drive back out and watch this thing—whatever it was—as long as we could. We grabbed our .22s from the cabin, jumped into the station wagon, and headed out to Division Road to the place we saw it last. It was gone. We looked all around—still nothing. There was a collective sigh of relief, and we started joking loudly and pushing each other around. It was over.

Then my brother Will suddenly shouted, "There it is!" It was slowly rising from behind a line of poplar trees bordering a farm field a little more than 100 yards (91 meters) from us. It stopped about

10 feet (3.4 meters) above the treetops and remained there, motion-less. We watched in stunned silence waiting for its next move. Then, at the base of the stand of trees, a bright red ball about 2 or 3 feet (.6 or .9 meters) in diameter began to rise straight up and apparently right into the thing. We were speechless. Then it was on the move again, heading south of us at about 5 to 10 miles (8 or 16 kilome-ters) per hour. We tried to follow it but ran out of roads. Because we were less than a mile (1.6 kilometers) from the cabin, we decided to return, climb up onto the roof, and watch it from there. We still kept our .22s close at hand: this situation was too weird to face unarmed.

By now the sky was completely dark. Transfixed and in silence, we watched the thing as it continued to cycle through its 30-second "dim-then-bright" pattern. In the bright portion of its cycle, it illu-minated the ground below it and the thinly overcast sky above. It proceeded south, then made an abrupt 90-degree turn to the west about a half a mile (.8 kilometers) away. At this point we had been watching for about 45 minutes. The object continued to move in its precise manner and then stopped. It was as if it was staring straight at us. We all leaned forward with rapt attention—suddenly it was right over us! In unison we reflexively leapt from the cabin roof—.22s, elbows, and knees flying in all directions. We picked ourselves up and frantically searched the sky in all directions. Gone! It was gone! For the next couple of hours we peered out the windows, periodically stepping outside to sweep the sky, but to no avail. As a group, we typically viewed everything in life with a cynical sense of humor, but that night nobody broke the tension with a joke. We were exhausted from the long day of carp hunting and our strange encounter had left us shaken and drained. We took one last look around outside and went to sleep.

The next morning we were quiet and thoughtful. What had we witnessed? We were sure we knew everything, especially about flying technology. This was so out of bounds that we were unable to come up with any plausible explanation. It was science fiction! We went into Fallon and asked a gas station attendant if anyone had reported seeing a light 20-plus feet (6-plus meters) in diameter flying about 100 feet (30 meters) off the ground. We got that look of "you're-putting-me-on-and-I-am-not-taking-the-bait." He then asked if we had been drinking.

During the next several weeks I kept going over and over our experience. Was it a group hallucination? Had we spent so much time and energy together that we created our own reality? Then there was the thing itself. Was it solid? I still couldn't say for sure. Even when it was right on top of us I didn't hear a sound. The haunting feeling that this thing was from another world kept returning. Had we been witness to an extraterrestrial intelligence? Had this object come light years through outer space to pull a frat-house prank on four teenagers? None of it made any sense. My once-comprehensible world was now in total chaos.

I was full of questions, but every time I tried to discuss what had happened, I was thwarted. There was a strong force-field of denial building around our friends and families. Talking of possible visitors from outer space made everyone uncomfortable. My parents skillfully deflected the topic. Even my brother Will cut me off with, "We saw a big, bright light. Let it go." I quickly learned to keep the experience to myself. Nobody really wanted to hear about it, and if I didn't bring the subject up, my social life was far more comfortable.

Stories of UFO sightings occasionally showed up in the press at that time. In the early 1960s, I saw a magazine with a picture on its cover of something that resembled what we had seen at Stillwater. It had been taken somewhere in the Midwest with more than 100 people watching. I poured over the article. We weren't crazy after all. We had not been hallucinating. During the next few years, I noticed more reports of airline pilots seeing the same sort of thing we had witnessed in 1958. I pointed out to my friends how similar these reports were to what we had experienced at Stillwater, but I only received a forget-about-it dismissiveness. They still wanted nothing to do with it. They couldn't emotionally afford to include our experience in their worldview. They couldn't reconcile it with their beliefs. However, I *knew* what I had seen, and I was determined to find out what was going on. I soon discovered that there was, in a myriad of books and articles, overwhelming evidence that aliens had been visiting our planet for hundreds, possibly thousands of years. More than one million sober, intelligent people have witnessed UFOs. Sightings by scientists, engineers, astronauts, pilots, presidents (Kennedy, Reagan, and Carter, to name a few), and even populations of entire cities have been documented.

When I tell my story today, the most prevalent response is that if UFOs were indeed real, the press would have uncovered the truth by now. I reply that newspapers and magazines have printed literally hundreds of stories that blow the lid off the UFO conundrum. Upon hearing that they usually regale me with one of their own stories of a UFO "sighting." In it, they typically describe a dusk or dawn scene in which a bright light streaks across the sky. They think they are witnessing a UFO, only to read in the paper the next day that a missile launch had strayed off course or that the space shuttle had returned to earth. To them, their experience is proof that UFOs don't exist. With a condescending smile, they then dismiss me and the entire subject altogether. This kind of denial undoubtedly has many facets, but I believe there are three major factors at work here— *status*, *consensus*, and *faith*.

Status

Everyone is concerned about status. Even Mother Theresa was concerned about her status with God. Outside of survival, status is our strongest motivator. Status is our handle on life, our coordinates within our community, and the underlying structure that both supports and guides our social interactions. With status we have self-confidence, the best mating possibilities, the best food, and the most creature comforts. Without it, we have self-doubt and depression. This is neither right nor wrong; it is just the way we are programmed. Essentially we are software-driven to keep our status intact—or, better yet, to reach the next status level.

An acquaintance of mine bristles at the word status. She maintains that she will have nothing to do with it. However, if you probe more deeply, you will find out that her house is in a fashionable rural area on two acres with a large garden, that she drives a Prius, and that she wears hemp clothing. She has accumulated all the necessary status symbols to be at the top of the local "green status ladder," yet denies that status is a motivating factor in her life. So it is with most of us—even when we deny its influence, status continues to motivate us on a subconscious level.

Everyone daydreams about winning a big chunk of status and respect. The adolescent boy shooting hoops in his backyard can be heard impersonating a sports announcer: "Five seconds left! The championship is on the line! We're two points behind! Bobby has the ball! He breaks free, but he is well behind the three-point line! He shoots—and scores! The crowd goes wild!" We all lust after status. We spend billions on lottery tickets. We will do foolish and even desperate things to get more of it. Securing and bolstering our status is a genetically programmed imperative that has us frantically competing against one another to acquire wealth, power, and prestige. When someone states that he or she believes that UFOs are real, most others see this person as automatically having a lower status. The majority of us cannot afford to challenge the official cultural stance concerning UFOs. If we do, we open ourselves to censure, rejection, and even verbal attack.

Consensus

We have all noticed that every culture has its trends, fads, and movements. *Consensus* is the general agreement and group solidarity of a belief or sentiment. When the cognoscenti embrace something, we automatically follow because we want both their status and their acceptance. In a psychological experiment that illustrated this point, a subject was led into a room with what appeared to be four other participants. The subject didn't know that the other "subjects" were actually in on the experiment. The group was shown four lines projected on a screen and then asked to pick out the longest line. (The lines were of similar length, but still different enough to tell which one was the longest.) The four other members enthusiastically endorsed line #3, even though it was clearly not the longest one. The experimenter then polled the group one by one, the subject last of all. After all the people in the room emphatically agreed that line #3 was the longest, the subject concurred and named line #3 as the longest, even though he could see that it was not. All of this illustrates my point that group consensus is a very powerful thing, indeed. We know that if we do not agree with the group, it will withhold acceptance and status from us. It's very easy to see how this is applicable to the UFO question. If people roll their eyes and dismiss us when we talk about UFOs, we instinctively know that we have stepped over that invisible line. We feel the sting of rejection and the implied suggestion that we ought to rethink our convictions if we want to be accepted. It seems that we need consensus, acceptance, and approval even more than we need the truth.

Faith

Faith is a belief or set of beliefs that does not depend on logical proof or empirical evidence. We have faith in ourselves, our family, our religion, our nation, and even our favorite sports team. Through faith, we establish a unified set of unquestioned beliefs— our convictions. These convictions are not open for debate. Having convictions enables us to reduce any incoming data to a mentally digestible scale. Without faith, without convictions, we would be in a constant state of energy-draining overload and confusion.

We have all witnessed a religious or political argument in which both sides obdurately restate their beliefs and refuse to listen to a word from the other side. Through faith, both are certain that they are right and the other is wrong; neither can give an inch (25 mm). If either side were to admit the possibility that they were in error, they would have to go through a long and painful rebuilding of their convictions. As you can see, once they are in place, our faith-based convictions hardly ever change. Indeed, some people would rather die than change: think of those who have sacrificed their lives in revolution or battle rather than change their faith-based convictions. It is my belief that we are genetically programmed to believe that we humans are special—the masters of the universe—and when we are confronted with evidence to the contrary, we instinctively take cover in our faith-based convictions that keep us from having to acknowledge any self-doubt and its attendant loss of status.

Denial

Denial is the refusal to grant the truth of a statement or allegation. Denial is also the censoring and withholding *from ourselves* any information that is at odds with our belief system and that of our milieu. It is a sort of personal assistant that blocks calls and deletes e-mails we can't handle. Even after Galileo demonstrated that the earth circled the sun, it was more than 100 years before that hypothesis was officially accepted as fact, and another 100 years after that before the general public came on board. We hold fast to our belief systems and engage denial when necessary to keep the faith. To change one's belief system as an adult is more than a challenge—it is all but impossible. And so it goes with UFOs. People who are raised in families that dismiss UFOs, and who ridicule those who do believe, generally cannot entertain even the *possibility* that they might exist. Indeed, the vast majority of these people, even when presented with logical arguments, photos, videos, and thousands of unimpeachable eyewitness accounts, will flat-out deny the existence of UFOs. Our old, programmed, human-centric view of the universe will not allow us to embrace the idea that we are not alone.

When Captain Cook discovered the Hawaiian Islands, he moored his ship in deep water and went ashore in a longboat. When he and his entourage landed, the natives exhibited a great deal of excitement over the longboat. They couldn't believe what a marvel it was. Through his interpreter, Cook asked the natives that, given how impressed they were with the longboat, what did they think of his large boat out in the bay, his ship? The natives literally could not see the ship *as* a boat. When pressed to explain what they saw, the natives guessed that it was an island or even a low cloud. Their minds simply could not admit a technology so far in advance of their own experience. And so it is with us. When we are confronted with UFOs, we can't understand what we are seeing. If it is true that we are being visited by beings in possession of a far more advanced technology than our own, we will instinctively hide in denial. People who reflexively deny the reality of UFOs would do well to imagine themselves as 18th-century Hawaiian natives seeing that tall ship for the first time.

I believe that all of these things—our fear of losing *status*, our tendency to follow the group *consensus*, and our use of *faith* and *denial* to override logic—have enabled us to reject the existence of aliens and UFOs. Even when a UFO witness comes forward to report his sighting (and less than one out of 10 people who encounter a UFO ever actually report it), he finds that his friends and coworkers ridicule and reject him. Even his own family members—even the ones who were there with him!—do not believe him. It's clear that we can't handle the truth.

There is good news, however. When Galileo figured out that we were not the center of the universe, humanity was humbled. This humility eventually opened the door to the new paradigm of *rational deduction* to describe the world around us. We were forced to reevaluate our mechanisms of perception. If we had been wrong about Earth's place in the cosmos, what else were we wrong about? This question was just one of many that led to the Enlightenment— the age of reason that gave birth to the sciences. We then had a much more accurate way to explore and understand the world, instead of relying on superstitions, spirits, and gods. So, humility can open the door to open-mindedness and a spirit of inquiry, despite the pressures of the collective, the need for status, and the urge to deny.

Today, hundreds of years later, we need to get beyond our natural tendency to reject and deny the idea that we are not alone. If we are to survive in the long run, we must move away from our reflexive instincts and instead embrace this same spirit of inquiry and brave quest for truth that we first latched onto all those many hundreds of years ago. We need to start thinking of ourselves in a larger context as citizens of our galaxy, not just as stewards of this beautiful planet. I believe that if an educated person were to set aside, even temporarily, his or her various inner and outer influences—the denial, the pre-existing beliefs and convictions, and that urge for status—and instead read some serious UFO history, he or she could only conclude that *yes, we have visitors.*

An Alien Intervention

By Jim Moroney

Dr. John Mack, a Pulitzer Prize–winning psychiatrist from Harvard University, was a leading authority on the phenomenon of alleged alien abductions. Mack initially approached the phenomenon with a belief that it was some sort of emerging mass psychosis or disturbance state. Ultimately, however, he concluded that the vast majority of the abductees he had interviewed were psychologically healthy individuals who were simply trying to contend with an extraordinary experience. Mack reported that abductees experienced such intensely powerful emotions during hypnotic regression that even a determined skeptic would find it difficult to deny that *something* extraordinary and emotionally shattering had taken place. Based on the large sample of people he interviewed, he concluded that the abduction experience is a worldwide phenomenon:

People of sound mind, hundreds of thousands if not millions of people from all over the world, not just in the Western countries, but on other continents and among indigenous people, are having what seem like authentic, incontrovertible encounters with some sort of beings that apparently enter into our physical world and communicate to us about ourselves, and seem in some way to be connecting with us (quoted in John E. Mack's *Passport to the Cosmos*).

With Mack's research and findings in mind, we must be prepared to listen to those people who have had direct experiential contact with the aliens if we hope to answer the most fundamental question of who they are and what their purpose is. Of course it's a difficult assignment, given that information can be easily obfuscated by misleading reports, but I hope that the narratives presented here will help begin to unveil some of the greater mysteries. However, as with any serious inquiry into any field of knowledge, the more we know, the more questions we have.

It is my contention that humanity is fast approaching a crucial turning point in its evolutionary development. Our surging technological accomplishments and propensity to destroy each other have simply outpaced our lagging spiritual development. Unfortunately, our collective actions have taken on a life of their own and created enough momentum to ensure that a crisis is now inevitable. It seems unlikely that we will be able to steer the ship of humanity away from the brink of this impending catastrophe without some form of intervention. Fortunately for us, something or someone in this universe has been watching this planet and decided they must do something to help.

It is my belief that the aliens (if that is what we want to call them) have decided upon a complex and multifaceted intervention plan to help us save us from ourselves. Although many details of this plan remain shrouded in mystery, we can be certain that a better relationship with ourselves and these beings will be of utmost importance going forward. A human-alien relationship will perforce be atypical, and, given our spiritual deficiencies, potentially very, very difficult. It leaves me wondering if this contact is occurring far sooner, maybe thousands of years earlier, than it was supposed to. As the encounters themselves so vividly demonstrate, the aliens clearly want to control not only how these encounters unfold, but also the very memories of the abductees. This is a sobering thought.

Ideally we will be able to develop a better understanding of who—or what—the aliens are. Because the world they inhabit is so fundamentally different from our own, however, it seems unlikely that we will ever be able to fully understand them. Sobering as that reality is, I'm convinced that we must at least *try* to understand them. Our future and the future of this world depend on it. And if we're to avoid destroying ourselves, we may well need to redefine who and what *we* are. Shattering our limited perceptual view of this reality will be the easy part, relatively speaking, but the development of a greater human understanding of our true place in the universe will be the hard part.

Creating a peaceful world will require some hard choices on our part. The changes required are almost unimaginable. If there is to be a new world, it will be our generation that will have the greatest difficulty living in it. Yet all is not lost. We have an opportunity, a wonderful, glorious opportunity to make changes. We can educate ourselves about these beings and how they have decided to interact with us; we can review the groundbreaking work of psychiatrists and psychologists; and, most importantly, we can listen to and read about the experiences of others. These remarkable experiences challenge our most fundamental beliefs about this subject and, indeed, about ourselves. I certainly believe that it would be in our best interest to listen to them before we pass judgement either way.

The Experiences

Abduction on North Canol Road

To respect the privacy of "Kevin" we will not share his real name.

I first met Martin Jasek at a UFO conference in Edmonton, Alberta, Canada. When I came across Martin's investigation into this abduction story I felt compelled to share it with others. Martin first met Kevin on July 8, 2000, while attending a UFO conference in St. Paul, Alberta. He had just finished a presentation on Yukon UFO sightings when a quiet and reserved man cautiously approached him. The man introduced himself and explained he had lived in Ross River, Yukon, where he had heard and seen some pretty strange things. Kevin provided his contact information before returning to his humble small town in Alberta. Martin later travelled to North Canol Road to take photographs of the area that Kevin had described in his story; the photographs were later matched up with Kevin's blow-by-blow description. Martin described Kevin as a very honest, sincere, and reserved individual, "not at all the type looking for attention," and went on to add, "I have no reason not to believe his entire story."

On a cool and damp September morning in Ross River in the Yukon, Kevin eagerly jumped on his motorbike. He was looking forward to spending three days moose hunting and fishing in the Sheldon Lake and Macpass area. He was also excited at the prospect of joining two other friends the following day. The plan was to stay in a small trailer in Dewhurst Creek. The isolation of the area made having this trailer extremely convenient. Kevin left just as the temperatures dropped and the skies opened up with first a drizzle of rain, then a deluge of water. Being exposed to the elements on a motorbike for a few hours is, of course, a much different experience than driving a car. By the time he arrived at Gravel Creek, he knew he needed to stop at a friend's cabin to put on warmer clothes. It seemed that that Mother Nature would nurture the forest with life-giving water for most of the day.

The sun had barely peeked out from behind the clouds and was just going down behind the mountains when he arrived at the somewhat dilapidated trailer. It wasn't much, but it was warm and dry and just the thing he needed in order to rest and warm up from his long, cold ride. He started a fire, cooked supper, and went straight to bed, dreaming about the hunting adventure the next day. During the night the rain stopped, leaving the forest damp and wet. The higher elevations of the mountains were capped with their white winter hats as the snow reflected the early morning sunlight.

Now fully rested and awake, he carefully and methodically loaded his gear and gun on the motorbike before starting down Canol Road. The sun was bright and the air was cool and clear. He took his time avoiding the potholes that were semi-hidden by the shadows of the trees stretching across the road. As he drove down the otherwise peaceful road he began to feel uneasy for some reason. He couldn't explain the feeling—it was unlike anything he had experienced before, and it grew in intensity. Because he had learned to trust his intuition and knew it was a valuable tool for survival in the wilderness, he began to anxiously scan the trees and hillsides for movement. Unfortunately his morning coffee was now working its way through his system and his bladder was sounding the alarm, so he stopped and got off the bike to relieve himself by the roadside.

Standing in front of the motorbike and staring at the tableau of the wild mountains in front of him, a movement out of the corner of his eye caught his attention. At first glance it appeared to be a low-flying airplane about the size of a DC-3, approximately 450 yards (411 meters) away. It was dangerously low, about 40 yards (37 meters) above the ground, and moving very slowly. As he gazed at the plane, he realized to his astonishment that it had no tail or wings. As Kevin watched the object, whatever it was, move slowly through the valley, it occurred to him that he should get a picture of it. After all, his camera was just inside his jacket in his shirt pocket and was easy to get to. Inexplicably, however, a sudden calmness washed over him and he thought better of it. *It's no big deal, don't worry about it. You don't have to take a picture*, he thought to himself. This seemed strange to him, but even stranger was the realization the object made no sound. To his disbelief the object appeared to partially dematerialize and then return to solid form as it moved above the rugged valley floor.

He knew it was a UFO and felt it did not want to be seen. Instinctively he crouched down on the road, hiding behind the long roadside grass. The craft silently floated and disappeared behind a cone-shaped hill. He jumped to his feet and tried to see if it would come out from behind the hill. As he stood there in the grass, he heard someone close a heavy trunk lid behind him. Somebody else had apparently come up the road, and he needed to tell them what he just saw. Half running and half walking along the edge of the gravel, he peered around the bend in the road. To his shock and horror he came face-to-face with two 5-foot-tall (1.5 meter-tall) grey creatures in what appeared to be blue jumpsuits. They had two arms and two legs, but their heads were large and insectile, with triangular faces and large eyes. He thought to himself, *They're not little green men— they're grasshopper people!*

Suddenly the one on the left raised an object that looked like a flashlight, which emitted a bright beam of light in his direction. Instantaneously, he lost all sense of time: "Nothing existed but me, like I was pulled from reality. There was the most absolute quiet I ever imagined. I was really scared and tried to yell 'No!' but all that came out was a gnarly [sic] growl." Time seemed to stand still as darkness engulfed him. There was a sensation of being stretched, as if his feet were on the ground and his upper body were 20 feet (6 meters) above the ground. He then felt as though he were hurtling skyward at a terrific speed. The next thing he knew he was standing on the road; the beings were nowhere to be seen. It occurred to him that he should get out of there before they "got to him" again. He turned around to grab his motorbike but it wasn't where he had left it—it was on the other side of the gravel road! Panicking, he rushed over and jumped on the bike, only to realize the keys were not in the ignition. He always left the keys in the ignition so he wouldn't looe them while hunting in the bush. (The risk of losing keys is far greater than anyone stealing your vehicle in this remote area of the world.) Stunned, he realized that he had had the keys in his hand the whole time. He started the bike and hightailed it back to the relative safety of the trailer.

"I was feeling scared and amazed at the same time and then noticed that all the shadows of the trees were now pointing in a different direction than they had when I had left in the morning. About 15 minutes later I was at the trailer. Half an hour later it was dark. I thought, *No way, I left here only an hour ago—what's going on?* I was really confused. I said to myself, *I'm not telling anybody about this, I'll just forget the whole thing.*" As he put on a pot of coffee he suddenly heard a soft humming sound that seemed to come from above the trailer. After about 10 minutes it stopped, but he continued to struggle with an ominous feeling that whoever or whatever it was, was still outside. Feelings of loneliness and vulnerability sunk in, and sleep eluded him.

As he sat there and sipped on his coffee he began having disturbing and troubling flashbacks. He recalled being in a dream-like state, watching scenery flash by underneath as if he were flying. He remembered moving above the beautiful green mountains, blue rivers, and dark primeval forests. "I became aware of other sounds that seemed to wake me up. I opened my eyes and could see nothing but black, a very deep and inky blackness." As he stared into the profound blackness, it appeared to be fading or pulling back. As he refocused his eyes, he realised that he had been staring into coal black eyes that were framed by a triangular, alien face. "I could hear in my mind a voice saying, 'There is nothing to worry about.' I could hear him talking in my mind."

The bug-like alien beings from the road were nowhere to be found, but there were three or four grey aliens moving about. Kevin asked the one nearest to him if they were going to perform experiments on him. The alien replied that they had already been done! Despite the bizarre scene, Kevin felt surprisingly well, except for a strange sensation in his hands. He kept rubbing them together as he scanned the strange environment around him. The same alien asked if he would like to see his home planet. Kevin eagerly agreed and walked over to a window where there was a machine that resembled a large photocopier. "He asked me not to touch it. I replied, 'Don't worry; I'm not touching anything in here.' He then said, 'That bright white star is your home.' I didn't know anything about astronomy at the time, but I always thought Earth was blue, so right away I thought, *He's lying*. He also explained to me about space, the stars, etcetera, but I can't remember any [specifics] now." I suspect that the aliens were actually showing him other planets besides Earth that were capable of sustaining life. These life-giving planets were represented as bright, star-like objects in space, which explains Kevin's initial confusion when the alien pointed at Earth as a bright object on the map.

The alien asked Kevin if he would like to go on a trip. He sensed that this offer was a great honor, but he refused, feeling that the time just wasn't right. When Kevin was told he would have to forget the entire experience, he was very disappointed. The first part of the experience was terrifying, but once he was with them he found them to be friendly and helpful. Even their odd appearance didn't bother him anymore. In fact, they felt more like old friends. Kevin was then offered a clear glass of a yellow liquid and was asked to drink it; he was told it would help him forget everything. When he told them that he did not want to forget such an incredible experience, they insisted that it was for his own good. Seeing that they were momentarily distracted, Kevin took only three small sips and put the glass down. That was the last thing he remembered before he found himself standing on the road beside his motorbike.

Kevin never felt very comfortable speaking of his experience, but felt that it was important that someone knew about it. "The next day [after the experience] I met up with the other two guys and never said anything to them. Every time I tell someone (and it's not that often), I feel like I just broke a promise I made to [the aliens] that I wouldn't tell anybody." Admittedly Kevin's experience is not as well-known as some of the other more celebrated encounter stories (Betty and Barney Hill, for example), but it vividly illustrates

the many different types of experiences, both positive and negative, that abductees are often subjected to. We will likely never
know what happened to the other two insectile aliens that he first
observed on the road. Were there two different species that were
working together in this case? Or, were these aliens "shapeshifters,"
capable of changing their form or altering their appearance? Again,
more unknowns in an already baffling story.

Tellingly, the initial experience of the actual abduction was
frightening to Kevin, but paradoxically he later states that this very
experience left him with feelings of comfort and friendship. It seems
reasonable that intelligent beings capable of emotions would want
to connect with us in some way, yet how do we account for the fact
that they took him by force and performed tests on him? The aliens
also seemed to be aware of what memories would be beneficial for
Kevin and what memories would not. However, it would seem that
their systems and procedures are far from flawless, as Kevin was
able to recall portions of his experience, despite his captors' earnest
wishes to the contrary.

A Mass Encounter

Another astounding encounter occurred on a hot summer day
in September 16, 1994, Ruwa, Zimbabwe. A total of 62 children of
various ethnicities, ranging from 5 to 12 years of age, from a private primary school in Ruwa were playing in a field during their
mid-morning break when they saw an object come down at the
edge of the field, about 109 yards (100 meters) from where they
were standing. A small alien being appeared on top of the object;
it walked a little way across the rough ground, seemed to become
aware of the children, and then disappeared. It then reappeared by
the object, which took off very rapidly and disappeared. The being
was dressed in a tight-fitting black suit, which was "shiny," according to one observant 11-year-old girl. It also had a long, scrawny
neck, huge eyes "like rugby balls" in a pale face, and black hair
falling below its shoulders. Some of the children reported that the
being had relayed a message to them telepathically during the brief

encounter. The message contained a warning that we were harming our planet with our technology and that the world was going to end! One of the young children said that the being seemed "astonished" by the children. The consistency of the reports from the children as well as the physical appearance and apparent telepathic abilities of the beings, provide further support to the idea that these beings are concerned for humanity. This extraordinary event still remains one of the most significant, well-documented, and intensely investigated mass encounters on record. Some of Dr. John Mack's interviews with the children can be found on Youtube.com.

My Story

Now this essay becomes all too personal. My own story starts on the cool summer morning of August 9, 1987, when I pulled into Deacon's Corner Truck Stop outside of Winnipeg, Manitoba, Canada. It was about 2 a.m. and there were already a number of rigs parked around the friendly little diner for the night. For some unknown reason I had an intensely uneasy feeling of foreboding that I just could not shake. I felt that I needed to be in a place where people could see me, so instead of parking in an out-of-the way, dark corner of the lot, I found a space conveniently right in front of the diner. I pulled in, grabbed my blanket from the back seat, and slid over to the passenger side. I was now able to push the seat all the way back, stretch my legs, and close my eyes. The chilly night air combined with the incessant attacks of local mosquitoes persuaded me to roll up my windows.

I was lying on my back with my eyes closed when a truck seemed to be pulling into the parking lot. It seemed awfully close as the bright headlights seared their way into my car. Strangely, the lights seemed now to be moving over the top of the car and coming through my sunroof. The air went dead, as if its density had suddenly changed. I could hear the engine of the truck behind me struggling. Two things happened simultaneously: I was overcome by sudden paralysis, and I felt an overwhelming sense of abject terror. The fear was sudden, stark, and totally unexpected. It seemed to come out of nowhere, a terror so raw and so crushing that I was unable to think clearly about what was actually transpiring.

I sensed that something was above my car, and the hair on my arms began to rise. Whatever it was must have been emitting an intense electromagnetic field. Then something brushed against my right arm. Even though my eyes were still closed, my other senses told me that something was in there with me! But how could it have passed through the solid windows and walls of the car? (Remember that I had closed all the windows.) It seemed impossible, but there wasn't another explanation.

The gentle movement against my arm suddenly stopped, and there was a sense of expectancy in the air, almost as though someone were waiting for me to do something. It occurred to me that my life might well depend on what I did next. At this point I still hadn't opened my eyes; I didn't think I could handle seeing some kind of creature peering at me thru the windshield while I was paralyzed. As well, I didn't want to lose whatever small amount of self-control I was clinging to and thus do something stupid that could jeopardize my life. All the while, I was struggling against a terror so intense that it threatened to completely override my rational, conscious mind. Nonetheless, I realized that my only option was to do *something* to show that I meant them—whoever or whatever they were—no harm and was more than willing to communicate with them. But, as in a nightmare, I found that I couldn't move my mouth! The extraordinary amount of force I felt restraining me suggested that they were very worried about my reaction. The situation was deteriorating rapidly. *Maybe I can slowly unlock the door and open it*, I thought. Maybe that would convey to them that I was willing to let them come in and talk to me, that I was no threat. With immense mental and physical effort, I managed to slowly move my right arm that endless few inches and unlock the door. It was so exhausting that the moment I succeeded, my arm dropped like a thousand-pound (454 kg) lead weight. I immediately felt a sensation of pressure around my head, as if some kind of band were being tightened—not an actual, physical band, but some kind of energy force that was bearing down on my skull. Strangely, as the pressure increased, I felt my consciousness drift further and further into a state of deep relaxation. The fear was dissipating, but if I put up any kind of resistance to the pressure, it caused an immediate and painful throbbing.

At this point, the memories become jumbled and disconnected. I was lying in a strange position and could hear an echo of myself screaming, but there was no pain. I was lying down and could feel something touch me behind my right ear, sending what felt like an electrical shock into my brain. I felt that whatever had touched me was both mechanical and alive. I could feel waves of energy traveling throughout my brain, branching out along specific neural pathways, when suddenly I was back in the car. The paralysis was over as soon as it had started, and the strange lights moved off to the right.

It wasn't until months later that I was able to recall, while under hypnosis, what had actually happened to me after I unlocked the car door. I remembered feeling myself moving forward and upward out of the car seat. The movement was accompanied by an excruciating pain, as if every fiber in my body were being torn apart. For a moment, it felt as though I were actually being ripped to pieces. The searing pain was agonizing. I wanted to scream but was unable to open my mouth. Then, just as abruptly as the pain started, it stopped, and I was standing next to my car inside a circular, amphitheatre-type of room with tiered steps. Each step in the tier was about 5 inches (127 mm) high and 2 feet (.6 meters) deep, which would be rather odd step spacing for humans. On the steps stood six stoic, identical-looking beings, all dressed in a kind of uniform. They had the typical large heads that many contactees have described, and stood about 4-and-a-half feet (1.4 meters) tall. They stared intently at me with large, blue eyes.

Despite the fact that I was clearly in some form of hypnotic trance at the time, the searing pain and fear I experienced was very raw, and very real. I wanted to make sure they didn't do anything that was going to kill me accidently. I felt that they had acted callously in causing me so much pain, and so I started screaming at them: "You could have used the door! I unlocked the thing for you! I did all of this so that I can *talk* to you guys, and you *hurt* me? What do you think you're doing!?" Upon which, one of the beings stepped forward and asked, "What do you need doors for?"

What did we need doors for? My surprise at hearing this spoken in perfect English was lost in the jaw-dropping strangeness of the response. My God—how was I going to communicate with these beings if the cultural gap was so huge that we didn't even have *doors* in common? Once again I became angry and indignant, scolding them about human rights, when suddenly a being stepped forward, and in the next instant I was completely calm again. It was obvious that they had the ability to directly influence, if not completely control, my emotional state. I then calmly asked them if the alien being who contacted me during my meditation a month previous was there. I thought her name was Althenia, and I sensed she was on the ship. There was a split second of hesitation as they quickly glanced at each other and then burst out laughing. The oppressive tension of the moment was suddenly broken by their outrageous, uncontrolled belly laughter. They were practically holding onto each other. I wondered what they thought was so funny, and then correctly guessed that I got the name wrong. I said, "Okay, go ahead and laugh at me, I'm just the stupid human." One of them, still struggling for composure, said, "No, no, it's not you, her name is_____." (I am still unable to remember her name.) When she had contacted me during my meditation, she must have already been planning this encounter. I now suspect that she gave them a stern briefing on how she had contacted me, how important it was, what they needed to do, how they needed to do it, when they needed to do it, and so on. They must have thought it amusing that the being in charge of their training was unable to provide me with her name in a way I could remember. Heck, maybe I insulted her accidentally by calling her "bubble head" in their language.

Two of the beings told me to come with them. With one walking in front and one behind, I was escorted to what appeared to be a shower facility. Inside the chamber, but fully clothed, I was subjected to a blast of light combined with something else that I couldn't identify. Although it was certainly uncomfortable, I was relieved that I didn't have to remove my clothes. I assumed that it was some kind of decontamination chamber. Next, we walked down a hallway. I noticed a certain automatic compliance in my own reactions, as if I were no longer in complete conscious control of myself. I recognized this, but thought, *Well, what else am I going to do?* They gave me suggestions and I followed them. It seemed perfectly natural to do what I was told. At no time while I was in the craft did I have any sense of it being in motion, although I suspect that it was. It's also notable that all the beings who spoke to me demonstrated a flawless command of the English language, though most used very short phrases. I don't recall them speaking any words or initiating any kind of communication between themselves, however.

The hallways were about 7 feet (2.1 meters) wide, and the walls were curved in such a way that they were slightly wider in the middle than at the top and bottom. Three people could easily have walked abreast in them. The halls had narrow support archways spaced about 10 feet (3 meters) apart. The lighting in the hallway I was in was indirect but bright. The light source was in the floor, but I couldn't see the actual source—just a glow of light similar to what comes from a track-lighting system. The ceiling was about 8 feet (2.4 meters) high, although I soon found out that it was higher in other areas of the craft. We then crossed another hallway that intersected ours at a perfect 90-degree angle. It was about 35 feet (10.6 meters) long, with only one door opening off of it, and it appeared to connect to another hallway running parallel to the one we were in. The cumulative suggestion of these details was that there was one large compartment in the space between them. There were no windows, so I couldn't determine my location within the craft, nor could I determine the relative size of the vessel. However, my sense is that it was very large. I now believe that I may have been picked up by a smaller craft and taken to this larger one.

Many of the design elements seemed to mirror human architecture. The general air temperature (which seemed to be about 72 degrees Fahrenheit [22 degrees Celsius]) and air quality were completely consistent with a large, well-ventilated building on Earth. However, there was no sense of air movement, no unusual odors, and no visible indication of a heating, ventilation, or air-conditioning system. As far as I could tell, the gravitational field strength was normal, too. I looked at the small being walking ahead of me. How likely would it be to find an alien species that voluntarily embraced the exact same environment that humans preferred? I compared the diminutive size of these beings with the more human-sized dimensions of the ship. The implications were staggering: the ship must have been constructed for the purpose of dealing with people. *I'm not the first person who's been here*, I thought. The colossal commitment to resources, design, and function was astonishing. What in the world were they planning?

As I walked, I had time to study the head of the being guiding ahead of me. It was large, bald, and almost bi-lobed, and I could distinctly see what looked like large arteries or veins pulsating beneath the thin skin. I didn't count the pulse rate, but there must have been a huge blood flow to the brain to create that kind of visible pulsing. The neck seemed far too small to be able to support the head, suggesting either a completely different internal structure than that of humans, or some sort of localized independence from the earth's gravitational field. In spite of their small necks and relatively large head-to-body size ratio, however, they moved with utter ease. We reached a room with two more beings in white outfits, and I was put into what seemed like a holding area. As I became more aware of my surroundings, I started to panic. The stress was beyond belief! I began crying uncontrollably. I still recall the feeling of utter hopelessness and devastating vulnerability that this engendered. I was just thinking about asking them to help calm me down when one of the beings apologized to me, and suddenly I was calm. Once again, they were able to connect with my consciousness to influence my emotional state.

I was later escorted into a gymnasium-sized room that contained an estimated 70 beds. Although most of the beds were empty, about 20 or so were occupied by other human beings. They were of different ages, and everyone was dressed in ordinary, everyday clothing—most in pants, shirts, and jackets, and some even in nightgowns. I vividly recall that one man had on a red flannel shirt. There were no blankets on the beds and no movement or sounds coming from any of the people. They seemed to be in some sort of induced sleep. I don't know how I would have reacted had one just sat up or cried out to me for help. It was very upsetting. I thought, *What is this? I don't want to see this!* One might have thought that seeing another human being would have been a comforting sight, but it certainly wasn't in these circumstances. I recall that there were aliens moving about the beds, as well. This momentary glimpse of large-scale contact, and the human helplessness it implied, was the most disturbing aspect of the entire experience. They obviously had the capacity for many more people with those empty beds. How could we not have known about this? *Clearly I am not supposed to be seeing this*, I thought. *There is no chance anyone will ever believe this! Am I ever going to make it back home? How am I going to get out of here?*

I eventually went through a series of painful medical procedures, some so painful that I couldn't stop myself from screaming in agony. After the first procedure, I remember asking two of the beings, who were dressed in what looked like white lab coats, if there was anything I could do to help them. They seemed completely astonished by my question. During the final medical procedure, I apparently lost consciousness. As I came to, I found myself staring into a bright light. The light drew back and I could make out a kind of crosshair, similar to what you see in a rifle scope. Another alien in a white lab coat was shining a type of retina scope in my right eye. As it pulled away I could make out two other very tall aliens, about 9 and a half feet (2.9 meters) tall, and dressed in tight, jet black uniforms, standing by the foot of the bed I was lying on. They looked anatomically identical to the others except they were extremely tall and lanky. They were staring at me with such watchful intensity I felt that they may have been guards of some kind. Just to my right there was another being, about 5 feet tall and dressed in a beige outfit. Although it didn't look any different, I sensed that this being was female. In an emotionless voice she said, "We don't understand your anger." It was as if a mannequin had spoken. There was no facial expression or body language for me to read, and certainly no hint regarding what the beings' intentions were.

Her statement made no sense to me. The whole time I was on the ship, from the decontamination chamber onward, I had been trying to cooperate, asking them if I could help them and what it was they wanted. She said it again and moved closer to me: "We don't understand your anger!" I was still trying to get my bearings as to where I was and what was happening and then it hit me: *I had yelled at them.* The process of initial transport up to the larger craft had been painful—I was scared and I yelled at them. I turned my head away and tried to explain what had happened, but I couldn't get it out. All I could manage was, "I'm sorry...." It was as if a veil had fallen away. She stepped forward and I was completely enveloped in an incredible sense of love and compassion. I tried to control myself, but the tears flowed freely from my eyes. I cried harder than I ever had before. It's difficult to explain, but there was a tremendous sense of relief and sudden salvation. The horror was over. I clung to her and cried like a child. She whispered gently in my ear, "It's okay to cry. The strong ones cry." I know that we spoke together at some length, but I can't remember what about.

The next clear memory I have is standing with her next to my car, which was still inside the craft. It felt as though we had known each other for a very long time. We warmly embraced each other and she gently pulled away to look at me. She said, "I wish I could stand beside you to face the things that you're going to have to face." And I said, "No, that's okay. I understand." In spite of the incredible feelings of warmth and love, I knew that I couldn't stay with them. She told me I needed to forget about what had happened. Upset, I told her I didn't want to forget about it; certainly, I didn't want to remember the pain, but I wanted to remember her and the other amazing things I had seen. I was very disappointed and felt determined that, no matter what, I was going to remember at least *some* of this.

Despite my newfound feelings of joy and acceptance, I knew that my place wasn't there with them. I had to go home. Several of the small beings were there, as well, and the mood was joyful and loving mixed with sadness. I knew this was a special moment, not just for me but for them, as well. We said our farewells, and as one of the smaller beings escorted me toward my car, I suddenly recalled my initial painful experience. I hastily jumped ahead of him and reached for the door. "It's okay," I said with a friendly smile that masked my relief, "I'll get the door," and I stepped back into the car's passenger seat. The next thing I knew, the lights were moving away and the paralysis was gone. I could not remember anything I had seen on the ship, and I could not recall the name of the loving, compassionate alien that seemed to know me so well.

I finally opened my eyes to a peaceful summer night and the irritating buzz of those incessant mosquitoes. There was nothing unusual about the scene—no lights in the sky, no people running around. The little truck stop and diner that I had pulled into earlier was still accepting its road-weary travellers. The transport truck that had parked between my car and the diner was still there. I stepped cautiously out of the car and glanced fearfully into the night sky. I wondered if anyone had seen what had happened. I checked my watch. It was after 3 a.m. and still dark—only an hour since I had pulled into the lot. How much time had really elapsed, though? I had no idea. A bit shaky but still calm, I walked into the diner where everything seemed so...normal. The bright fluorescent lights washed out what little color was in the faces of the people who looked in my direction. There was no panic, no running around, and no excitement. It was just a peaceful little place in the middle of nowhere, with a few tired truckers and vacationers straining to stay awake.

In the cool restroom, I splashed warm water on my face and took a hard look in the mirror. The fluorescent lighting in there didn't compliment my pale skin any better than it did the people in the diner. Other than looking like a person in desperate need of a blood transfusion, I felt completely normal. *What now? Did anyone see anything? Should I even ask?* Even though I had only fragmentary flashes of memory, I was determined to try and remember what had happened. Back in the diner, I cautiously approached the waitress and asked, "Excuse me, Miss—did you see anything outside?" She said that she hadn't. *The trucker,* I thought—*what about the trucker who had parked beside me and blocked my car from view of the diner? He must have seen something!* But when I looked out the window, my car was clearly visible outside. The truck was gone!

"Honey," the waitress said, studying my face, "were you looking for somebody?"

"Never mind," I mumbled, "they probably already left." What was I going to do—call the police and report it? Hardly. Besides, what could they possibly do? They would have thought I was crazy.

"Oh," the waitress said, breaking the awkward silence. "Do you want a coffee?"

I hesitated as I struggled with what to say and what to do. I only had fragments of memory. From those fragments I was certain I had been taken on board a craft that was now somewhere out there. I sensed at a deeper level that my life would be changed forever and that something very important had happened. I wanted to remember more, but no matter how hard I wanted to recall every detail I just could not. I didn't feel sore or hurt but the thought of going back into that dark lonely parking lot with some alien ship in the night sky, no matter how benevolent they might be, just made me uneasy. I needed time to sort things out and I needed sleep. I was going to struggle with this so sleep was just going to have to wait. Getting away from that place seemed like a very good idea.

"Yes." I replied slowly. "Could I have a large coffee...cream... sugar...and make it to go?"

With my eyes tracking slowly towards the window and peering into the night, lost in new thoughts, I quietly added, "Thanks."

Beyond a doubt, the experience changed me. Reading and hearing about the experiences of others helped me understand that I wasn't alone and that I could cope. I'm aware that there's another reality, one that's much different from the reality that I knew and that most people are familiar with. Yet I don't feel special or unique because of this. This is a worldwide phenomena occurring without reference to race, culture, or class distinctions. The most tragic thing about the phenomenon of alien contact and abduction has been our inability to accept the truth. As my own experience illustrates, contact experiences can be traumatic, and it's tragic that some contactees will be harmed all over again by a society that offers no support or validation.

Our fearful and aggressive response to the phenomenon is understandable and even predicable. In many ways it's a sad reflection of our world's problems (our ignorance and fear of the unknown) and humanity's present state of spiritual development, or lack thereof. If we were more spiritual, more insightful and less fearful, the hard scientific evidence and anecdotal evidence that we've accumulated would have galvanized the public and encouraged independent organizations and governments to allocate resources to investigating the UFO and alien abduction phenomenon.

We spend billions on military endeavors and space exploration but we haven't spent a penny on finding out the truth about alien contact and disseminating this truth to the public. It is sad that we have misdirected our resources toward agencies that are determined to cover up the truth, even if it means ridiculing and isolating those who are brave enough to come forward with their experiences.

I believe we still have a chance to change our paradigm and develop a more measured and sensible response. I personally have been graced to meet many courageous people who have had the bravery to report on this great mystery, at great personal expense and risk to themselves. We have a real opportunity to build a new bridge of love and understanding that will extend not only across our world, but into a new world. We owe it to ourselves, to our children, and to all life on this planet to do this. Regardless of whether we're afraid, we should be looking at this intervention as a magnificent opportunity. Above all, we need to remember that those who make the best use of any opportunity are those who have prepared for it. It is no longer a question of *when* extraterrestrials will contact us, but rather the much more difficult question of *how* they will interact with us. It is my belief that at the core of the phenomenon is the aliens' struggle to build a relationship with us. It's a new type of relationship, to be sure, with a depth and purpose that few could have ever imagined. But if I am right in my conclusions, it's a kind of relationship that many more of us will be experiencing in the future.

Alien Abduction: Fact or Fiction?

By Kathleen Marden

Alien abduction has captured the public's imagination for more than 45 years through literary works, television programs, and motion pictures. But many scientists assert that it is no more than a modern myth created in the minds of fantasy-prone individuals, with the aid of hypnotic regression or hypnagogic/hypnopompic hallucinations and/or sleep paralysis experienced by the scientifically naïve. Critics claim that there is no tangible evidence worthy of consideration, only unacceptable anecdotal information. But serious researchers assert that some UFO abductions are, in fact, real. They bolster their claims with detailed correlating data given by multiple witnesses in hypnotic regression, along with the analysis of physical evidence, psychological evaluations, multiple witness reports, military radar reports, medical reports, character assessments, and conscious continuous memories of close encounters and subsequent abductions by more than a third of alleged abductees.

The age of alien abduction was ushered in with a series of startling newspaper articles that appeared in the *Boston Traveler* in October of 1965.[1] A year later, *The Interrupted Journey* by John G. Fuller, a *New York Times* best-seller, chronicled the hypnosis sessions of Betty and Barney Hill, then 41 and 39, respectively, a Portsmouth, New Hampshire couple who, on September 19, 1961, allegedly had a close encounter with a UFO and a subsequent period of amnesia

Betty and Barney Hill. From the Hill family archival collection.

in New Hampshire's White Mountains. The year 1975 brought the made-for-TV movie *The UFO Incident* starring James Earl Jones and Estelle Parsons. In their 2007 book *Captured! The Betty and Barney Hill UFO Experience*, Stanton T. Friedman, M.Sc. and I (I am Betty's niece) added more than 50 years of previously undisclosed information about Betty's life and the meticulous examination of evidence in the case.

As the story goes, Betty, a highly regarded social worker for the State of New Hampshire and Barney, a postal employee and political civil rights activist, were relaxed and enjoying the night sky on their drive along U.S. Route 3, northern New Hampshire's major north-south route. Atop Mount Washington, visibility was at about 130 miles (209 kilometers), and the waxing gibbous moon was about two- thirds full. It was the last leg of their journey home to the New Hampshire coast after a brief getaway to Niagara Falls and Montreal.

Betty's interest was aroused by a star-like object that darted upward in the night sky before stopping beside the moon. As it grew larger, the enigmatic object rapidly changed direction, ascended and descended vertically, and then hovered motionless in the sky. As the Hills approached closer, the mystifying object seemed to be pacing their blue and white 1957 Chevy Bel Air. As they motored south of Indian Head in North Lincoln, almost directly in their path the couple encountered what resembled a huge, flattened circular disc with a row of intensely illuminated blue-white windows along its front edge. Barney immediately brought the car to a halt in the middle of the road, and grasped his binoculars as he opened the car door for a less obstructed view. The silent hovering object loomed less than 200 feet (61 meters) overhead. Rapidly, in an arc-like movement, it glided from the right to the left side of the road and continued to descend above the adjacent field. The silent enigmatic craft was huge, maybe 60 to 80 feet (18 to 24 meters) in diameter. As Barney approached it, two red lights at the end of short, fin-like structures parted from the sides, which now tilted in Barney's direction.

Peering through his binoculars Barney spied a group of strange figures that, in his estimation, seemed determined to carry out a plan. With military precision, all but one figure moved away from the window toward what Barney thought was some kind of a panel on the rear wall of the curved corridor. Finlike wings appeared to extend from the sides of the craft as it descended and tilted in his direction. As the craft tilted downward and began to descend toward him, one of the figures at the window communicated a frightening message to him telepathically. Barney had the immediate impression that he was in danger of being seized right there in the field. Tearing the binoculars from his face he raced back to the car. Breathless, trembling, and in near hysterics, he told Betty that they needed to get out of there or they were going to be captured.

Buzzing tones that sounded like some sort of rhythmic code bounced off the trunk of their vehicle, causing a penetrating vibration to pass through the car and their bodies. About 35 miles (56 kilometers) south of the field, they once again heard another series of buzzing sounds. After the fact, they had vague memories of encountering a roadblock, of seeing a huge, fiery, red-orange orb resting on the ground, and of feeling a strong desire for human contact. They looked for an open restaurant to no avail, so they made a beeline to Portsmouth, expecting to arrive at approximately 3 a.m. But dawn was already streaking the sky.

The night's events became even more perplexing when the couple discovered 12 to 18 shiny circles on the trunk of their car. Strangely, when a compass was placed on top of the area, the needle whirled around crazily (the same compass worked normally on other surfaces of the car). Additionally, Betty's best dress was torn in several places, and there were scrapes on the toes of Barney's dress shoes. The watches that they were wearing were inexplicably broken, as was the leather strap on Barney's binoculars.

On October 21, 1961, an NICAP investigator by the name of Walter Webb undertook an extensive investigation which ended up spanning several years. His confidential report, titled "A Dramatic UFO Encounter in the White Mountains of New Hampshire—September 19-20, 1961," clearly and exhaustively recounts the details that Betty and Barney were able to remember. He summarized Barney's close encounter as follows: "He knew it was no conventional aircraft he was observing but something alien and unearthly containing beings of a superior type, beings that were somehow not human."[2]

It was Barney's intractable health problems that led the couple to Dr. Benjamin Simon, a prominent psychiatrist celebrated for his successful treatment of WWII veterans suffering from PTSD (post traumatic stress disorder, also called "shell shock" or "battle fatigue"). He knew almost nothing about UFOs, but was skilled at deep-trance hypnotherapy to resolve psychogenic issues related to traumatic amnesia. Early in 1964, the Hills began what would amount to six months of separate hypnotherapy sessions with Dr. Simon. Dr. Simon hypnotized them separately and reinstated their amnesia at the end of each session. What emerged was an uncannily consistent dual recall of the abduction and correlating positional and numerical data. With the exception of a few important differences, Betty's recall was strikingly similar to her dream account, which had been previously recorded in November of 1961. Barney's recall was similar to Betty's but without the richly detailed information found in her account. He was also able to recall some detailed information that was not in Betty's dream record. Dr. Simon suspected that Barney might have absorbed some of the information in Betty's dreams when he overheard her talking about them with UFO investigators and her friends. But new information has emerged that casts some doubt on Dr. Simon's hypothesis. Additionally, both Betty and Barney recalled specific detailed information that was *not* a part of Betty's dream account, which suggested to Dr. Simon that they experienced a real event. For example, Betty dreamed that the car was surrounded by her captors, but under hypnosis both she and Barney recalled that their captors divided into two groups of three, one for each side of the car. As well, Betty dreamed that she and Barney were returned to their car together, but under hypnotic regression, they both recalled that Barney was already seated on the driver's side when Betty returned to the car. They also recalled correlating detailed information about the craft's environment and occupants that were not in Betty's dream account. Importantly, psychiatrists deemed the Hills free from mental illness and personality disorders. In 1983, Betty even passed a polygraph exam administered by Ed Gault, President of the American Polygraph Association. Barney was never able to take an exam, as he died in 1969.

The abduction would probably have remained a secret forever, if it were not for a violation of confidentiality. On October 25, 1965, the Hills' greatest fears were realized when a Boston newspaper published, for five consecutive days, a detailed account of the Hills' UFO encounter and abduction experience. A year later, *The Interrupted Journey* revealed much of the information on the Hills' hypnosis tapes. In 2007, *Captured!* added previously unpublished biographical information about the Hills' lives, the scientific investigation of the evidence, and the never-before-told investigative findings. The Hills' UFO encounter has stirred worldwide interest for nearly 50 years because, clearly, it cannot be easily dismissed.

oᶜᵒᵉᶥᵒ　oᶥᶥᵒ　oᶜᵛᵝ

The world would soon learn that Antonio Villas-Boas, a 23-year-old Brazilian farmer, had reported his 1957 abduction by non-human entities to Joao Martins, a journalist, and Olavo Fontes, a medical doctor and professor from Rio de Janero. But it was not widely publicized in the United States until after the Hill case received its unfortunate notoriety.

In a thoroughly detailed account, Villas-Boas testified that on October 5, 1957, he and his brother had observed what appeared to be an intense white searchlight over their family's corral. Nine days later, an intense, pale red light that was approximately the diameter of an ox cart wheel hovered only about 300 feet (91 meters) above the northern part of the field. When Villas-Boas approached it, however, the light shot to southern end of the field. This pattern repeated itself each time he attempted to move toward it. On the evening of October 15, he saw the object again; this time it hovered approximately 150 feet (46 meters) directly above Villas-Boas, bathing him and his tractor in an intense beam of pale red light. Three metal protrusions dropped out of the bottom of what appeared to be a craft as it made its descent. His tractor's engine died and the lights cut out. He attempted to flee but was caught by several small beings clothed in close-fitting, gray, one-piece suits, gloves, and oversized helmets. The entities appeared to be wearing goggles which made their eyes appear smaller than those of humans. Villas-Boas reported that he was forced into the elongated, egg-shaped craft and into a small room, where two entities removed his clothing and extracted blood from his chin. When the creatures left the room it filled with noxious smoke.

Villas-Boas's strange tale might have been relegated to the annals of UFO hoaxes were it not for the medical evidence. Villas-Boas reported that he experienced overwhelming fatigue, nausea, eye inflammation, headaches, body aches, and loss of appetite for days after the alleged abduction. Dr. Fontes noted coin-sized scars on Villas-Boas's chin, and multiple fresh lesions on his arms, legs, and hands that had a strange purplish discoloration around them that resembled the effects of radiation poisoning. Despite living through these traumatizing events, Villas-Boas completed his education and worked as a lawyer for many years. But he never rescinded his alien abduction claim.

With these two famous accounts, the age of alien abduction had begun. During the next several years, several alien abduction reports were well-publicized in the popular media, but most lacked the supporting evidence necessary for scientific credibility. One of them, however—the 1968 abduction of two teenagers at a summer camp on Lake Champlain—has withstood the test of time.

By the time that Michael Lapp (not his real name) phoned Walter Webb of the Hill case fame at Boston's Charles Hayden Planetarium in October of 1978, Webb had become a seasoned abduction investigator. Michael told him that he had had a UFO close encounter, followed by a period of amnesia, on August 7, 1968. The 16-year-old Michael, a waterfront maintenance worker, and his friend, 19-year-old Janet Cornell (not her real name either), a water skiing instructor, were lounging on the dock at the Bluff Ledge girls summer camp on Lake Champlain. That evening the champion swim team was vying to uphold its undefeated title at a state competition in Burlington, Vermont. A college student at Smith, Janet had landed a summer job as a camp counselor and water skiing instructor. Michael, a local high school student, was employed as a boat and ski maintenance worker. It was the teenagers' first opportunity to spend time alone together that summer.

The sun had just dipped below the horizon when Michael noticed that what he had misidentified as the planet Venus had swung, in a rapid arc-like motion, to a position low in the sky and come to a complete stop. As it drew closer, the glowing cigar-shaped object released three small, illuminated, disc-shaped objects and then disappeared up into the sky. The oscillating trio maneuvered in close formation, zigzagging like falling leaves, and stopped dead in the sky before resuming their unconventional flight pattern. Two of the discs departed, but one remained hovering over the lake. As the pair watched, the disc approached the dock with its multicolored lights pulsating one color at a time. By now Janet and Michael watched in wonder as the disc ascended vertically until it became only a dot in the sky, and then rapidly descended again and plunged into the lake. Shortly thereafter, it emerged from the water and glided right toward the dock where the couple was standing in shock.

Now just 60 feet (18 meters) away, the 40- to 50-foot-diameter (12-to-15-meter-diameter) disc hovered above the water. It was topped with a translucent dome through which an intense, blue-white light shone. As it approached the stunned couple, Michael recalled observing two slightly built, hairless figures dressed in what looked like grayish or silver uniforms, with large frog-like eyes that extended around the sides of their heads like goggles, slits for nostrils, and small, rounded mouths. As Janet stood trancelike and unresponsive, Michael asked the entities why they were here. In response, he received a telepathic message that they would not be harmed, and that this was their first return to Earth after the detonation of our first atomic bomb.

Within seconds the object was directly overhead. It emitted an intense, cone-shaped beam of light which engulfed the teens. Sensing that he was about to lose consciousness, Michael instinctively grabbed Janet and dropped to the deck. What seemed like only a second later, the disc was once again hovering above the dock in its previous position, but it was now after dusk, indicating that an unaccounted-for period of time had elapsed. Janet and Michael suddenly heard the voices of two campers who stood at the top of the steps leading to the beach. The craft made a rapid departure, but not before its rapid-fire flashes were observed by additional witnesses. After the encounter, Janet and Michael conversed briefly about their overwhelming fatigue and desire for sleep, but surprisingly, neither discussed the UFO incident. Michael reported it to friends and family and the Plattsburgh, New York, Strategic Air Command base. Other than one or two brief encounters, the teens' paths never crossed again that season. Soon the summer ended, and the pair went their separate ways.

It was 10 years before Michael finally contacted Walter Webb, and the investigation ensued. After much searching, they were able to track down Janet, who was now a college fund-raiser living with her husband, a physician, in Atlanta. Eventually, both Michael and Janet underwent 12 hours of separate hypnosis sessions with Harold J. Edelstein at the New England Institute of Hypnosis in Wakefield, Massachusetts. Because they had never had an opportunity to discuss their close encounter or the information that was recovered during hypnosis, Webb was able to conduct a statistical analysis of their statements. In hypnotic regression, Michael and Janet described their abduction in remarkable correlating detail—70 percent on recall of the close encounter, and 68 percent on the abduction experience.

Michael Lapp's sketch of the alien that allegedly abducted him. Image courtesy of Walter Webb.

Under hypnosis, Michael recalled observing Janet lying on a rectangular table surrounded by two non-human entities. A third entity appeared to be monitoring test results on several screens. Skin samples, bodily fluids, and ova were extracted. Michael underwent an examination, as well, on a table next to Janet's, but he lost consciousness immediately after he was placed on a table. Both of them also described the interior of the craft in great detail. Additionally, their testimony regarding their positions onboard the craft, as well as those of their captors, matched in prefect correlating detail.

Both tested normal on the Minnesota Multiphasic Personality Inventory (MMPI), a psychological screening test. Janet's profile revealed her as self-aware and self-confident, socially well-adjusted, and not prone to confabulation or excessive fantasizing. Michael's profile indicated that he was outgoing, optimistic, energetic, and not prone to excessive fantasizing. However, his score indicated that he might be prone to exaggeration.[3] This doesn't necessarily discredit his testimony, but it does indicate that he might have, consciously or unconsciously, embellished some of his descriptions. As might be expected, Janet passed a polygraph test, but Michael's result was inconclusive for the abduction part of the event. As is often the case in alleged alien abductions, there was no physical evidence that could be analyzed in a scientific laboratory. However, Webb's meticulous investigation produced multiple witnesses, excellent character references, confirmatory statistical evidence, and the in-depth psychological profiles.

Seven years passed before any further credible abduction accounts emerged in the popular media. This next one was highly publicized and surrounded by a circus-like atmosphere, probably because a young man who was reported missing reappeared five days later, along with the strange account of his abduction by aliens.

⚬⫘ ⚭ ⚭

The November 5, 1975 abduction of 22-year-old Travis Walton is one of the best documented, most convincing UFO abductions ever reported. Travis was part of a logging crew that was riding in a extended cab truck driven by the business owner, 28-year-old Mike Rogers. Also riding in the cab were Allen Dalis (20), John Goulette (21), Ken Peterson (25), Dwayne Smith (17), and Steve Pierce (17). They had just finished a day's work clearing debris in the Sitgreaves National Forest outside Snowflake, Arizona (about 100 miles [160 kilometers] northeast of Phoenix).

They were traveling on a forest service road at twilight when they observed a glowing, disc-shaped object less than 90 feet (27 meters) away from the road, hovering about 20 feet (6 meters) above the ground. It wobbled and changed brightness, glowing a yellowish-white color. Travis exited the truck and approached the object, which by that time had started to rotate. A bright blue light suddenly shot out from the bottom of the craft, striking Travis and throwing him into the air and backward 10 feet (3 meters). Fearing for their lives, his coworkers fled the area, but returned 15 minutes later when Mike Rogers observed what he believed to be the outline of the glowing object leaving the area. They searched in the frigid night air for Travis, but he was nowhere to be found.

Travis Walton. Photo courtesy of Travis Walton.

Mike then drove the 10.5 miles (16.9 kilometers) along the rough forest service road into Heber and reported the incident to the sheriff's department. The men's UFO report was initially met with incredulity, but the fact that a young man was missing in rugged terrain and in potentially lethal weather conditions prompted a full-scale search. Men scoured the area on foot and horseback, but to no avail. Finally, Jeeps and helicopters were called in, but there was no trace of Travis.

Suspecting that he had been murdered and buried somewhere in the vast expanse of the Turkey Springs area of the Sitgreaves National Forest, the sheriff's department asked the six suspects to submit to polygraph exams. The first three questions probed the men's possible involvement in Travis's disappearance. When asked, "Did you tell the truth about actually seeing a UFO last Wednesday when Travis disappeared?"[4] all but Allen Dalis, an agitated and belligerent accused burglar, were deemed to have given truthful corroborating testimony. Allen's exam was inconclusive due to his edgy emotional state.

Five nights later, Travis's sister received a phone call from a phone booth in Heber. It was Travis. He told her he had "come to" lying down on the pavement and that he had seen the craft depart. He was dehydrated and had lost a significant amount of weight. Later he remembered waking up on a table with a 3 × 1.5 foot (.9 x .45 meter) luminous rectangular object suspended above his body. A curved, dark gray appliance was folded over his chest cavity. The air was close, humid, and uncomfortably warm, and pain and weakness wracked his body. But when his eyes focused on a horrifying sight— enormous dark eyes set in a huge, hairless cranium—he struggled and began to lash out. He saw that he was surrounded by non-human entities slightly less than 5 feet (1.5 meters) tall and dressed in what looked like brownish-orange coveralls. He described their skin as having a pale, marshmallow-like appearance and texture. Their facial features reminded Travis of fetuses—small noses, slits for mouths, and no visible ears. By now nearly hysterical, Travis jumped up and assumed a defensive stance. The object that had been folded over his chest fell to the floor as he staggered into a corner in search of a weapon. The entities immediately scurried out the doorway, leaving Travis alone in the wedge-shaped room.

Travis fled down a curved hallway until he spotted an opening on the inside wall. He entered a round room that contained a single pedestal chair. As he approached the chair, the room darkened and he suddenly saw stars everywhere. When he moved a lever on the chair, a screen that was attached to the chair signaled movement. Realizing that his reckless experimentation might prove fatal, Travis left the chair and inspected what appeared to be a door that conformed to the shape of the circular room. Suddenly, what appeared to be a normal man (except for his strange amber eyes) wearing tight blue coveralls and a crystal clear helmet entered the room. He took Travis by the arm and led him into a tiny cubical that connected to what appeared to be a hangar. As he passed through the hangar, Travis observed three or four disc-shaped craft ranging in size from 45 to 60 feet (13.7 to 18.3 meters) long. He was led through an automatic door into another room. Seated at a table were three more people, two men and a woman. Without speaking a word, they assisted Travis onto a table and covered his face with a mask-like apparatus. His next conscious memory was of waking up on the cold pavement near Heber. Although Travis remembered only a two-hour ordeal, a total of five days had passed since his disappearance.

Naturally Travis wanted medical tests. Immediately, a representative from Ground Saucer Watch, a UFO investigating group, contacted Travis and arranged for him to see a doctor who was also a hypnotist. Coral Lorenzen, the co-founder of the Aerial Phenomena Research Organization (APRO), arranged for a confidential house call with two physicians. They performed a thorough physical exam and sent Travis's urine sample to a laboratory for analysis. An examination determined that Travis wasn't suffering from any major physical injuries. However, he was dehydrated, extremely distressed, had lost anywhere from 10 to 14 pounds (4.5 to 6.4 kgs), and had what appeared to be a one- to three-day-old puncture wound in the inner part of his right elbow.

Although they were advised that Travis's lack of rest and distressed emotional state would yield inconclusive results, authorities rushed Travis to submit to a polygraph exam. However, he passed two tests—one in 1976 and the other in 1993—with flying colors. Allen Dalis, the only man whose first test results were equivocal, passed a follow-up polygraph exam in 1993, as did Mike Rogers, whose integrity had been questioned by debunkers. Additionally, according to his MMPI results, Travis was emotionally healthy, had good self-awareness, and was adequately skeptical. A Rorschach (ink blot) test indicated that he was not highly suggestible. The late Dr. James Harder, a professor of hydraulic engineering at U.C. Berkeley and a trained hypnotist, attempted to recover more information from Travis through hypnotic regression, but only a few additional details about his abductor's physical appearance and the craft's interior emerged.

An ample amount of misinformation caused many twists and turns in the final outcome of this case. Some skeptical individuals intentionally lied, while others embellished the facts to create their own versions of the story. Despite a protracted effort by debunkers to discredit Travis Walton and the witnesses, however, no one has been able to successfully refute the case once they've examined the evidence. Now married with children, Travis has established a solid reputation as an honest, intelligent man who continues to swear that his abduction was real. This, combined with the fact that all seven men passed polygraph exams swearing that they didn't take part in a hoax, and that Travis's psychological evaluation was normal, lends credibility to his claim.

As a side note, there seem to be some similar patterns in how these abductions are actually carried out. For example, both the Hills and Antonio Villas-Boas reported that they were taken aboard a craft by non-human entities. Conversely, Lapp and Walton lost consciousness after being struck by some kind of light beam and could not recall how they arrived on the craft. Others reported being captured by a smaller craft that later docked with a "mother ship" that was several stories high. More recent abductions have introduced yet another common *modus operandi*: Credible abduction witnesses have reported being *floated*, via a cone-shaped beam of light or transport device, up through an illuminated opening on the underside of the craft.

Two months after the Walton abduction, three women from Casey County, Kentucky, became the next multiple witness abduction victims. Late on the evening of January 6, 1976, Louise Smith (44), Mona Stafford (36), and Elaine Thomas (48) had traveled 35 miles (56 kilometers) north of Liberty, Kentucky to have dinner at a restaurant near Lancaster in celebration of Mona's 36th birthday. At the restaurant, the three amateur artists engaged in some sketching and conversation with other patrons, but did not drink any alcohol.

After their quiet but enjoyable celebration, they headed for home at about 11:15 p.m. Louise took the wheel of her 1967 Chevy Nova, with Elaine in the front passenger seat and Mona between them. Little did they know that what they anticipated would be a routine drive to Liberty would become a life-altering event.

The three women suddenly glimpsed a brilliant red object in the sky that at first appeared to be an airplane in a freefall. The now huge object suddenly stopped at treetop level several hundred yards away from the awestruck women. They later described it as a metallic gray disc with a glowing dome and rotating red lights around a convex center. Suddenly a bluish light beam projected from the underside of the now gently rocking craft. Now on the driver's side of the vehicle, it flipped on its side and traveled right next to the car. A bluish-white light shot into the car's interior, creating a hazy effect that burned the women's eyes. Next they all felt a tingling sensation followed by a sudden, severe headache.

Although she had already taken her foot off the accelerator, Louise lost control of the car as it careened ahead at speeds in excess of 85 miles (137 kilometers) per hour. As the craft moved to the rear of the vehicle the car suddenly changed direction and went bumping in reverse into a pasture. The engine stalled, but the car still continued to speed along what seemed like a wide, straight, well-lit road. What felt like only an instant later, the women found themselves back on the road that would take them home.

The astonished women arrived at Louise's house nearly 90 minutes later than anticipated. All were traumatized and suffering from severe headaches, eye irritation, and extreme thirst. They also had strange patches of raw flesh on the backs of their necks. The minute and hour hands on Louise's watch whirled around continuously, while Elaine's watch had stopped altogether. Dubious about the missing time, the women woke up Louise's next door neighbor, only to have their worst fears confirmed: They had indeed somehow "lost" one and one-half hours sometime during their trip home. The neighbor then suggested that they retire to separate rooms and sketch the object from memory. Their illustrations were remarkably similar.

During the next several days, the women experienced skin inflammation and burning, headaches, eye swelling and irritation, mental confusion, and weight loss. Each had 3 x 1 inch (7.5 x 2.5 cm) burns on the backs of their necks. In addition to the physical problems, they were also suffering significant emotional distress over the incident as well as the missing time and apparent amnesia. Two days after the incident, Louise's car had to be serviced due to electrical malfunctions. Her battery had inexplicably lost its charge, and her turn signals and taillights weren't working. Additionally, the car's paint was blistered in places.

Feeling more and more convinced that she had to report the event, Louise phoned the state police. Her call was met with disbelief. The only other local authority that she could call was the Navy Recruiting office, but, again, no assistance was forthcoming. In direct violation of the women's desire to keep this confidential, the Navy recruiter reported the encounter to a local television station. A month later, much to the women's dismay, the *Casey County News* even ran a feature article on the event.

Investigators from the Mutual UFO Network (MUFON) initiated a formal investigation, starting with separate interviews with the trio on February 29. They all reported a feeling of dehydration and extreme nervous tension related to the incident. Louise Smith had lost 11 pounds (5 kgs), and Mona Stafford's eyes were still inflamed. Additionally, Louise's healing burn was still visible. As a strange side note, on the night of the close encounter, Louise's 4-year-old pet parakeet had suddenly become terrified only of her. The investigators noted that the bird merely budged on its perch when they placed their hands into its cage, but it panicked at Louise's approach, flapping its wings and attempting to flee. It died a month later on March 31. The previous day Louise was hospitalized due to her ongoing weight loss, vomiting, and fatigue.

Mona consented to hypnotic regression by University of Wyoming psychologist Dr. Leo Sprinkle on March 7. Eventually all three women underwent hypnosis, but not until July 23 and 24, and only after the *National Inquirer* agreed to pay for more hypnosis sessions and lie detector tests. (Funding for the investigation had always been a major problem, and despite its tabloid status, there was no other viable money source.) As a result of the hypnosis, remarkably consistent details of an alien abduction emerged. Mona Stafford and Elaine Thomas recalled warm liquid being applied to their faces and bodies. All three women were subjected to painful experiments involving joint mobility. Mona remembered being in a chair-like device, and Elaine recalled being in some kind of a capsule with a noose around her neck, which would tighten when she attempted to speak. Initially only Elaine recalled the 4-foot-tall (1.2-meter-tall), dark-eyed, gray-skinned creatures that communicated with her telepathically. Mona's most vivid memory was of passing through a dark tunnel toward an intense light, and then observing a woman on an examining table surrounded by four non-human entities. Louise later stated that she was lying on a table with her face covered; she remembered feeling unbearably hot, and screaming and begging for her captors to uncover her face. This they did briefly, which gave her a glimpse of the hazy room. She recalled looking directly at one of the aliens, which had no hair, no ears, and very large, piercing eyes. It was dressed in what looked like a long, dark robe.

Finally, all three women passed polygraph exams, which were administered by James Young from the Lexington Police Department. Because an honest, nervous person can tell the truth and still fail a polygraph, and a sociopath can lie and still pass, these exams are not admissible as evidence in a court of law. However, when multiple witnesses pass a polygraph exam that asks the same questions, it is a significant indicator of truth.

A follow-up investigation found several other witnesses to the event. A couple, who wished to remain anonymous, testified that they observed the craft from their living room window, which was only several hundred yards from the abduction site. Two teenagers and a farmer also observed the craft. The farmer owned the land at the abduction site. He reported that on the evening of the event or the following evening (he wasn't certain which), he observed a glowing object which emitted a beam of bright white light toward the ground.

Most abductees report subsequent close encounters after the initial contact, but the early abductees tended to only report subsequent *sightings* but no additional encounters or abductions. In a bizarre twist, in 1976, Louise Smith awoke on July 28 or early on the 29th feeling a strong compulsion to return to the abduction site. A male friend drove her there but remained in the car while she walked onto the field. She later stated that she felt terrified at the time but was unable to flee. Feeling concerned, her friend got out of the car to look for her and eventually found her, unconscious on the ground. After the fact, Louise recalled feeling a tugging on her hands prior to losing consciousness. When she returned home, she discovered that her three rings were missing. She again sought assistance from the police, but to no avail. Amazingly, two of her rings suddenly reappeared at her front door two months later. Mona Stafford reported later terrifying experiences, as well. The lingering terror led both Louise and Mona to relocate outside of Kentucky. Sadly, Elaine Thomas died only two years after the event.

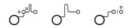

Abduction reports were isolated events in the 1960s and '70s, but by the '80s they were becoming more widespread. By 1985, 300 abduction accounts could be found in published literature, and between 1985 and 2000, approximately an additional 1,000 accounts emerged, with nearly 2,000 more that are currently being investigated.[5] The accounts I've chosen to discuss here make it clear that at least some abduction claims have a foundation in reality. Despite the many possible psychological explanations, not every abduction story can be explained away as a personality aberration, a psychological abnormality, a hoax, a sleep anomaly, a hypnotic confabulation, or a misinterpretation of less fantastical events.

That said, physical evidence and eyewitness testimony in more recent cases are often more elusive than they were in the historical cases discussed here. More recently, only 40 percent of suspected abductees report ever seeing a UFO, but a full 30 percent recall the abduction experience without hypnosis. For example, many abductees report that they have been surreptitiously taken from their bedroom in the middle of the night. Typically, the abductee is awoken by a strange light shining through his/her window or the presence of non-human entities in the bedroom. The abductee becomes paralyzed, and he/she is somehow transported through a solid surface, such as a roof or window, and onto a waiting craft. Many abductees also report that their otherworldly experiences began with a close encounter and "missing time" while driving, fishing, or camping while they were alone. With these people, the initial contact is often followed by subsequent serial nocturnal bedroom abductions. Evidence in these cases has included the presence of anomalous substances on articles of clothing; testimony from neighbors, bed partners, and family members; unusual, unexplainable marks on the abductee's body; the presence of dermal and subdermal florescence under black ultraviolet light; correlating detailed information given in hypnotic regression (typically not released to the public); and even the surgical removal and scientific analysis of suspected tracking devices. (Dr. Roger Leir and Derrel Sims have this laboratory evidence. I wrote about it in Chapter 14 of *Science Was Wrong*.)

The nocturnal bedroom abduction phenomenon has aroused the interest of some academic psychologists. Years of systematic study have suggested that alleged alien abductees exhibit no more psychopathology than the general population. Additionally, they can be found in every demographic throughout the world, ranging from peasant farmers to professionals to prominent individuals in positions of power. In the absence of a primary psychiatric disorder, such as depression or schizophrenia, experimental psychologists have searched for alternative explanations. Several experimental studies conducted in the past 30 years have attempted to delineate personality traits or tendencies that may separate abductees from non-abductees—for example, boundary deficit disorder, false memory syndrome, and fantasy proneness. (Hypnosis researchers Dr. Theodore X. Barber and Sheryl C. Wilson coined the term "fantasy prone personality" in 1981 to describe an individual who has the tendency to confuse fantasies with real experiences.) A personality disorder can be loosely defined as a set of traits that causes people to feel and behave in distressing or socially unacceptable ways. They may be overly negative, hostile, or needy, or exhibit antisocial behavior. People with personality disorders carry these traits throughout their lifetime, but symptoms may fluctuate in severity and duration.

During the 1990s, however, empirical evidence seemed to indicate that suspected abductees who met the clearly defined criteria for an abduction experience (criteria that includes multiple witness testimony, missing and being actively searched for, credible evidence that is deemed anomalous by qualified scientists, and conscious recall of at least part of the abduction by a credible witness) were no more fantasy prone than the general population. Self-identified abductees (many of whom did not meet the criteria for alien abduction and had not been vetted by abduction investigators) scored mostly within the normal range on a variety of false memory formation indicators. However, they scored slightly higher on the false recognition section of a rote memory test, and exhibited slightly higher levels of creativity, a stronger belief in psi phenomena, and greater imagination and absorption than did the general population. Further, alleged abductees did *not* exhibit the social or psychological maladjustment so characteristic of boundary deficit disorder (characterized by a difficulty in differentiating between fantasy and reality; poor sense of self; poor social adaptation with frequent feelings of rejection; suicidal tendencies; feelings of powerlessness; and unusual alertness to sights, sounds, and sensations). There was a slightly higher incidence of dissociation as a coping strategy among suspected serial abductees than among the general population, but this finding could be expected in individuals who have experienced the continuous trauma of systematic abductions.

Another explanation that has been offered is that alien abduction phenomenon, particularly when it occurs during sleep, could be caused by hypnagogic and hypnopompic sleep anomalies among fantasy-prone individuals. However, abductees with compelling cases that meet the criteria (the presence of physical evidence, witnesses, and so on) report subtle but significant differences between their experiences and those resulting from normal sleep anomalies.

Finally, hypnosis by underqualified individuals who lead the witness toward confabulated memories of UFO abduction has long been a suspect in the generation of false memories of alien abduction. Of course, this can only occur when no real memory of the experience exists. Responsible abduction researchers and therapists refuse to hypnotize individuals who fall into this category. The primary requirement for hypnosis is substantial evidence that the experience was *not* merely a hallucination or a fantasy.

In sum, alien abduction presents a greater challenge to investigators than any other area of the UFO phenomenon. Newer, more sophisticated technology is currently being implemented with promising results, but it has not yet convinced mainstream science that the alien abduction phenomenon is real. For more than 20 years, academic research grants have supported experimental studies of suspected abductees' personality traits, but not the scientific evaluation of evidence. Official government denial has complicated UFO investigators' pleas for an official inquiry. Additionally, abduction investigators have broken off into two camps: those who are attempting to collect and scientifically evaluate physical evidence, and those who want to focus on the so-called alien agenda based solely upon eyewitness testimony and hypnotic recall. Clearly, alien abduction investigation is firmly planted on the frontier of science. As in any science, the careful, methodical collection and evaluation of credible evidence over an extended period of time, along with political change, might bring about a paradigm shift. But until then, the controversy will rage on.

For a complete account of the Michael and Janet case, read Walter Webb's excellent book, *Encounter at Bluff Ledge.*

For a complete account of the Travis Walton case, read *Fire in the Sky* by Travis Walton.

For more on the possible psychological explanations for the nocturnal abduction phenomenon, see my essay "The Conundrum of Alien Abductions" in *Science Was Wrong*, written by Stanton T. Friedman and myself.

Notes

1. The Antonio Villas-Boas abduction in Brazil in 1957 had been reported to Dr. Olavo Fontes in Rio de Janeiro, but had not been publicized in the U.S. at the time of the Hills' abduction.

2. Webb 1961, pp.19–20.

3. Webb 1994, p. 244

4. From a letter by C. E. Gilson, polygraph examiner, to Sheriff Marlin Gillespie, Navajo County Sherriff's Office, dated November 13, 1975.

5. From "Emergence of the UFO Abduction Phenomenon," in Hall 2000, p. 515.

Bibliography

Appelle, Stuart. "The Abduction Experience: A Critical Evaluation of Theory and Evidence." *Journal of UFO Studies.* n.s. 6 1995/96: 29–78.

Bartholomew, Robert E., Keith Basterfield, and G.S. Howard. "UFO Abductees and Contactees: Psychopathology or Fantasy Proneness? *Professional Psychology: Research and Practice.* Vol. 22, No. 3 (1991): 215–22.

Blackmore, Susan. "Abduction by Aliens or Sleep Paralysis?" *Skeptical Inquirer Magazine.* May/June 1998. *www.ufoevidence. org/documents/doc817.htm.* Accessed7/2/2009.

Bryan, C.D.B. *Close Encounters of the Fourth Kind: Alien Abduction, UFOs and the Conference at MIT.* New York: Alfred A. Knopf, 1995.

Clancy, Susan A. *Abducted: How People Come to Believe They Were Abducted by Aliens.* Cambridge: Harvard University Press, 2005.

———, et al. "Memory Distortion in People Reporting Abduction by Aliens". *Journal of Abnormal Psychology.* Vol. 3, No. 3 (2002): 455–461.

Donderi, Don C, PhD "The Scientific Context of the UFO/Abduction Phenomenon." Dec. 28, 1996. *www.ufologie.net/htm/donderi.htm.* Accessed 7/2/2009.

Hopkins, Budd. "The Faith-Based Science of Susan Clancy." *www. intrudersfoundation.org/faith_based.html.* Accessed 7/9/2009.

———. *Witnessed.* New York: Pocket Books, 1996.

"Famous UFO Cases." Travis Walton case investigation files at *www. mufon.com.* Accessed 6/14/10.

Fontes, Olavo, MD and Joao Martins. "Report on the Villas-Boas Incident." *Flying Saucer Occupants.* Edited by Coral and Jim Lorenzen. New York: Signet Books, 1967.

Friedman, Stanton T, and Kathleen Marden. *Captured! The Betty and Barney Hill UFO Experience.* Franklin Lakes, NJ: New Page Books, 2007.

———. *Science Was Wrong.* Pompton Plains, NJ: New Page Books, 2010.

Fuller, John G. *The Interrupted Journey.* New York: Dial Press, 1996.

Hall, Richard. *The UFO Evidence. Volume II.* Lantham, Maryland and London: The Scarecrow Press, Inc., 2000.

Jacobs, Devid, PhD (editor). *UFOs and Abductions: Challenging the Borders of Knowledge.* Kansas University Press, 2000.

Kottmeyer, Martin. "Abductions: The Boundary Deficit Hypothesis 1988." *www.think-aboutit.com/abductionsTheBoundaryDeficitHypothesis.* Accessed 7/6/2009.

LeLieuvre, Robert B., PhD, Lester Valez, and Michael Freeman. "Omega 3: Revelation or Revolution—A Comparative Study of Abductees/Experiencers & Community Control Participants." Unpublished white paper written in 2010.

Lorenzen, Coral and Jim Lorenzen. "Abducted!—The Story of the Casey County Kidnapping." *Saga UFOReport.* Vol. 5, No. 6 (June 1978): 20–23,60–67.

———. *Encounters with UFO Occupants.* New York: Berkley PublishingCorp., 1976.

———. *Flying Saucer Occupants.* New York: Signet Books, 1967.

Mack, John, Caroline McLeod, Barbara Corbisier. "A More Parsimonious Explanation for UFO Abduction." *Psychological Inquiry* 7:2 (1996).

Parnell, June O. and R. Leo Sprinkle. "Personality Characteristics of Persons Who Claim UFO Experiences." *Journal of UFO Studies.* 2 (1990): 45–58.

Powers, Susan Marie. "Fantasy Proneness, Amnesia and the UFO Abduction Phenomenon." *Dissociation.* Vol. 5, No. 1 (March 1991): 46–54.

Ring, K. and C. Rosing. "The Omega Project: A psychological survey of persons reporting abductions and other UFO encounters." *Journal of UFO Studies* 2 (1990): 59–98.

Rodeghier, Mark, Jeff Goodpastor, and Sandra Blatterbaur. "Psychosocial Characteristics of Abductees: Results from the CUFOS Abduction Project." *Journal of UFO Studies* 3 (1991): 59–90.

Rueger, Russ A. "Villas-Boas Abduction". *The Encyclopedia of UFOs.* Edited by Ronald D. Story. New York: Doubleday & Company, Inc., 1980.

Spanos et al. "Close Encounters: An Examination of UFO Experiences." *Journal of Abnormal Psychology* 102 (1993): 624–32.

Stringfield, Leonard. *Situation Red*. Garden City, NY: Doubleday & Company, Inc. 1977.

Walton, Travis. *Fire in the Sky*. New York: Marlowe & Company, 1996.

Webb, Walter. "A Dramatic Encounter in the White Mountains, NH Sept. 19-20, 1961." Unpublished confidential NICAP report. 10/26/61.

———. "Encounter at Bluff Ledge: A UFO Case History." *MUFON 1988 International UFO Symposium Proceedings*. Versailles, Missouri: B-W Graphics, Inc., 1988.

———. *Encounter at Bluff Ledge*. Chicago: J. Allen Hynek Center for UFO Studies, 1994.

Wilson, Sheryl C. and Theodore X. Barber. "The Fantasy Prone Personality: Implications for understanding imagery, hypnosis, and paraphysiological phenomena." *Imagery, Current Theory, Research and Applications*. New York: Wiley, 1983, 340–390.

Cosmic Peeping Toms: UFOs and Invisibility

By Micah Hanks

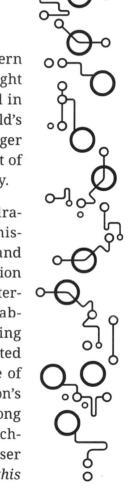

Throughout the Cold War era, it was a common concern that humanity, for all its sophistication and civility, might still succumb to the forces of destruction as evidenced in the proliferation of nuclear weapons among the world's superpowers. Now, though the old Soviet tensions linger mostly as remnant ghosts, concern regarding the threat of nuclear war nonetheless remains very much alive today.

It's probably no surprise, then, why the release of dramatic footage showing the test launch of an Iranian missile in 2009 became an overnight media sensation, and reignited old fears and engendered rampant speculation around the world. As the drama played out before an international audience, viewers were able to watch the Shahab-3—a medium-range ballistic missile capable of reaching distances of 800 miles (1,287 kilometers)—as it blasted upward into the heavens, leaving a thick white plume of exhaust in its devastating wake. With all the weapon's destructive potential, the American government, along with nearby Israel and other nations, were no doubt watching with interest—and concern. However, upon closer inspection of the filmed launch, the various nations of *this world* may not have been the only interested parties.

In the footage that was shown on Fox News in the United States, the Shahab-3 could be seen flying upward for approximately 38 seconds without incident. Then, something unexpected occurred: As the missile hurtled steadily toward a bank of clouds in the distance, the clouds seemed to part abruptly, as though severed by some tremendous unseen force that was moving just ahead of the projectile. The distinct impression given was that a large, invisible object, moving with tremendous speed, had torn through the clouds, leaving an easily distinguishable path of its departure as it seemed to evade the approaching missile. In an article in the British tabloid the *Sun*, UFO expert and former Ministry of Defense official Nick Pope surmised that the launch had apparently been observed by a "craft" that was tracking the Shahab-3. Pope further commented that "the speed and acceleration seem[ed] phenomenal. I'm not convinced we've got anything capable of such maneuvers."[1]

The extraordinary speed of the object was only half the equation, however. Taken at face value, what was seen—or perhaps more appropriately, what was *not* seen—was something that was clearly capable of some kind of advanced cloaking technology, revealed for only a second or two for the camera as the unseen object made its swift departure through the clouds above. Although this may sound strange, this was not the only instance in which this kind of cloaking had apparently been employed by a UFO. As recently as October of 2010, a report filed with the Ohio area Mutual UFO Network (MUFON) detailed a peculiar UFO sighting that involved a triangular array of lights hovering in the evening sky. Apparently part of some larger object, the body of the UFO remained obscured; the author of the report, clearly struggling with words, attempted to describe an object that escaped clear detail "because it looked invisible." Although a triangular shape had been discernable, the witnesses maintained that the object "was invisible [...] because we all agreed we could see through it."[2]

So we are left to ponder whether extraterrestrial craft might be lingering in our airspace without our knowledge, thanks to an advanced technology that renders them invisible to the naked eye, and perhaps even to advanced radar equipment, as well. But what would happen if such cloaking technology were to temporarily malfunction? More importantly, what incredible evidence of visitors from other worlds might we stumble upon if this were ever to occur? One extraordinary encounter suggesting that this sort of thing may have already happened was related to me in October of 2009, when a man identifying himself only as Steven called in to a local Saturday evening talk radio program I was guest-hosting, *Speaking of Strange with Joshua P. Warren*. Initially, Steven seemed fascinated with a previous caller's recollection of seeing a large, triangular UFO in the summer of 1988, and he asked us what the significance of that particular year was in relation to the story. The reason for his interest in the date of this incident soon became apparent, as he began relating a similar experience he had had early one morning, just before dawn, halfway across the globe; his encounter had taken place the very same month and year as that of the previous caller.

It was July of 1988, and Steven had been stationed on an island in the North Pacific called Johnston Atoll. Although the island would later be deactivated and removed from active military use in 2002, Johnston Atoll had served in a variety of U.S. Air Force operations throughout the decades. These included its role as launch site for the first operational ballistic missile in the United States arsenal, the PGM-17 Thor—one of only three missiles the Air Force used to launch live nuclear weapons during tests conducted in the early 1960s.[3] Steven told us that while he was stationed there, a variety of aging chemicals used for biological weaponry over the years had also been kept on the island, awaiting destruction (which eventually took place between 1992 and 2002). "There was a small security force of military police out there, along with a lot of civilians," Steven said. "About 1,000 people total on the island," consisting of both Army and Air Force military personnel. "We did anywhere between 12- and 24-hour shifts out there, and I was a downrange security police officer for the Army-Military Police Corps."

"We saw a lot of strange things out there," Steven admitted. He proceeded to tell us how on this particular occasion, during the summer of 1988, he and several others were coming back from a 24-hour shift on the downrange area of the island, which at the time housed a maximum-security prison. Steven and his company were to be relieved by the oncoming shift, and were headed back to turn in their weapons, have breakfast, and sleep for a few hours. The island's highest elevation was 7 feet (2.1 meters), according to Steven, who referred to it as being "basically a piece of concrete and coral" jutting out into the Pacific. Looking out across the ocean, he and his company could see the beginnings of a golden-pink halo of daylight rising over the horizon, where the sun hadn't quite broken over the water yet. As they drove eastbound along the island, one of the officers noticed what looked like a small, dark, metallic ball hovering in the sky above; it appeared to be heading north. Steven was immediately concerned because Johnston Island is a highly secure location; anyone attempting to fly into the airspace would be easily spotted on surface or air radar. Additionally, Steven and his fellow policemen knew that anything out of the ordinary was to be reported to their superiors; if a situation ever became a matter of defense, they could rely on the support of both the Navy and the Air Force present on the island.

All this flashed through the minds of those present, as the mysterious little ball moved slowly in the air above them. Steven tried to determine whether it was something very small and nearby, or something very large and far away. Although it was vaguely metallic in appearance, it didn't appear to reflect light as much as it absorbed it. Steven recalled that this became increasingly irritating, as it was difficult to discern exactly how close he and his convoy actually were to the strange object. Whatever it was, nobody could identify it, which left them with only two options: find some way to identify the object very quickly, or prepare for offensive action.

Steven and his crew quickly moved to their radios, and within moments the downrange area was put on alert. The word from the island radar station wasn't reassuring, either: "We can't paint this thing," the report hissed across their radios (Steven explained that "paint" was military slang for spotting an object on radar). The next person to radio Steven and his convoy was the base commander who, incidentally, was entertaining a two-star retired general that morning at his house on the island. The two had apparently been breakfasting on the commander's deck overlooking the ocean when the initial radio exchanges were taking place. "Alpha One [the base commander] jumped on the radio," Steven told us, "and said he's got a two-star sitting there. He told us we'd better find this thing because the two of them were looking at it also."

With the top brass now weighing in, most of the available personnel awake at that hour had begun scrambling to try and identify the mystery object, which had been slowly moving in a northerly direction. Suddenly, the object stopped directly over the middle of the island and seemed to begin a slow descent; the tiny metallic ball now appeared to be growing larger. Steven described how the surface of the object seemed to show only the slightest discernable change of texture as the thing—whatever it was—kept getting closer and filled more and more of the sky. This continued for several more minutes as the morning light grew faintly brighter, and the sun threatened to peek over the water on the horizon.

"The object got bigger, and bigger, and *bigger*," Steven said, recalling the tension that had grown amongst the company as they continued to watch this enormous, unidentified object literally close in on them. He said that even though people generally think of UFOs as being the size of a large vehicle, such as a school bus, this object dwarfed even the largest known aircraft used by the Air Force at the time. "The best way I can describe it to you is if you were standing underneath a piece of glass—a large piece of glass—and someone had a bottle of black ink, and they poured it slowly onto the glass.... That's what this thing ended up looking like." Steven said that by now the object's circumference could easily have been the length of the island, though he still couldn't tell for certain whether it was round or flat, because it seemed to be absorbing light. Steven made sure to emphasize the tremendous size of the object as he related his bizarre story: "As the [daylight] got brighter, this thing got blacker, and *bigger*," he said. "When you live on [an island] that's two miles (3.2 kilometers) long, you really start to appreciate the size of things." By now, radio communication, which only minutes earlier had been a near-continuous stream of excited chatter, had fallen silent. Personnel all over the island had apparently just *stopped*, watching in awe as this silent behemoth loomed overhead, seemingly inching closer every second. The silence was broken abruptly by his coworker George blurting out, "If this thing lands, where are we supposed to go?" George's panicked question only expressed what was on all their minds at that point: *Is it going to land? If so, where will something that big go, and what will it do to us?*

As the black void loomed above, Steven said that the water and the air on the island became charged with electricity. "You could almost taste it. The best thing I could use to describe it would be like if you were in your shower with salty, steamy water vapor that was ionized; I could smell the ozone, like when you electrocute something, or when something burns and shorts out." Steven and his crew knew they didn't have the kind of weapons needed to deal with this—*thing*—had it decided to attack. Tension had grown to a near-breaking point; at any moment, life as they knew it might come to a screeching halt. "Then, if this wasn't weird enough already, the moment the sun cracked the horizon, this thing vanished. And I don't mean it flew away; I don't mean it went left or right. This thing just *wasn't there* anymore!" Steven said that according to the Coast Guard Station that provided the weather reports for the island, the cloud ceiling was at 10,000 feet (3,048 meters) that morning. "We could see the cloud deck behind it where we couldn't see anything before. The shadow that had been over the island was no longer there, either. This thing didn't fly anywhere else. It just went—it *disappeared.*"

The producers in the studio and I stared at one another in amazement as Steven related this incredible twist in an already crazy story. What can take up nearly two miles (3.2 kilometers) of open sky and then suddenly vanish into thin air? At this point, I asked Steven for clarification about the shadow that had been cast over the island while the object had been present. "Oh yeah, there was something over us [...] this was not a light anomaly. This thing was taking up *space*." So what in the world—or to be exact, what *out of this world*—could it have been? Steven left us with one final assessment. "[What] I really want to say about this is that I think all technology—no matter how advanced—that is built by any being, entity, or anything with some degree of intelligence, has its limitations and the potential for failure. And I think that whatever this thing was—whatever "they" [were]—I think we witnessed a malfunction. I think something went wrong with this thing's technology for a moment, and it was at the wrong time [in] the wrong place [but] the right time and the right place for us."[4]

According to Steven, whatever he and his fellow servicemen on the island had seen, it had remained, even after it had seemingly and inexplicably vanished. "It's a wild assumption—as wild as the story itself—but I think we actually witnessed a [technological] malfunction," he told us, "and if you think about it, even if they're a million years ahead of us, at some point things break, or mistakes are made, so I really think we were [in] the right place [at] the right time to see this." Steven ended his call by flatly stating, "They *are* out there, and they're *huge*. Some of these things are enormous." Evidently, in spite of their size, these objects, whatever they are, might be hanging around more often than we realize, unseen to both the naked eye and sophisticated radar equipment. But what *are* they, and what might cause their occupants (if there are any) to take such an interest in remote locations the likes of Johnston Atoll in the North Pacific?

Throughout the history of experimental military weapons exercises, there have been numerous instances in which strange aircraft moving at high speeds have suddenly appeared. These mysterious interlopers have sometimes even intercepted nuclear devices and missiles, disabling them in midair. This seems to suggest that the military operations of various world superpowers are being monitored by an interested third party that is, well, not of this world. As strange as this may sound, such stories are hardly a secret among UFO enthusiasts today, with the publication of books such as Robert Hastings' *UFOs and Nukes*, among others.[5] For many, it seems obvious why visitors from elsewhere in the cosmos would take such great interest in our use of weapons of mass destruction; after all, how much longer before our terrestrial war games begin to spill over into other realms, reaching beyond the confines of this planet alone?

Noted ufologist Stanton Friedman, author of *Flying Saucers and Science*, was kind enough to speak to me in October of 2010 about this incident. He seemed to share this sentiment, as well: "Johnston Island, as I recall, was involved in nuclear weapons tests. If there had been tests of missiles and nuclear weapons, they might have been paid attention to by [...] alien visitors [...] trying to check out what's going on. When you look back at the progression of our weapons programs—bombs, especially—you start off peacefully. In 1943 or so you have a 10-ton blockbuster," Stanton said, joking sardonically about "what a mess" people initially thought this weapon—comparatively small by today's standards—would make, noting that it took a B-29 to carry it. By 1945 we had moved on to atomic bombs. "They released the energy not of 10 tons [9 metric tons] of TNT, but *15,000 tons* of TNT," Friedman noted. "The real granddaddy came just a few years later in 1952. We exploded our first H-bomb—we called it Mike, for whatever reason. There was a three-mile-wide (4.8 kilometer-wide) fireball out in the Pacific, and it released the energy of *10 million tons [13,607 metric tons] of TNT*. So in less than 10 years, in other words, you go from 10 tons [9 million metric tons], to 15,000, to 10 million!" As if the massive scale of the United States' nuclear proliferation during this period weren't staggering enough, history tells us there were other high bidders around the world seeking to cash in on the mother of all weapons. "Of course, the Russians outdid that, and had one that was 57 million tons [51.7 million metric tons] of TNT energy released," Friedman pointed out. "Don't ask me what you want to do with *that*, but I can just imagine the aliens saying, 'What in the heck is with these idiots? They've got one heck of a mess of a planet, and they're testing these *huge* weapons.'"

"Now, there's another part to that story," Friedman continued. "H-bombs are nuclear fusion devices, and you can use nuclear fusion for propulsion systems for deep-space travel." According to Friedman, fusion can be looked at as a sort of "ultimate universal energy," as nuclear fusion is the energy source that powers the stars. "Everybody out there," Friedman said, referring to the possible extraterrestrials elsewhere in space, "must know about fusion, because they'll want to know what goes on in their sun [...] so I think one could expect there would also be considerable interest in the locations where nukes were tested."[6] Friedman admitted that his knowledge of fusion for use in space-age propulsion systems stemmed from a study he had been involved with in 1962, while working as an engineer for defense contractors such as McDonnell Douglas. Ironically, 1962 was also the occasion of one of the most controversial nuclear tests ever performed by the United States government, code name "Starfish Prime." Starfish Prime was one of five high-altitude nuclear tests that made up Operation Fishbowl, and it was the first successful high-altitude nuclear explosion achieved during a series of tests that were part of the larger Operation Dominic. The resulting blast created a massive electromagnetic pulse (EMP) that was much larger by far than studies had anticipated.[7] Many of the instruments used to measure the effects of the Starfish Prime blast were driven off the scale, and widespread electrical damage was sustained as far away as Hawaii, nearly 900 miles (1,448 kilometers) from the site of the explosion. According to one declassified document detailing effects of the blast, "the large amount of energy released at such a high altitude by the detonation caused widespread auroras throughout the Pacific area, lasting in some cases as long as 15 minutes; these were observed on both sides of the equator." Observers in Honolulu reported that on the evening of the launch, the overcast sky "was turned into day for 6 minutes" immediately after the blast.[8]

The after-effects of the Starfish Prime explosion would rank it far beyond most any other nuclear blast that has ever occurred on Earth, due in part to the resounding EMP shockwave it produced. Additionally, artificial radiation belts were created by the release of highly energetic charged particles at the time of the blast, and later held in place outside Earth's atmosphere by the planet's magnetic field. In the months after the explosion, these radiation belts managed to disable a number of satellites that were operating in low orbit around Earth, lofting its effects beyond our planet and into the realm of space. At this point in the story it should come as no surprise that the location for the Starfish Prime launch had been none other than Johnston Atoll, where Steven claimed his frightening encounter with a UFO occurred 16 years later. Could this event have triggered the interest of wary extraterrestrials and caused them to keep a close watch over Johnston Atoll (and a variety of other nuclear test sites) for decades after the blast, should any potentially dangerous experimentation of this sort continue?

Even if we were to suspend our disbelief and assume that this scenario was a likely one, we have yet to understand the bizarre cloaking technology that allowed the object appearing over Johnston Atoll in the summer of 1988 to suddenly vanish. There are, however, some clues that might steer us toward a few startling conclusions in this regard, perhaps even revealing the key to how these UFOs operate. According to Steven's testimony, the object only vanished after it was struck by direct light from the sun. Perhaps this detail is inconsequential; or perhaps, as Steven had guessed, it indicates that some kind of malfunction had occurred. If we look at other more widely reported UFO incidents, however, we find literature in which similar scenarios have been described, especially during one of the most dramatic astronomical events that obscures the light of the sun, the solar eclipse.

On July 11, 1991, sky watchers all around Mexico City gathered to observe a dramatic total eclipse of the sun, many armed with video cameras hoping to capture footage of the rare event. As the eclipse began, people in various parts of the city began to report seeing strange, metallic objects hovering in the sky. Appearing on the Travel Channel's *Weird Travels* TV program in 2006, ufologist Ed Sherwood revealed that the metallic objects began to appear in the sky "just as the eclipse was taking place, and remained in the sky as the eclipse was finishing." Remarkably, 17 individuals in the city, each watching from a different vantage point, managed to film the event.[9] Could the fact that these UFOs appeared just as the sun was disappearing behind the moon be a mere coincidence, or is there something more to this peculiar story?

During my discussion with Stanton Friedman, he recalled hearing of various projects throughout the years that seemed to indicate that scientists were working on aircraft that were capable of this kind of invisibility. Apparently, aerospace engineers hope to one day find ways to control electromagnetic radiation and manipulate portions of the light spectrum, in order to achieve invisibility. Ostensibly this would be done by building on and exploiting various technical processes and tools that, in terms of our present understanding, still remain in their infancy. These tools do already exist, however, and the hope is that they will one day be implemented in advanced cloaking devices that use artificial composite materials called *metamaterials.* This brings us to the forefront of a vast new scientific frontier called transformation optics, in which scientists seek to learn the secrets of "bending" space and light around objects. If light could be controlled and redirected as simply as bending a wire, imagine what fascinating potentials may exist. Perhaps we will one day be capable of rendering aircraft completely invisible to the naked eye.[10] As mind-numbing as the prospect of bending light around an aircraft may be, there is also the distinct likelihood that advanced extraterrestrials are doing it already; for all we know, they may have had this ability since time immemorial.

Where, then, does all this leave us? Are these curious aerial interlopers, whether extraterrestrial, interdimensional, or something wholly different from anything we've yet imagined, a potential threat to humanity? If their apparent interest in remote nuclear test sites is any indication, they may be more concerned with our own self-destructive nature than they have any interest in harming us themselves. Whatever the curious purpose behind their visits may be, one fact remains irrefutable: They only allow us to see them at times of *their* choosing. Nonetheless, on occasion we may still be able to catch a fleeting glimpse of these odd, enormous shapes in our skies, shapes that may represent an intelligence far more invested in our existence than we realize. Perhaps they are more invested in our existence than we would *want them to be*, if their intentions were ever fully known. Perhaps, in the grand scheme of things, we are trapped in an intergalactic game of cat-and-mouse; or, considering how these UFO craft display such a tendency to remain invisible, perhaps "hide and seek" would be a better comparison. But how close to these inexplicable visitors must we get before we're too close for comfort, especially given the fact that we seem to be dealing with a variety of cosmic Peeping Tom we may never be able to fully see?

Notes

1. Soodin, Vince. "UFO tracks Iranian missiles." *The Sun*, October 6, 2009. *www.thesun.co.uk/sol/homepage/news/2670396/UFO-tracks-Iranian-missiles.html*

2. Marsh, Roger. "Four UFOs over Ohio seem to emerge from 'black hole'." Examiner.com, accessed October 18, 2010. *www.examiner.com/ufo-in-national/four-ufos-over-ohio-seem-to-emerge-from-black-hole*.

3. *Air Force Missileers*. Association of Air Force Missileers. Paducah, KY: Turner Publishing, 1998, page 23.

4. *Speaking of Strange with Joshua Warren*. Clear Channel Communications. WWNC, Asheville. Oct. 3, 2009.

5. Hastings, Robert. *UFOs and Nukes: Extraordinary Encounters at Nuclear Weapons Sites*. Bloomington, Indiana: Author House, 2008.

6. From the author's personal interview with Stanton Friedman. October 23, 2010.

7. Defense Atomic Support Agency. Project Officer's Interim Report: STARFISH Prime, Report ADA955694. August 1962.

8. Harland, David M., and Ralph Lorenz. *Space Systems Failures.* New York: Praxis, 2005.

9. "Alien Encounters." *Weird Travels.* Travel Channel, Authentic Entertainment. Scripps Networks: Knoxville, January 27, 2006.

10. Kyzer, Lindy and Richard Hammond. "Invisibility Research" (teleconference transcript). U.S. Army. Accessed August 19, 2008. *www.defense.gov/dodcmsshare/BloggerAssets/2008-08/08200809314320080819_DrHammond_transcript.pdf.*

The Kingman Affair

By Nick Redfern

Within the realm of UFO research, and even within the media and the general populace, there are very few people who have not heard of the so-called Roswell Incident. It is a strange, sensational saga of conspiracy and duplicity that suggests that nothing less than an alien spacecraft, complete with crew, catastrophically crashed on a remote ranch in the New Mexico desert during the summer of 1947. As of this writing, the Air Force's official position on Roswell is that the affair can be explained in wholly conventional and down-to-earth terms: The unusual wreckage found at the crash site, says the military, originated with a secret high-altitude balloon project, called Project Mogul, which was designed to monitor early Soviet atomic bomb tests. As for the strange bodies found at the scene, according to the Air Force they were nothing stranger than some crash-test dummies that had been used in military parachute experiments. Needless to say, die-hard UFO researchers scoff at such assertions and accuse the U.S. government of engaging in a cover-up of *X-Files* proportions in order to hide the decidedly extraterrestrial truth. Roswell is not alone in this. Indeed, there are far more than a few reports that suggest aliens may have visited the earth, only to fatally crash and burn. One such event is alleged to have occurred in 1953 in a desert locale on the fringes of the town of Kingman, Arizona. The Kingman case is a truly unique one that contains a near-infinite number of curious plot lines and countless characters—some named and speaking on the record, and others wholly anonymous and Deep Throat–like in nature. Numerous twists and turns abound. As you will soon see, this story ultimately reached a final conclusion that few would have suspected or even imagined.

The genesis of the story can be traced back to early February of 1971. Jeff Young and Paul Chetham were two new and enthusiastic UFO investigators who, at the time, were digging into a truly sensational story that, if true, strongly suggested that intelligent life existed outside of the confines of our own world. These amazing revelations came from a man named Arthur Stansel, who was a good friend of Young's family and who claimed to have had personal, firsthand knowledge of a crashed UFO and alien body recovery near Kingman on May 21, 1953.

During the course of a face-to-face, tape-recorded interview with Young and Chetham, Stansel—who held a master's degree in engineering and who took part in the D-Day landings at Normandy, France, during the Second World War—recounted that in 1953, he was working at the ultra-secret Nevada Proving Ground. This was the location of a recent atomic bomb test that had been a part of a larger series of tests known as Operation Upshot-Knothole. This operation was just the latest in a whole series of atmospheric nuclear weapons-based tests that fell under the jurisdiction of the Atomic Energy Commission (AEC), all of which were conducted at the Proving Ground from March 17 to June 4 of 1953.

Stansel told the astonished but excited duo that late one night, he and a colleague observed nothing less than an honest-to-goodness UFO soar across the skies near the site. Ultimately, however, Stansel had much more to impart than a sketchy story of a hard-to-define aerial encounter. As he felt more and more comfortable telling his story, he gradually divulged the details of what would become known as the Kingman affair to the unsuspecting Young and Chetham. Stansel stressed that the incident had taken place during his brief tenure with the U.S. Air Force's UFO investigation

*One of the Atomic Energy Commission's Operation
Upshot-Knothole tests at the Nevada Test Site, May 1953
(Copyright: U.S. Department of Energy).*

program, known as Project Blue Book. Previous to his time there, he had received a telephone call from the base commander at Wright-Patterson in Dayton, Ohio, with orders for him to fly to Phoenix, Arizona. From there, Stansel was driven to the crash site of what he was told was a secret Air Force project gone awry. Upon his arrival at the site—which he was certain was situated on the fringes of Kingman—Stansel could not fail to see the unusual object. This was no classic flying saucer, however; rather, the object was shaped like a cross between a teardrop and a cigar. Moreover, it was small, barely 12 feet (3.7 meters) long. But that was not all: There was a body. According to Stansel, this was no human body. Yes, it had arms, legs, a torso, and head, but it was only about 4 feet (1.2 meters) tall, its skin was dark, and its facial features were manifestly different than those of a human being.

That, in essence, is the basic story told to Jeff Young and Paul Chetham in early 1971. Aside from being mentioned in an April 23, 1973 article in the Massachusetts-based *Middlesex News*, not much else came of the account. However, a man named Raymond Fowler, a well-respected UFO investigator and author, read the article and was intrigued. As Fowler began to dig into the story, he discovered that both he and Stansel were currently employed by the very same company. Needless to say, Fowler wasted no time contacting Stansel, and the pair met in Stansel's office at noon on May 4, 1973. The Kingman case was about to be taken to a whole new level.

Fowler had some concerns about both the witness and his story, since it soon became clear that the tale Stansel told to him was radically different from what had been imparted to Chetham and Young two years previously. Stansel explained, somewhat awkwardly, that this discrepancy arose from a basic confusion regarding the dates as well as from the fact that he had been under the influence of four martinis when he was interviewed back in 1971. Stansel admitted that when the booze kicked in, he was often prone to exaggeration. Although these issues raised some justifiable suspicions, the Stansel account, as related to Fowler, was still one that cried out for scrutiny and investigation—which is precisely what Fowler did. On June 7, 1973, Fowler procured a signed affidavit from Stansel, albeit one in which Stansel's name was changed to the pseudonym of Fritz Werner—which, of course, rendered the affidavit wholly meaningless and worthless. Nevertheless, the very fact that Stansel had at least been willing to put something in writing was encouraging.

According to Stansel's new—or, rather, modified—version of events, it was while on a very short assignment with the Air Force's Project Blue Book that, on May 21, 1953, he was flown to Phoenix, Arizona, and then driven in a bus with blacked-out windows to a location not too far from the nearest significant landmark: Kingman. When Stansel spoke with Fowler, however, what he had originally described as a 12-foot-long (3.7-meter-long) teardrop/cigar-shaped object had been transformed into an oval-shaped craft with a diameter of at least 30 feet (9.1 meters)—a definitive flying saucer, in other words. The exterior of the vehicle resembled brushed aluminum, Stansel added, and the craft had only penetrated about two feet (.6 meters) into the ground. The affidavit also described some kind of a hatch, about 3 feet (.9 meter) high and a foot (.3 meters) wide, on the side of the craft that provided entrance to its interior. Looking inside, the investigative team spied an oval-shaped cabin, two swivel chairs, and a variety of instruments and screens that did not resemble conventional aircraft technology. Most significant of all, a small body was retrieved from the interior of the vehicle and was taken to a nearby, hastily constructed tent. Very human-like, if small in stature, the presumed pilot had two eyes, two nostrils, a small mouth, and two ears. It wore a silver-colored, one-piece suit, and atop its head sat what appeared to be a small skullcap made out of the same material as the suit.

Naturally Fowler had concerns about the differences between the two narratives, but he did not discount Stansel's story entirely. In fact, quite the opposite: he continued to investigate it—and Stansel—with vigor. What he uncovered added a degree of credibility to Stansel's new or modified version of the events. Fowler was able to confirm that between June 1949 and January 1960, Stansel held a variety of engineering and management positions at Wright-Patterson Air Force Base in Dayton, Ohio, and that during the period in which the incident supposedly took place, Stansel worked within what was known at the time as the Air Materiel Command Installations Division, within the Office of Special Studies. In other words, Stansel certainly did not appear to be a fool or a fantasist; quite the opposite, in fact. Of course, these welcome discoveries with respect to Stansel's career did not negate the fact that he had clearly told one story to Young and Chetham (after having had a good old time quaffing a few martinis) and a very different one to Fowler. Most UFO researchers would have been inclined to walk away from the sorry saga, shaking their skeptical heads and uttering weary sighs. However, something happened that kept the Kingman candle burning: Other sources came along with their own accounts of crashed UFOs in Arizona in 1953. A dubious case with just one solitary source suddenly became something much more.

In a 1978 research paper titled "Retrievals of the Third Kind," presented at the annual Mutual UFO Network (MUFON) Symposium of that year, former intelligence officer Leonard Stringfield related the story of a researcher named Charles Wilhelm, whose father had, in turn, heard an account by a certain Major Daly of Daly's flight to the site of a UFO crash in April of 1953. Daly described how he was then blindfolded and driven out to a desert location. Once there, his blindfold was removed and he was shown an undamaged metallic craft, close to 30 feet (9.1 meters) in diameter. Of course all of this sounded very similar to what Fowler had heard from Stansel. Granted, the date was a month off, but Stringfield, a dedicated collector of crashed UFO stories, suggested that there might be a connection to the Stansel revelations.

Two years later, in 1980, Stringfield revealed how, midway through 1977, after lecturing on UFOs at the administration building of Cincinnati's Lunken Airport, he was approached by a pilot who claimed to have been present at the site of a UFO crash in Arizona at some point in 1953. Stringfield's informant was unsure of the precise location of the crash, but he did add that it was a desert environment and that an unknown number of alien bodies had been transferred from the site in sealed crates to the Wright-Patterson Air Force Base. Like Stansel, the pilot claimed that these bodies were around 4 feet (1.2 meters) tall, and possessed eyes, a nose, and a mouth. He also claimed that one alien reportedly survived the initial impact but died shortly afterward, despite the best efforts of military medical personnel. A full 14 years later, in 1994, Stringfield was still reporting on the Arizona events of 1953. In February of that year, Stringfield revealed the testimony of a new source—only identified as J.L.D.—who claimed knowledge of two UFO crashes in Arizona in 1953. Were these events connected with the Kingman case? We may never really know the answer to that question, as

Stringfield passed away that same year, steadfastly refusing to ever reveal the true identity of J.L.D.

And still the Kingman saga rumbled on. In the 1990s, the UFO investigator Don Schmitt spoke with a woman named Judy Woolcott, who had an intriguing tale of her own to tell concerning the Kingman crash. Her story centered on a strange letter that she had allegedly received in 1965 from her husband, who she said was serving in Vietnam at the time. In his letter, her husband expressed his fears that he would not be returning home alive. He also told her about something strange he had seen 12 years previously. While she could not be absolutely certain of the exact month, Woolcott was positive that her husband had mentioned Kingman, Arizona, as the location. He was a military officer and was on duty when an unidentified flying object was picked up on radar. It soon began to lose altitude, however, and summarily vanished from the radar screen. Woolcott said that her husband felt sure that something had crashed, adding that there had apparently been casualties of the extraterrestrial kind. She further claimed that her husband's fears had proved to be ominously correct: He never did come home from Vietnam. The tale of Judy Woolcott had the potential to take the Kingman case to a whole new level. After all, here was an outside source, with no ties whatsoever to Arthur Stansel, speaking on the record about a crashed UFO in 1953—and in the vicinity of Kingman, Arizona, no less. Unfortunately, her story ultimately crashed to the ground, too. Midway through 2010, the UFO investigative author Kevin Randle revealed his findings on the now-deceased Woolcott's claims, and those findings cast significant doubt on the Kingman story: Her tale utterly collapsed upon investigation. There was no husband killed in Vietnam, and even Woolcott's own daughter, Kathryn Baez, admitted that her mother was prone to embellishing and sensationalizing stories and certain aspects of her personal life.

This did not put an end to the Kingman controversy, however. One of the most intriguing figures to surface vis-à-vis this affair was Bill Uhouse, a retired mechanical engineer from Las Vegas who claimed to have worked on classified projects at certain governmental locations in Nevada that focused upon the reverse-engineering of recovered UFO technology. Uhouse's story is a strange one, and much of it is beyond the scope of the Kingman story. However, the UFO researcher Bill Hamilton dug deep into the claims of Uhouse, who also asserted that no less than *four* alien entities had been found alongside the Kingman UFO and that all of them had survived the crash, albeit with varying degrees of injury. Somewhat ominously, Uhouse also asserted that several members of the team involved in the retrieval were later afflicted by what was suspected of being an unknown biological agent. In 2006, new and provocative data surfaced regarding this last statement via an unnamed source who claimed a background within the United States' Intelligence community. According to the information on the Website, the Kingman crash did indeed occur, and, just as Bill Uhouse claimed, four aliens had been found at the site, two severely injured and two in reasonably good condition. As well, a number of the military retrieval team suffered adverse physical effects by their exposure to the craft and the bodies. While a number of researchers believe that the data on this site are government-generated disinformation, the fact that some of it dovetails with what I have written here warrants further scrutiny.

The year 2006 was notable for one other reason: on December 3, Arthur Stansel passed away at the Good Shepherd Health Care Facility in Jaffrey, New Hampshire, thus taking with him to the grave whatever it was that he really knew about the Kingman conundrum. He was laid to rest at the Central Cemetery in New Ipswich, New Hampshire.

In 2009, three new revelations surfaced regarding the Kingman affair. All three were equally fascinating, but unfortunately they only served to further obfuscate the facts of what did or did not occur on that fateful day way back in May of 1953. First, there is the story of Marion Shaw. In her early 80s as of this writing, Shaw worked in the heart of the Pentagon during the 1950s as a secretary with a high-security clearance. There she rubbed shoulders with some significant and well-known figures in the military arena of the day. She claims to have typed a lengthy classified report on the Kingman crash and body recovery that detailed the nature of the crash, the appearance of the recovered device, and an autopsy of an alien corpse at a medical facility in Arizona two days after the incident had occurred. Research is currently underway to test the validity of Shaw's admittedly brief and fragmentary story, and the particular nature and point of origin of the vehicle and the body.

Then there is the story of a man named Truman Bethurum, whose testimony relative to UFOs extends more than half a century into the past, but whose relevance to Kingman I only came to appreciate in 2009. Beyond any shadow of doubt, the number of people who can claim that aliens wrecked their marriage is infinitely small. But such claims have been made, the most memorable being that of the construction worker Bethurum. His idea of a "close encounter" was apparently quite different from those of other UFO witnesses and abductees: His alleged 1952 liaisons atop Nevada's Mormon Mesa with Space Captain Aura Rhanes, a supposed citizen of the planet Clarion, ultimately led his outraged wife to file for divorce!

Mormon Mesa is a 1,893-foot-high (577-meter-high) summit that dominates Nevada's Moapa Valley. Between the mesa and its two near-identical neighbors are two huge chasms created by the Muddy and Virgin rivers, which carved the mesa eons ago. The visually stunning Mormon Mesa was about to become a veritable hotbed of alien activity—literally—when, in the latter half of 1952, Bethurum was contracted to do some work in the area. Because the area had been covered by ocean during prehistoric times, after he finished his shift one particular night, Bethurum headed out to the Mesa to see if he could find any fossilized shells as a gift for his wife, an avid collector of seashells. (She had decided not to accompany her husband to Nevada, and instead elected to remain at their home back in Santa Barbara.) Bethurum searched in virtual darkness for a couple of hours but failed to find anything, so he returned to his truck to catch some welcome sleep. It was while snoozing—or perhaps, one might argue, in an altered state of consciousness—that Bethurum was visited by the inhabitants of another world: the Clarionites. An hour or so after falling asleep, said Bethurum, he was awakened by what he described as mumbling. As he began to stir, Bethurum was shocked to see that his truck was surrounded by between eight and 10 men. They were all olive-skinned, around 5 feet (1.5 meters) tall, and wearing uniforms and black baseball caps.

On the night of November 2, 1952, Bethurum was out in the desert, actually very near to the town of Kingman, Arizona. Anxious to see his gorgeous Captain Rhanes again, Bethurum fired into the air one of several flares, supposedly given to him by his alien friends as a means of contacting them at any time. Sure enough, Rhanes and her crew were quickly on the scene. For what was to be the final time, Bethurum was invited aboard the saucer, and the pair chatted at length about life on their respective worlds, their hobbies, and much more of a friendly nature. Rhanes escorted Bethurum out of the saucer and back to the desert floor, where they bid one another farewell. In a few moments, Bethurum was alone, standing in the stark desert darkness and watching in awe as the huge alien craft rose silently in the starlit sky.

It must be said at this juncture that much of Bethurum's tale is, frankly, unbelievable. His description of his encounters with the shapely Captain Rhanes read like a cross between *Star Trek* and *Baywatch*, or a wild science-fiction novel. It would be easy to relegate Bethurum's story to the realm of fiction and nothing else; indeed, many people within the UFO research community have done so without hesitation. Despite this, however, there is one particularly intriguing aspect to Bethurum's otherwise fantastical tale that may have a bearing on the story of Arthur Stansel, and may even suggest that Bethurum wasn't quite the fantasist that so many believed him to be.

When Arthur Stansel described the alien body found at the Kingman site in his 1973 affidavit, it was about 4 feet (1.2 meters) tall, dark brown in complexion, and had two eyes, two nostrils, two ears, and a small, round mouth. It was also clothed in a silvery, metallic suit and wore a skullcap of the same type of material. Compare that with the aliens that Truman Bethurum claimed to have encountered in late 1952, mere months earlier, very near to Kingman: they were all olive-skinned, around 5 feet (1.5 meters) tall, and wearing uniforms and black caps. The location, the Kingman region, is the same in both stories, and the aliens in both accounts are short in stature. Both Stansel and Bethurum said that the aliens wore uniforms and caps. As well, the body that Stansel saw had dark skin, and Bethurum's aliens had olive skin. The similarities between the two accounts are striking.

The wholly skeptical commentator might say that Bethurum simply made up his story after hearing of the Stansel revelations in the 1970s. However, there is an insurmountable problem with this particular theory: Bethurum's account was published in 1954, less than one year after the alleged events at Kingman occurred, and nearly two decades before Arthur Stansel even related his story to Jeff Young and Paul Chetham. Perhaps Bethurum was not the hoaxer that many people thought he was. All we can say with absolute certainty is that we have one controversial case—the Kingman affair—which seems to be somewhat corroborated by a highly controversial UFO story—the Bethurum affair.

At the time of this writing, there has been one further addition to the Kingman cauldron. This new development may not be the one that many devotees of crashed UFO stories wish to hear, however. I have uncovered U.S. Air Force files showing that in the same precise time frame of the Kingman crash—specifically, during the Atomic Energy Commission's Upshot-Knothole tests that Arthur Stansel played a role in—the military was secretly test-flying drone aircraft in the Nevada/Arizona area with monkeys on board. While the image of an unmanned drone aircraft packed with a crew of monkeys flying across the deserts of the Southwest might sound laughable and bizarre in the extreme, official papers establishing that such tests were indeed undertaken have surfaced.

They were recently released into the public domain via the terms of the Freedom of Information Act, and are housed at the National Archives, Maryland, where they can be viewed and studied by the general public.

A document titled "Early Cloud Penetration," dated January 27, 1956, and prepared by the Air Research and Development Command at Kirtland Air Force Base, New Mexico, states in part:

In the event of nuclear warfare the AF is confronted with two special problems. First is the hazard to flight crews who may be forced to fly through an atomic cloud. Second is the hazard to ground crews who maintain the aircraft after it has flown through the cloud.... In the 1953 Upshot-Knothole tests, monkeys were used so that experiments could be conducted on larger animals nearer the size of man. QF-80 drone aircraft were used, their speed more nearly approximating that of current operational aircraft.

The QF-80 aircraft were actually modified USAF P-80 "Shooting Star" aircraft that had been converted to drone status via an operation known as Project Bad Boy, which fell under the jurisdiction of a contractor called Perry Gyroscope. And that's not all. The document clearly states that the monkeys on board the aircraft were dressed in "various types of protective clothing" and wore skullcaps. A closer match to Stansel's admittedly embellished description of the creature he saw would be very difficult to find, indeed. Moreover, an elderly man named Albert Barker, who formerly worked in the U.S. Army's Psychological Warfare Center, has shown me copies of additional documentation that refers to the secret recovery of one such drone aircraft that went wildly off course and crashed approximately 33 miles (53 kilometers) outside of Kingman in May of 1953. According to these documents, the recovery of the device and the bodies of the dead monkeys was the subject of stringent security because the crash was tied to the Upshot-Knothole atomic tests undertaken in Nevada.

So this is where we stand today with this curious cosmic case. We have initial testimony from a military source that seemed credible (the story of Arthur Stansel, as related to Jeff Young and Paul Chetham in 1971), but which was subsequently thrown into a significant degree of doubt when it was revealed that Stansel had changed his story and exaggerated the facts after having imbibed his favorite beverages of the boozy kind. Of course, all of this means that we really have no choice but to look at the whole thing with a firm degree of caution. However, the additional data on the

Ham, a chimpanzee utilized in a NASA space-flight in 1961—evidence that primates, dressed in rudimentary flight-suits and helmets, were routinely used in aviation-based experimentation. (Copyright: National Aeronautics and Space Administration).

Kingman story—from Leonard Stringfield's insider sources, from Pentagon secretary Marion Shaw, and from Bill Uhouse—still suggests that we should give Stansel the benefit of the doubt. And what about the bizarre story of Truman Bethurum? In retrospect, it does seem to fit in with certain salient points in the Stansel revelations. But, that Bethurum stuck to such a bizarre tale of ethereal dalliances only adds even more controversy to the tale!

The question must be asked as to where I stand. Admittedly, for a significant period of time I believed that a UFO of extraterrestrial origins crashed near Kingman, Arizona, in May of 1953. Today, I am far less inclined to go down that path, and far more inclined to believe that the object found in Kingman was indeed one of the secret drone aircraft remotely flown through the ominous mushroom clouds born out of Operation Upshot-Knothole. After all, recall that Stansel was informed by his superiors that the Kingman craft was a secret experimental vehicle of the U.S. military. Moreover, during the course of his interview with Young and Chatham, Stansel described the vehicle as being barely 12 feet (3.7 meters) long, metallic aluminium in color and appearance, and teardrop- or cigar-shaped. The resemblance of this description to a piece of fuselage of one of the QF-80 aircraft utilized in the Upshot-Knothole "monkey flights" can't be ignored. Indeed, one only has to take a look at the photograph of one of these aircraft to get a sense of the resemblance:

In May 1953, a modified, remotely-piloted U.S. Air Force P-80 Shooting Star aircraft, with several monkeys on-board, crashed near Kingman, Arizona (Copyright: U.S. Air Force).

And finally, is it really feasible that a UFO piloted by a small alien entity should happen to crash in the same location and within the same time frame as a secret Air Force aircraft with a number of small primates aboard? The answer is surely no. Although I don't usually subscribe to the false "either-or" dichotomy, in this case it simply has to be one or the other.

That said, even though the Kingman UFO tale seems to have been borne out of exaggeration of a real but wholly down-to-earth event, which has largely been amplified by unnamed whistleblowers of the type that contacted Leonard Stringfield in the late 1970s and early 1980s, we should perhaps not totally discount the story. We should always strive to be grounded, methodical, and, above all, logical in our pursuits of the UFO kind. And we should avoid falling into the trap of *wanting* to believe that the Kingman crash had alien origins; after all, this kind of bias or predilection is a huge impediment to getting to the truth of any matter. My own biases and interests aside, the subject of UFOs is a truly strange one: It is filled with halls of mirrors and smoke, and with conspiracies within conspiracies, and truths that may be lies and lies that may be truths.

Kingman R.I.P.? Perhaps, but not quite yet.

Bibliography

Note: All Websites were accessed in October of 2010.

Bethurum, Truman. *Aboard a Flying Saucer.* Los Angeles: DeVorss & Co., 1954.

"Documents newly disclosed, reporting confusion, sickness and disorientation when entering a disk at the Kingman crash site," author unknown, *www.serpo.org/consistencies.html*

"Early Cloud Penetration." Air Research and Development Command, Kirtland Air Force Base, New Mexico, January 27, 1956.

Fowler, Raymond. *Casebook of a UFO Investigator: A Personal Memoir.* Englewood Cliffs, N.J.: Prentice-Hall Trade, 1981.

Hamilton, Bill. "The Strange Story of J-Rod. An EBE, 1999."

www.eboards4all.com/866799/messages/18.html

Middlesex News, April 23, 1973.

"Operation Upshot/Knothole, 1953—Nevada Proving Ground."

www.nuclearweaponarchive.org/Usa/Tests/Upshotk.html

Randle, Kevin. *A History of UFO Crashes: Documented Proof of UFO Visits to Earth*. New York: Avon Books, 1995.

Randle, Kevin, *Crash: When UFOs Fall From the Sky*. Pompton Plains, N.J.: New Page Books, 2010.

Redfern, Nick. *Contactees: A History of Alien-Human Interaction*. Pompton Plains, N.J.: New Page Books, 2009.

———. Interview with Marion Shaw. May 14, 2009.

Stringfield, Leonard. "Retrievals of the Third Kind." Mutual UFO Network Symposium Proceedings. Seguin, Texas, 1978.

———. *Situation Red: The UFO Siege*. London: Sphere Books, Ltd., 1977.

———. "The UFO Crash/Retrieval Syndrome, Status Report II: New Sources, New Data." Mutual UFO Network Symposium Proceedings. Seguin, Texas, 1980.

———. "UFO Crash/Retrievals: Search for Proof in a Hall of Mirrors: Status Report VII." Published privately. Cincinnati, Ohio, 1994.

Roswell in Perspective: The Human Response to an Extraordinary Event

By Donald R. Schmitt

Eyewitness testimony is in need of a reinstitution of relevancy. It has been weakened by revisionists and cynics who establish a double standard in the process of determining what is accepted as fact. For example, criminals are still being convicted solely based on the testimony of very human witnesses, while the very same sort of testimony is decried as "subjective" and outright false in the case of UFO reports. Of course, reports of UFOs have always been and should always be held to a much higher scientific standard of acceptance due to the extraordinary nature of the phenomenon. Skeptics notwithstanding, those of us who still profess to be objective should allow witnesses every opportunity to tell the facts as they know them—even if, or perhaps particularly if, we don't like what they're saying—lest we become nothing more than story gatherers who fall into the same complacency trap that most contemporary journalists find themselves in today vis-à-vis the subject of UFOs.

For these past 21 years, a concerted effort has been underway to find a resolution to the one of the most perplexing and enduring mysteries of all time—namely, that apparently insurmountable question of what actually fell out of the sky outside of Roswell in 1947. The government has tossed out possible explanations like excuses coming from a 5-year-old; UFO investigators have debated not *if* it happened, but *where*, and even *how many* of these crashes there were; and debunkers continue the same damage control tactics—all to no avail. After eliminating every alternative explanation, only two possible scenarios remain: 1) that certain parties involved in the Roswell incident have perpetuated a grand campaign to cover up some super-secret government project gone awry; or 2) something extraterrestrial really did crash there, as all the witnesses say it did. It is amusing how many people subjectively dismiss hundreds of eyewitness accounts and simply insert a random hypothesis in their place, then seek to make all the known facts magically fit the new pair of shoes, the theory of the month, if you will. Such would prefer that someone fabricated the entire affair in order to cloak the truth, with the proviso that someday, hopefully in their lifetime, a more open government will release the files and the true nature of this event will come spewing forth. Unfortunately, officialdom keeps fumbling around in the dark and has actually created more suspicion than solutions. Apparently, this "fumbling" has always been for effect only, and has not arisen from any real quest for the truth; it certainly hasn't come from any sense of obligation to the public. Control of information is still the government's primary precept, and this need for control is motivated by our government's own fears and ignorance of the facts.

With disclosure *not* at hand, UFO research—specifically, inquiry into the 1947 Roswell event—has arrived at a crossroads. I will ask readers to don their best detective caps and reexamine the origins of the plot. Without prejudice or bias we will ignore the minutiae and instead focus on the human aspect of this story. The names of the players, though important, will not be central to the plot. For the past 20 years I have published and exhaustively catalogued and cross-referenced the entire body of sources for this story; indeed, most of them are on public record. However, I believe that a reinvestigation of the verbal and behavioral *responses* of those involved will demonstrate the full scope of this now iconic case. We shall attempt to separate the "story" from what the eyewitnesses state and swear as fact. We will reexamine Roswell through the eyes of the novice and see where human perspective begins and a jaundiced eye intervenes, where eyewitness accounts are countered and often silenced by an official position. We shall conduct a pragmatic investigation of the case from start to finish and observe if the human response matches our expectations for a mundane event or a truly extraordinary one. And lastly, we will examine the immediate aftermath and decide whether the authorities effectively buried the Roswell saucer story or not. Was it really "case closed," as the Air Force continues to insist even today?

We begin with the hot, lazy summer of post–World War II in 1947. The flying saucers officially arrived the last week of June and became instant celebrities on all news fronts. Mass hysteria was not the issue; it was clear that someone else was invading our airspace. Never ones to miss an opportunity, advertisers and pranksters jumped on the bandwagon and attempted a number of hoaxes. All were easily identified as such, but people continued to anxiously scan the skies nevertheless. For the military this was no laughing matter. With each passing day, it failed to identify the intruders, the Pentagon was pressed for answers from both the White House and the general public. Witnesses were observing and photographing aircraft that outmaneuvered, outperformed, and outflew anything we "scrambled" after them. Nervous tension replaced amusement as military officials provided no explanation for what had happened. Given this situation, how could we expect an average, relatively sophisticated and rational population to react? For those who have suggested that the entire country was caught up in a sort of collective flashback to the 1938 Orson Welles *War of the Worlds* broadcast, history proves otherwise. According to major newspapers at that time, polls revealed that the percentage of the population that actually thought we were facing an extraterrestrial intelligence was a mere 2 percent. These are hardly the numbers that would support the "hysteria" of those who peacefully resided in and around

Roswell, New Mexico, in July of 1947. The fact is that none of them had anticipated the life-altering events yet to come.

According to Project Blue Book, there were more UFO sightings at that time in New Mexico than anywhere else in the nation. The Land of Enchantment was clearly the subject of someone's curiosity. Was it Russian spy planes? Top secret atomic testing? Whoever was behind the activity, New Mexico was clearly tracking unknowns at a growing rate. Moreover, we already had the bomb. "We didn't need any more excitement than that," as one officer, Captain Sheridan Cavitt, put it. The vast portion of the central part of the state is open grazing land. Ranchers were more than casual bystanders of the constant demonstrations of military might in that area. So when these civilians reported hearing an explosion amidst thunderclaps during the night of July 3, suspicions were immediately aroused. They had good reason to be concerned, for the very next morning, as ranch foreman W.W. Brazel rode out at dawn as he usually did to inspect the rainfall from the previous night, he stumbled upon a scene that would forever change his life. We know that Brazel had no knowledge of all the saucer excitement spreading throughout the country, so it was no surprise that he didn't race to that conclusion. Being a responsible citizen he normally would have gathered up any garbage and kept it out of the grazing path of the cattle and sheep. To this day you can still see the now-overflowing water tank at the main ranch house, brimming with weather balloons; ranchers continue to deposit such refuse in this receptacle. But Brazel didn't just gather this material from the grazing land of his livestock and dispose of it as he should have. Later, he would describe how he had to circle the sheep two miles (3.2 kilometers) around this pasture, which suggests the extent of the debris. He also stated that the sheep were afraid of it. What transpired next was most unusual. The confused rancher brought samples of the wreckage to his neighbors asking for help. Still in search of answers, he then went into the nearest town of Corona and placed a call to his boss over in Texas. Pieces of the crash started to circulate around town, including the local pub, which left the patrons just as puzzled as Brazel. Artifacts would even steal the show at the annual 4th of July rodeo in Capitan. From all accounts no one could cut or burn, let alone identify, this strange material. That same evening a frustrated Brazel returned to the debris field to drag a large section of the strange wreckage to a livestock shed three (4.8 kilometers) miles away. Night fell, and that was the first day.

Word was spreading quickly throughout the surrounding region, and with it, souvenir hunters made their way to the scene of all the speculation. This was hardly the typical behavior of these hardworking, no-nonsense, salt-of-the-earth individuals whose handshake was their bond and who disliked being crossed even more. They weren't about to be fooled about this—they needed to see for themselves. They found that the rumors were true and, like kids in a candy store, they grabbed the most exotic pieces they could find. Neighbors hid their bounty in caves, water tanks, under floor boards, in sacks of feed, in fruit cellars, and even inside jars of peaches. One obvious question is, who were they hiding this evidence from and why were they so secretive about it? Still, for something so seemingly sensitive and important to national security, none of the authorities were looking for anything. Nothing was reported missing. And night fell on the second day.

Having not a clue about the source of the crash, Brazel was compelled to find a final resolution. Completing his end-of-the-week chores, he headed for Roswell to price out some sheep's wool. He would report the wreckage to the sheriff there. Not even a Lincoln County police officer who was supposed to know about everything that was going on in his jurisdiction knew what this stuff was. Brazel's idea was to report it to the authorities in Roswell. Up to this point not a single individual had described a conventional piece of material. Unfortunately for Brazel, neither the sheriff nor any of his deputies could offer any help. Nonetheless, the sheriff was so impressed with the box of scraps sitting on his desk that he dispatched two of his deputies to head north and check out the story. But so far Brazel was batting a big zero.

What happened next created the nightmare scenario that officialdom fears most—the press, albeit serendipitously, had gotten wind of the growing story. The radio station KGFL talked to the rancher over the phone while he was still at the Chavez County courthouse. After asserting that someone was responsible for cleaning up all that wreckage, he poured some gasoline on an already smoldering fire: *"They weren't human,"* he proclaimed. In stunned disbelief, the reporter urged the distraught man to contact the Army at the RAAF (Roswell Army Air Field). It sounded like something they needed to know about immediately. Keep in mind that this was the Sunday of a Fourth of July weekend. Now imagine that not only the head of intelligence of the most elite military unit in the United States, the 509th Atomic Bomb Wing, gets involved, but also the commanding officer of that very base unit. Well, you can stop imagining. The base commander, Col. William Blanchard, couldn't identify the debris either, and there were absolutely no reports of any downed aircraft, secret tests, or rocket launches on the clipboard. If anything had happened around Roswell, they would have been the first to be notified. Moreover, the RAAF was always on alert, given the bomb and the attendant security issues. Whatever this material was, and wherever the rest of it had gone, it sure got the senior officers attention. Why else would Blanchard have dispatched the head of intelligence, Major Jesse Marcel, and the equivalent of foreign intelligence, Captain Sheridan Cavitt (the latter in the event that it was something foreign)? Why else was the head of the CIC sent? And if that weren't cause enough for concern, with a box of the true wreckage in hand, why did Blanchard immediately go up the chain of command and alert his boss in Fort Worth? And if that doesn't suggest the seriousness of the situation, why did his boss immediately contact *his* boss in Washington? The growing interest in the unusual material had now advanced all the way to Washington. The Pentagon wanted to see everything firsthand, so it quickly ordered that some of the material be flown east. Total ignorance remained the prevailing situation. Clearly, these high-ranking military officers found themselves in the same state of disorder as the rancher. The general state of affairs could be summed up as follows: "What is this stuff? And heaven help us if it isn't ours!" Now running out of daylight, Brazel and the two officers arrived back at the ranch. Night fell on the third day.

Sunrise found the two officers anxiously exploring the now ransacked arroya, as the wreckage had already scattered with the prevailing wind. Brazel just wanted all of this to end so that he could get back to running his farm. The army, on the other hand, wanted the wreckage to be one of our own secret devices in the worst way. But there was so much debris and it extended for almost a mile (.6 kilometers)—much more then they could load into two vehicles. They quickly determined that it was a mid-air explosion that had caused the components to rain down in a fan-shaped pattern. They then proceeded to gather up all they could while Brazel returned to his duties.

 Back in Roswell the press was getting antsy. What if the story about the crash of the flying saucer were true? They had to find the rancher, get his name from the sheriff, and grab him for the exclusive of the century. KGFL conspired behind military ranks to undercut their authority; freedom of the press would not be stifled! It would take the better part of the day to find the target of their manhunt. Brazel would spend the night at the radio station on a wire recorder talking about "little men." Not far from there, returning from the ranch, Major Marcel would rouse his wife and 11-year-old son, to share with them an experience none would ever forget: I-beams with strange symbols on them, and talk about materials not manufactured on this earth. Washington remained watchful late into the evening as night fell on the fourth day.

The very next morning, while Brazel sipped a cup of coffee in the kitchen of the majority owner of the radio station KGFL, the

RAAF base commander assembled his senior officers for an extra-early staff meeting to assess the escalating situation. But before his two intelligence officers could report on the debris field 65 miles (105 kilometers) northwest of town, there had been a new development just 40 miles (64 kilometers) to the north—the remains of a small ship and even bodies! And sound the alarm for the sheriff, the fire department, the press, and the other civilians who were already at the scene. The situation could have gotten completely out of hand, but the colonel was relieved to report that the entire area had been cordoned off, roads had been blocked, and witnesses had been warned not to talk.

Subterfuge is a military specialty. Washington had already had the material in hand for two days. No knee-jerk reaction there. They had to admit to something, but cooler heads chose the old scarecrow technique: first build it up, then tear it down. The press release was carefully written. Timing was crucial—after all, the later it hit the wires, the less chance it would have to make all the afternoon paper editions. As it turned out, only the *San Francisco Chronicle* managed to print the original press release. It was quite masterful, really. The base commander's boss was ready to fly back to Fort Worth to put the next phase of the investigation into effect. Within a matter of hours the slow evolution from saucer to weather balloon would begin, while mechanical engineers at Hangar P-3 pounded on a larger piece of the real wreckage with a 16-pound (7.3-kg) sledge-hammer. "Still no dent," lamented Major Marcel. Washington would support the initial press bulletins. They had this one opportunity to make it work, and so the cover-up went into a full-court press. Meanwhile, back at the ranch....

Fifty to 60 men descended on the sleepy, open range with a mission of recovery and cleanup. "If it doesn't move, pick it up," directed Sgt. Earl Fulford. Shoulder-to-shoulder they marched with burlap sacks, some even on hands and knees, in the 100-degree (38-degree-Celsius) desert sun. They deposited the artifacts in wheel barrows which were then rolled over to check points where each remnant was tagged and numbered. Lastly, trucks were loaded with wooden crates and driven back to the base in Roswell—only to return for another load and another.... "Looks like you had a crash here," said mortician Glenn Dennis, who was in charge of ambulance and mortuary services for the Roswell Army Air Field (RAAF).

The situation 40 miles (64 kilometers) north of Roswell was much more urgent. Heavier equipment was required, including a flatbed truck, and the amount of security seemed to indicate an incident of utmost national security. Most involved in the recovery operation were not allowed within specific parameters. Outside personnel and specialists, including engineers and crash investigators, were also called to the scene. Photographers were recording every move of the operation, including when the ambulance trucks arrived. The RAAF base commander conveniently announced his leave of absence after the press release went out. In reality, his vacation amounted to a picturesque tour of the high desert plains and overseeing the entire retrieval process. The Army Field Manual provided no mention of such a strategic project. All of this was uncharted territory.

An immediate search for Mack Brazel ensued and, fortunately for the authorities, they located him in short order, suspecting as they did the natural tendencies of the local press. The wire recording was also appropriated by the military police, in total defiance of the First Amendment. From beginning to end of this affair, the law didn't seem to apply. The military's main focus was to confiscate every last piece of physical evidence. People's rights were secondary. People were simply obstacles. However, the evidence didn't cooperate; it provided no answers. No serial numbers or return tags offering $5 rewards upon return were ever found amongst the wreckage. Reaction and response took on unprecedented proportions, but the most extreme reaction was yet to come.

Personnel at Roswell were ordered not to report to their normally assigned buildings as outside officers, MPs, photographers, and even doctors and nurses arrived from parts unknown to take over the entire campaign. As RAAF nurse Rosemary McManus said,

"Something big had clearly happened." But no one was talking. Men were called in to perform specific duties from individual units, to prevent any talking after all the dust cleared. Emotions were cast aside as the actors performed like machines in overdrive; alcohol certainly helped in this regard. Time was their enemy as the assigned floundered for unyielding solutions.

It was clear that attention had to be diverted from Roswell. Only the intelligence officer was specifically named in the press release, and he was being sent to "higher headquarters." The base commander went on vacation (*after* his real vacation, I might add) and the rancher who had started the whole commotion was nowhere to be found. It was all very contrived. Next, the press had to be shut down. Calls came from the FCC in Washington with threats to sanction media outlets within 24 hours. "You are not to release any more news on this situation," warned federal agent T.J. Slowie. Dennis Chavez, a senator from New Mexico, followed up with the obligatory, hand-washing call about it all being "out of his control." On a grander scale, the FBI would intercept a national wire transmission that was attempting to report the true nature of the incident, and stop it dead in its tracks. A news blackout was in effect until a new story could be substituted. Synchronization of this process was crucial. A scapegoat was also needed. The stage was being set for the press conference of the century in Texas. Would the military unveil for all the world to see the actual wreckage brought in by Brazel (the same wreckage, incidentally, that had been sent to Washington for high-level scrutiny just two days before)? The answer to this is an emphatic no. They had ample time to rewrite one of the biggest stories of all time; all the chosen actors had to do was stick to the script. Incidentally, all of this was occurring while Brazel was being harshly interrogated. No customary phone calls were allowed to family or legal counsel, and with no arrest, due process was no longer mandatory. The reality was that the military had no real authority over this civilian, which made the full body search he endured all the more undignified.

Unbeknownst to the head of the 509th intelligence office, disguised packages were being loaded into the cargo haul of the waiting B-29, nicknamed *Dave's Dream*. Originally the final destination was to have been Wright Field in Dayton, Ohio, but this special shipment, wrapped in brown paper, was intended for display at the late afternoon press conference in Fort Worth. And Blanchard's boss, Gen. Roger Ramey, wanted the main actor to be there to take his bows. A change of props and scenery was about to take place in Texas: Strewn over the general's floor was a pile of rotting Neoprene rubber, wooden sticks, blank masking tape, string, and some one-sided reflective foil. One lone reporter allowed into the officer's room would comment about the strong rubber stench. Major Marcel was ordered by Ramey to pose for two awkward photos and then instructed to exit the stage and keep his mouth shut. Proclaiming there was no longer any need to bring to Dayton what had proven to be such commonplace materials, the general canceled the show. The curtain was about to come down. However, the material was secretly shipped on to Ohio. The FBI office in Dallas confirmed that in a special bulletin, which went out at 6:17 p.m. CST that very evening.

Back in Roswell, reality proceeded in high gear. Wreckage continued to truck in at the base, and the remains of the object of unknown origin arrived on a flatbed through the east gate. All of these items were examined under the strictest security at the military hospital. Because everyone was working on pure adrenaline, human emotion got the better of some. Eli Benjamin described how one of the senior officers became uncharacteristically intoxicated and had to be relieved of his duties. Fear was put aside with the call to arms, but this kind of situation was never anticipated in *anyone's* army. Personnel followed orders under the premise that someone actually knew what was going on, but ignorance prevailed. All the Pentagon could do was stall for time—for years if necessary—while it tried to contain the story. A tent would be set up within a new chain-link fence on the far southwest end of the tarmac. Guards were posted at an unusual location, right next to the garbage incinerator. Someone commented that it was the perfect place to disguise an unknown odor. Rotting rubber it was not. Nervous eyes glanced skyward as night fell on the fifth day.

A relief detail arrived at the site at dawn but everything had already been cleared out. The tent, its contents, and metal fence were all gone. The only evidence left behind was a set of large plane tracks in the dewy grass where something unknown had been secured overnight. The weather balloon explanation had teeth and served as a banner headline throughout the nation. The press bought the retraction, and the public was relieved. Life was good, and now everyone could return to the normal rituals of summer. But even for the first atomic bomb wing in the world, nothing in their training seemed to apply to the mission still at hand. And with the balloon story taking effect, the "loose lips sink ships" policy that was promulgated during World War II took precedence. *That* part they lived every day.

As more of the remaining evidence was hurriedly transported from Roswell, additional troops were dispatched to finalize the cleanup at multiple sites north of town. Every last piece of debris needed to be secured, and that included the pieces that had fallen into civilian hands. So while the MPs were collecting every trace of the paper trail within the local media outlets, others were pulling up floorboards, tipping over water tanks, slitting open sacks of feed, and sampling the jarred peaches while the ranch families could only watch in total bewilderment. And no one had heard from or seen Brazel for days.

The White House resembled a war room as unscheduled meetings were called to discuss what had fallen out of the sky in New Mexico. The Deputy Army Air Force Chief sat through meetings with the Secretary of War, the head of the Armed Forces Special Weapons Project, the chair of the Joint Chiefs, and the President. Multiple meetings overlapped and interrupted each other throughout the entire day. Apparently they never received the weather balloon memo! Two secret service emissaries were dispatched to oversee the recovery operation and report back directly to the Commander-in-Chief. Familiar faces such as Generals Eisenhower, LeMay, and Twining had to remain in the shadows. The public was forced to accept the conventional explanation, but all of the actions of those who were directly involved continued to suggest otherwise.

Mack Brazel was now ready to denounce his original story. Friends of the rancher and others witnessed military officers escort their next pawn to the main newspaper and the two radio stations. Brazel recanted and stated that his story was simply a misidentification of a weather balloon. Next time—if there was a next time—Brazel wouldn't say a word if he "found anything besides a bomb," he said during an interview with the *Roswell Daily Record*. Undoubtedly, the main reason for his detention served a greater purpose than the halfhearted retraction of his story. Brazel had seen more than anyone else had, so they had to enlist him as an apparent willing member of the sideshow. More to the point, 64 years later, his haunting remark resounds louder than ever: *"They weren't green."* Another unscheduled flight later that afternoon would seem to corroborate the veracity of his stunned statement. What was secured the night before in the tent was now in a guarded crate loaded into a B-29, named *Straight Flush*, from atomic bomb Pit No. 1. Almost 24 hours after the general had "emptied the Roswell saucer," as reported in the banner headline on the July 9 edition of the the *Roswell Daily Record*, Ramey, other officers, and a mortician eagerly awaited the arrival of additional remains contained within that large wooden box. The recovery operation was quickly winding down on all fronts, and the Roswell townspeople were persuaded to put the entire incident behind them. And night, along with reality, faded into the sixth day.

The confiscation of media reports; the oaths of secrecy to military personnel; the commissioning of both elected and civil officials to perform proxy deeds of suppression and intimidation; and, in perhaps the most heinous violation of the U.S. Constitution, the use of the military to physically threaten the very lives of its citizenry should all serve to remind us how important this single historic event really was. Military search teams would continue to recover remnants for years after the story was buried. Just two years after the incident, the military retrieved material that Brazel's son Bill had discovered. One need only examine the mistreatment of Brazel himself to understand that he did not discover a mere weather balloon. According to all sources, the humble cowboy was robbed of his very spirit. The sheriff didn't fare any better, either; family members stated that the incident "destroyed" him to the point that he would not run for reelection. Even the RAAF PIO, who was destined to go all the way to the rank of general, resigned. So did the intelligence officer. Some officers were immediately transferred, while others were promoted for being good soldiers. No one was reprimanded, and no one was demoted. The RAAF base commander went on to Washington to get his four stars—not for misidentifying a weather balloon device, but for managing to pull off one of the greatest cover-ups in U.S. history. Civilians, on the other hand, were clearly the victims of the harshest treatment to ensure their full cooperation. Although the military is pretty much a dictatorship, civilians have rights guaranteed by our forefathers. But in this case at least, these rights fell by the wayside.

The crux of this entire historic event was the physical evidence. Even now, in the year 2010, we have yet to develop a near-indestructible, paper-thin metal that has perfect memory. Another important aspect of this event is the growing number of death-bed testimonies about "little men" and "little people." Rest assured that this isn't about short-statured humans or crash-test dummies; all of the witnesses have been very clear about this. Last confessions are admissible in a court of law for a reason, and if we throw out the ones we don't like, we have to toss out all of them. Roswell should be no exception.

As a collective sigh of relief was breathed over the country (and the world, for that matter), New Mexico was left to recover from a full scorched-earth policy which left its residents bitter and angry at the very people who had been entrusted with their safety and well-being. The relationship between the RAAF and local Roswellians would be forever strained. A dark cloud hung over the entire situation, but the Pentagon was far from finished with their damage control. Forget all of those flying saucer reports and the people who see them!

The next page in the military's damage-control "handbook" called for a nationwide attempt to dismiss *all* flying disc sightings. It was reasoned that if the balloon story could explain away actual physical evidence at Roswell, why wouldn't it be able to provide a long-standing solution for the entire phenomenon? As a result, balloon launch demonstrations were publicly conducted at military facilities all across the country. From New York to California, witnesses saw firsthand that a balloon with an attached radar kite at 10,000 feet (3,048 meters) could easily be misconstrued as something extraordinary. The irony was that the very same weather device that had burst the balloon, figuratively speaking, at Roswell next served to deflate the entire saucer mystery. No one in the media ever explained how anyone could possibly misidentify a weather balloon sitting on the ground right in front of them. While this public charade was taking place, the very officer who would later become the Air Force's "saucer man" was hitting the airwaves and mocking anyone who would even see such things. During an El Paso radio interview, Gen. Ramey was asked about the wave of sightings throughout the entire nation, to which he responded that yes, it was true that there had been reports throughout every state in the country, "except Kansas, which is a dry state." The UFO ridicule factor was officially born.

"Upstairs" in Washington, the government remained in a frantic state of confusion as it stalled for time, seeking out answers from the truckloads of unidentifiable wreckage. Experts in various fields were immediately dispatched to rewrite scientific history as they knew it, with hopes that the sun would still rise in the east the next morning. The renowned meteorite expert Dr. Lincoln La Paz arrived in Roswell within a few weeks after the incident with orders from Washington. His assignment: to determine the *speed* and *trajectory* of the crashed craft of unknown origin. (Note to reader: balloon crashes are not evaluated according to either of these factors.) In addition to T-2 (the Foreign Technology Division at Wright Field), metallurgists and engineers were enlisted from the Bureau of Standards, General Electric, Rand Corporation, and Hughes Aircraft. Just down the road in Columbus, Ohio, Battelle National Laboratories was contracted by Wright Patterson AFB in Dayton to conduct developmental research on this "self-healing" metal.

Air Intelligence in Washington sought their own resolution to the mystery. They urgently requested a report from the Air Material Command (AMC) at Wright Field under the command of Lt. Gen. Nathan F. Twining. The Pentagon wanted to get to the bottom of the entire "flying disc" affair. Just two months after the physical evidence of the crash was transported to Dayton, Ohio, Gen. Twining held a secret conference with personnel from the Air Institute of Technology; Intelligence from T-2; the Office of Chief Engineering Division; and the Aircraft, Power Plant and Propeller Laboratories of Engineering, Div. T-3. If the general was attempting to identify the materials he couldn't have asked for better consultants. Clearly, these were nuts-and-bolts experts, not lights-in-the-sky speculators waiting for the next UFO sighting to provide some answers. Given what Twining knew firsthand to be the truth about the recovery at Roswell, and given the late-breaking status reports he gleaned from these consultants, Twining decided how best to respond to the growing concern. On September 23, 1947, Twining sent a secret memorandum to Brig. Gen. George Schulgen, Chief of the Air Intelligence Requirement Division (AIRD), which concluded that: 1) "the phenomenon reported is something real and not visionary or fictitious"; and 2) "there are objects approximately the shape of a disc, of such appreciable size as to appear to be as large as man-made aircraft." The two and one-half page document concluded by recommending that the "Army Air Force issue a directive assigning a priority, security classification and code name for a detailed study of this matter...." But Schulgen wasn't totally convinced with that assessment, so the AIRD sent out a draft of collection memorandum on October 28, 1947. What they were attempting to "collect" was specific information from all intelligence sources from outside the United States, including England, France, Sweden, Finland, the USSR, Turkey, Greece, Iran, China, Norway, and the Philippines, as well as other U.S. facilities and installations around the world. The document was a further attempt to gather technical insights as to what had crashed months before in New Mexico. This final process of prosaic elimination cited "unusual fabrication methods to achieve extreme light weight and structural stability" as well as "the presence of an unconventional or unusual type of propulsion system...." The military's response to Twining's report has never been disclosed.

On December 30, 1947, Major General Lawrence C. Craige, the director of Air Force Research and Development issued an order establishing the first official U.S. government UFO investigation, code name Project Sign (or Project Saucer). The project was officially initiated on January 22, 1948, as a branch of Air Technical Intelligence Center (ATIC), headquartered at Wright Patterson. And it was without any surprise that the newly formed project was given a 2A priority (1A being the very highest in the Air Force). It should also be emphasized that the top people at ATIC were assigned to the project with the intent of providing the answers that physical evidence alone had failed to yield. The rest, as they say, is history. Bear in mind that this entire full-scale response was over a mere weather balloon device—or so they say.

This story should remind all of us of the great tragedy of Roswell, and the human element that was at play in dealing with something potentially non-human. No other explanation would make much sense given the depth of the emotional response. Confusion and chaos, and the resulting anxiety and fear, all led to overreactions of extreme proportions—emotions that clearly do not make sense within the context of a simple and plausible event such as the crash of a weather balloon. We are now asked by the government to accept the most recent of four official explanations, but it has yet to provide one witness to the last three of these "explanations." We are told that all records and documents pertaining to the event have mysteriously disappeared or been destroyed. And ever-reluctant witnesses tell us that they were sworn to secrecy over the recovery of a balloon project which was officially declassified almost 40 years ago. In his book *Report on Unidentified Flying Objects*, 1956, the Blue Book director Capt. Edward Ruppelt stated, "By the end of July [1947] the UFO security lid was down tight. The few members of the press who did inquire about what the Air Force was doing got the same treatment that you would get today if you inquired about the number of thermonuclear weapons stockpiled in the U.S. atomic arsenal. At [ATIC there was] confusion to the point of panic." What an amazing admission. Recall that wonderful scene in the movie *Roswell* in which the oversight committee is brainstorming the entire affair. The general asks, "What if the people discover that we are no longer in control of the skies?" The secretary of war very stoically replies, "They'd be right."

Secrets become the responsibility of those entrusted with the truth. After 64 years, that final truth still remains in the hands of those who know what really happened in Roswell. And our job should be to extricate that truth from the darkness and bring it to light, not become willing accomplices in the cover-up. If I am wrong about this, it will change nothing, but if I am right, it will change just about everything. The dead continue to cry out the truth while governments seldom proclaim *any* truism unless it advances their cause. For the government to concede its position and take responsibility for the multitude of constitutional violations to American citizenry, as testified by witnesses who have decried the extreme measures undertaken to conceal the truth and bully them into silence, will probably never happen. To fail to see the hidden agenda of the self-styled keepers of the Holy Grail besmirches those who bravely stepped forward and opposed them. History itself is compiled of the testimony and personal accounts by people such as these. It is time we stop revising *their* history to fulfill our own motives and desires. If you have read this essay with an objective open mind, as I have requested, at the very least it should leave you wondering: What if they are *right*?

Star Travel: How Realistic Is It?

By Stanton T. Friedman

One of the most common objections to the notion that some UFOs are intelligently controlled extraterrestrial vehicles is simply this: "You can't get here from there." That is, it would take too much energy, it would take too long, and the laws of physics (especially those relating to Einstein's theory of relativity) would prevent it. Even when these sorts of objections are uttered by well-educated people, they rarely arise from serious attempts to determine feasibility. It as if the details don't matter; it is simply impossible. However, the fact is that that the devil is in the details, at least as far as science is concerned. What's more, aerospace engineers have long since performed the "impossible," such as flying faster than the speed of sound, sinking battleships with bombs dropped from the air, and flying non-stop around the earth. So, clearly, the "impossible" argument is specious.

Here is a concrete example of how easy it is for intelligent people of science to go astray in these matters. The astronomer Dr. John Campbell published a paper[1] in 1941 attempting to determine the required initial launch weight of a rocket that would be able to send a man to the moon and back. He had pages of equations and concluded that the initial launch weight would have to be a million million tons. In 1969 NASA sent three men to the moon with a Saturn 5 multistage chemical rocket whose initial launch weight was "only" 3,000 tons (2,700 metric tons). Because of his numerous incorrect assumptions, especially the use of a single-stage rocket, he was wrong by an incredible factor of 300 million! He had not studied the considerable engineering literature that had been published by such very competent engineers as Konstantin Tsiolkovsky, Hermann Oberth, Robert Goddard, and many others. His assumptions clearly indicated that he knew nothing about the practical side of space flight to the moon. Everybody who was seriously considering deep-space travel at that time was aware that a multi-stage rocket offered enormous weight savings. In a multi-stage rocket, once all the fuel in the first stage is used up, the empty stage is simply jettisoned. That means that it no longer must be accelerated. The same goes for the second stage. For reasons unknown, Campbell also assumed a very low exhaust velocity for the propellant sent out of the nozzle. (The higher the exhaust velocity, the shorter the time and the less energy required to get up to speed.) He also assumed an acceleration of only 1 G, which is 9.8 meters per second/per second, or 21 miles (34 kilometers) per hour/per second. The higher the acceleration, the faster one gets into orbit, and the less the effect of earth's gravitational field on the rocket. There is a very large body of experimental work done on rocket sleds and centrifuges that shows that the amount of acceleration that a human can stand depends on the object's magnitude, duration, and direction. Astronauts routinely withstand 5 Gs during flight to the moon, and even higher values under certain circumstances. For example, the acceleration of the escape rocket on the Apollo Command Module, if it had ever been used, would have been 13 Gs. Astronauts are launched on their backs because humans can withstand much more acceleration back to front than they can foot to head, as in an elevator. As a matter of experimental fact, a properly constrained pilot can perform a complex task while being accelerated at 14 Gs for two minutes. That is about 300 miles (483 kilometers) per hour/per second. (By way of comparison, a "hot" automobile would be one accelerating at 1 G, which would get it to 63 miles [101 kilometers] per hour in only three seconds from a standing start.)

Dr. Campbell also assumed that the rocket itself would have to supply all the energy to get the craft to the moon and slow it down upon re-entry into the earth's atmosphere. This was a very foolish assumption. In the first place, a rocket launched to the east near the equator is already moving at 1,000 miles (1,600 kilometers) per hour. In the second place, if one is launched at the correct time (during a "launch window"), the gravitational field of the moon will attract the rocket, thus saving the fuel that would otherwise be required. Campbell correctly realized that the return rocket would be moving at about 25,000 miles (40,234 kilometers) per hour and would have to be slowed down before it could land safely. However, he wrongly assumed that a retrorocket would be required for that purpose. Of course, this part would be dead weight during the launch, during the landing on the moon, during takeoff from the moon, and during the approach to Earth. Smart engineers realized that they could use the earth's atmosphere to slow down the rocket if they provided a heat shield to keep the command module from burning up. The dramatic return of Apollo 13 clearly illustrated how important it was to get the correct angle of re-entry. If it had come in at too steep an angle, it would have slammed into the earth at much too high a velocity and killed the astronauts. Conversely, if the angle had been too shallow, the module would have gone right by the earth and been lost forever. The same rules and laws apply to our deep-space probes: We use the gravitational fields of the planets to assist them on their way out of the solar system. The Pioneer and Voyager spacecraft are now outside the solar system and have used the gravitational fields of Jupiter and other planets for this purpose. The Cassini spacecraft has been orbiting around Saturn for years. It got a free gravity assist from Venus, which sent it back past Earth, which gave it another free gravity assist, which sent it out toward Jupiter, which gave it another free boost back toward Saturn. This "cosmic freeloading" is standard practice in space travel.

As far as the "impossibility" of space travel goes, it is interesting to note that in a paper presented to the British Association for the

Advancement of Science in 1926, Professor Alexandre Bickerton, a New Zealand astronomer, "proved" it would be impossible to provide enough energy to put *anything* into orbit around the earth. In this he followed in the footsteps of America's most noted 19th-century astronomer, Dr. Simon Newcombe. In 1903, Newcombe proclaimed that "the demonstration that no possible combination of known substances, known forms of machinery, and known forms of force can be united in a practical machine by which man shall fly long distances through the air seems to this writer as complete as it is possible for the demonstration of any physical fact to be."[2] The first flight of the Wright Brothers took place only two months after Newcombe made this statement, mute testimony to the incredible arrogance and ignorance of this otherwise accomplished scientist.

Going to the stars is a much different proposition than traveling to the moon or other planets in our own solar system, however. The first step is, of course, deciding where one wants to go. Many naysayers seem not to understand how many potential targets there are within a mere 55-light-year radius. There are roughly 2,000 stars within this radius, five percent of which are very similar to our sun. Our solar system is only a few light hours across. It takes light from the sun only eight minutes to reach Earth, about 42 minutes to reach Jupiter, and a little more than five hours to reach Pluto. The next star over is 4.3 light years away. Most people have no idea how little time it would take to get close to the speed of light at only 1 G acceleration. I have had professors guess 1,000 or 100 or 10 years. The correct answer is *one year*. To give you a sense of this, if an astronaut were approaching the speed of light, time would slow down to such an extent that at 99.99 percent of the speed of light, it would take him or her only six months pilot time to go 37 light years. The closer something gets to the speed of light, the more time slows down.

That said, our galaxy, the Milky Way, is a flattened spiral pancake about 100,000 light years across and maybe 15,000 light years thick. It has more than 100 billion stars. The next similar galaxy, Andromeda, is a little more than two million light years away, and the universe itself is about 13 billion light years across. For reasons unknown, interstellar travel skeptics want to talk about how difficult it would be to go to Andromeda. This is hardly a rational consideration at this point in time. At our primitive stage of development, surely we need not be concerned with flights to other galaxies or even across our own! A more likely target would be a unique pair of sun-like stars, Zeta 1 and Zeta 2 Reticuli, which are only 39.3 light years from us, are visible from the southern hemisphere, and are only about an eighth of a light year apart from each other. They are also at least one billion years older than the sun. (More about these stars and their place in the history of UFOs can be found in *Captured! The Betty and Barney Hill Experience.*[3])

An excellent example of how *not* to go to the stars was provided by Dr. Neil de Grasse Tyson, the head of the Hayden Planetarium in New York City. In a very biased "documentary" on UFOs, hosted by Peter Jennings on ABC TV on February 24, 2005, he stated that our fastest craft, Voyager, would take 70,000 years to get to the nearest star. He neglected to mention that it has been coasting since it was launched in 1977 because it has no propulsion system. Sending Voyager to the nearest star would be like tossing a bottle into the ocean or releasing a balloon into the air to see how long it takes to get somewhere. He and most other astronomers need to do some serious homework!

Fusion and Fission as Paths to the Stars

Almost all skeptics contend that the only possible propulsion system for deep space travel would be a chemical rocket, such as those we have been using for more "local" travel. These rockets utilize the combustion of hydrogen and oxygen or kerosene and oxygen. On the other extreme, we have people postulating matter/antimatter annihilation as means for propulsion, which sounds both exotic and unrealistic—mostly unrealistic, because antimatter is very difficult indeed to both make and store. Both of these groups are seemingly unaware of the rational and realistic alternatives: nuclear fission and nuclear fusion. The major advantage of a system powered by fission or fusion would be the ability to fly for thousands of hours without refueling, thus requiring far less weight. There are nuclear fission–powered aircraft carriers in operation today that can operate for 18 years without refueling. Nuclear fission reactors can also produce electrical power in space to provide energy for weapons such as lasers (and perhaps even particle beams in the future), sideband radar, and ion or plasma propulsion systems. In contrast, solar energy conversion systems are large and heavy, and produce less energy the farther they are from the sun. All of this clearly illustrates a primary aspect of technological growth: Technological progress comes from doing things differently in an unpredictable way. The future is not an extrapolation of the past.

Nuclear Fission Systems

In 1958, the General Electric Aircraft Nuclear Propulsion Department spent $100 million in trying to develop an aircraft that was propelled by nuclear power. The program employed 3,500 people, 1,100 of whom were engineers and scientists. Jet *engines* had been operated on nuclear power before, but unfortunately these scientists and engineers were never able to achieve their goal before this classified (but not "black budget") program was cancelled in 1961. Eventually, however, it became obvious that we would be able to use the incredible energy density in uranium to power rockets. Scientists decided that liquid hydrogen would be very attractive as a propellant because it has the lowest atomic weight (1) of any element and is the most abundant and lightest element in the universe. No heavy oxidizer, such as liquid oxygen (which has an atomic weight of 8), would be needed. The lower the atomic weight of the exhaust, the higher its velocity, and thus the greater the velocity of the rocket. Several different programs were in the works during the 1960s, including Kiwi, Phoebus, and NRX, to name a few. Several systems were tested by the three primary organizations involved: Los Alamos National Laboratory in Los Alamos, New Mexico; Westinghouse Astronuclear Laboratory in Large, Pennsylvania;

and Aerojet General Corporation in Sacramento, California. Such systems were designed to function as the upper stages of rockets, not as vehicles for launching from the surface of the Earth. The energy density is truly incredible in these systems. They could more than double the payload to be sent to Mars, for example. Westinghouse's NRX A-6 (which I worked on) operated at 1,100 megawatts—in laymen's terms, half the power produced by the Grand Coulee dam—but was less than 6 feet (1.8 meters) long and 6 feet (1.8 meters) in diameter. LANL's Phoebus 2B was a little larger and operated at 4,400 megawatts. Actual tests on these systems were performed during the late 1960s at the Nuclear Test Site about 75 miles (121 kilometers) west of Las Vegas, Nevada. This is a very remote area not far from the notorious Area 51. Despite the successful operation of reactors by all three contractors, the programs were all cancelled because there was essentially no leadership provided by NASA.

Nuclear Fusion Systems

Controlled nuclear fusion systems have also been considered for deep-space propulsion. Many people are skeptical of fusion as a means of space travel because such systems have not yet been developed for producing power here on earth. A number of very powerful fusion devices have been tested in the form of H-bombs. However, fusion plasmas operate in a vacuum, and Mother Nature has provided a very good vacuum chamber in outer space. It takes a lot of energy to produce this kind of system at sea level. Aerojet General Nucleonics, in San Ramon, California, did a study in the early 1960s for the USAF of a fusion propulsion system. The director was Dr. John Luce, who had been head of the fusion research work at Oak Ridge National Laboratory. A major advantage to these types of systems was the combination of elements used: hydrogen and helium are the lightest and most abundant elements in the universe; uranium, by contrast, is the most dense and is much more rare. Of course, it would not be inexpensive to develop a full-fledged fusion propulsion system for deep-space travel. The stealth fighter, the nuclear submarine, the atomic bomb, the supersonic aircraft—all of these were very costly to develop. The Apollo program alone cost $20 billion. Such a development would also require a major program, not just a few professors and graduate students, and would likely have to be planetary in scope rather than restricted to just one country. Of course, in today's world it would be difficult to justify such an effort.

Quantum Travel?

Considering that we are less than 100 years into the nuclear age, it is unlikely that nuclear fusion will be the penultimate or even the ultimate deep-space travel technique, despite its promise, and despite the fact that it is vastly more advanced than chemical propulsion (which seems to be the only technique that astronomers and SETI specialists are aware of). Perhaps quantum mechanics will one day hold the key. When one goes down in size by a factor of 10,000, from the big, fat atom to the much smaller nucleus, one goes *up* in energy per particle by a factor of 10 *million*. This makes one wonder how much energy is contained in quarks, which are thought to make up the nuclei of atoms. Will the energy per particle go up rapidly, as well? Again, technological progress comes from doing things differently in an unpredictable way. Such progress has proven itself to be both speedy and unceasing. Witness the laser: it was invented only 50 years ago but it now appears all over world, from checkout counters to CD players to medical devices. And Moore's law, the doubling of the number of transistors on a microchip every two years or less, still marches on.

o[⌀]   o[⌀]   o[⌀]

The biggest obstruction in developing exciting and totally new technologies is the attitude of the noisy negativists who focus on trying to prove that the new systems won't work, instead of looking for new techniques to solve old problems. The British Astronomer Royal, Dr. Richard van der Riet Wooley, famously proclaimed in 1956 that "space travel is utter bilge." There are numerous examples throughout history of technological progress being delayed or derailed by the impact of false claims of impossibility from well-educated prominent people who were not at all knowledgeable about the details of the technical areas (aviation, space flight, radio, television, climatology, and so on) about which they made their pronouncements. The Dr. Campbells, Bickertons, and Newcombes of this world cover their own ignorance by proclaiming it is impossible, rather than admitting that they don't yet know how it can be done! It is unfortunate that the press always seems to turn to astronomers who know nothing about large-scale research and development programs, deep-space travel, or advanced technology, and who have trouble admitting that they have consistently been wrong about the situation within our own solar system, let alone travel to the stars. The press also seems unaware of the huge amount of advanced expensive research done outside of academia, often in classified or "black budget" programs that are never published in scientific journals.

Nuclear fusion is what produces the energy of stars throughout the universe, so it seems likely that any advanced civilizations out there would know what it is and how to harness it. There may even be a network of fuel depots, rest and relaxation centers, and even libraries throughout the galaxy for these interstellar itinerants. Just think of how our own earthly highway system has changed in the past 100 years. Who knows? Perhaps my young great-grandson will see the day when our first star travelers depart for Zeta 1 or Zeta 2 Reticuli. The enormous amount of evidence out there (much of which is cataloged in my book *Flying Saucers and Science*[4]) and in such government documents as Project Blue Book[5] clearly indicates that aliens are not only real—they are visiting our earth. Given our own technological progress, which shows no signs of slowing or abating, the stars may soon be within our reach, as well.

Notes

1. Campbell, John. "Rocket Flight to the Moon," *Philosophical Magazine* 7, no. 204 (January 1941): 31–41.

2. Newcombe, Simon. "The Outlook for the Flying Machine." *The Independent* October 22, 1903.

3. Friedman, Stanton T. and Kathleen Marden. *Captured! The Betty and Barney Hill UFO Experience.* Franklin Lakes, N.J.: New Page Books, 2007. (Order for $18.99 postpaid from UFORI, P.O. Box 958, Houlton, ME 04730-0958.)

4. Friedman, Stanton T. *Flying Saucers and Science.* Franklin Lakes, N.J.: New Page Books, 2008. (Order an autographed copy from UFORI for $19.00.)

5. Project Blue Book Special Report. No. 14, Battelle Memorial Institute for the USAF, October, 1955. (Order a copy from UFORI for $20.00.)

The UFO Problem: Toward a Theory of Everything?

By John White

In June 1947, Kenneth Arnold, a civilian pilot flying near Mt. Ranier, Washington, reported seeing nine strange objects in the sky. He likened their flight pattern to a saucer being skipped across the water. Within a few days, the term *flying saucer* was born, coined by a reporter to name the mysterious objects, and the media and public alike immediately speculated that Earth was being visited by extraterrestrials. Since then the term has been changed to *UFO* ("unidentified flying object"), and the study of them is called *ufology*. Since that day, UFOs have been widely investigated, hotly debated, and eagerly viewed by witnesses all over the world. Here's how the civilian research group called MUFON (Mutual UFO Network) defines the situation in their mission statement in the *MUFON Journal*:

UFOs are objects observed in the skies or on the surface of the Earth which defy conventional explanation after a thorough study and investigation by competent people. Some of the things reported as UFOs are balloons, planets, meteors, satellites, stars, advertising aircraft, falling aerospace debris, and the like. These are IFOs—identified flying objects. The "hard" sightings which are yet to be explained are daylight discs, objects with unusual lights which are simultaneously tracked visually and on radar at fantastic speeds, objects which leave physical evidence after landing, authenticated photographs, and an increasing number of cases involving visitations or close encounters by humanoids or entities. It is this category which serious ufologists are trying to gather additional evidence in our quest to resolve the UFO phenomenon.

But what exactly are UFOs? Where do they come from? What is the source of their power? Are they actual physical objects with mass and form, or are they something else altogether? And what do they want with us? Their reported characteristics—size, shape, color, material, type of occupants and their behavior, and so on—vary widely, so what, if anything, can we say about them with any certainty? The answer unfortunately is not much, but based on the evidence, it seems clear that no single explanation can cover every experience and event, or bring them together under a single monolithic label of "the UFO phenomenon." Likewise, there is no single answer to the previous questions. It would be nice if there were a neat, simple explanation, but as I survey the evidence, I find that there isn't. The UFO phenomenon, such as it is, is actually complex and multifaceted, and it can't be explained away with such facile generalizations. Little green men in spaceships with Martian license plates may be part of the puzzle, but that is only one piece of it. There is much more to it than that.

In my judgment, the evidence of ufology falls into three major categories, and so it stands to reason that there are three qualitatively different solutions to the UFO problem. These solutions are genuine, but partial at best. None is comprehensive of everything that could be included under the umbrella of "the UFO phenomenon." Collectively, they pertain to what can be called different levels of reality or different aspects of our existence. Just as we humans have a body, mind, and spirit, so, too, does the cosmos have a physical, mental, and spiritual level or aspect to it. With regard to UFOs, these levels or aspects are *terrestrial*, *extraterrestrial*, and *metaterrestrial*. The latter is a term coined by the astronomer-ufologist

Dr. J. Allen Hynek to denote an unseen world existing beyond or alongside of our familiar three-dimensional world. (He also coined the phrase "close encounters of the first [or second or third] kind.") This three-part solution for the UFO problem is the overview I offer here. There is not enough space to go into the evidence in detail, so I'll just sketch it in very broad strokes to give the reader a basic idea of what I'm talking about. I'll start with the most common idea— namely, that UFOs are extraterrestrial in origin.

The Extraterrestrial Solution

This idea is the most common simply because it's been around the longest and has gradually gained widespread acceptance. The idea of ET visitation was actually fairly common years before Kenneth Arnold's sighting. Almost 10 years earlier, Orson Welles' famous 1938 radio program, based on H.G. Welles' novel *The War of the Worlds*, frightened radio listeners with a tale of Martian invaders. But even before that, in the latter part of the 19th century, the renowned scientist-inventor Nikola Tesla claimed to have received radio signals from space—from a nearby planet, he thought. And still earlier, there had been an ongoing debate in astronomy over whether there were canals on Mars, and whether such canals might be indicative of a Martian civilization. So the idea of ETs in contact with Earth was already a familiar one when ufology was in its incipient stages. The real question, however, is whether there's any truth to it. I think there is.

Some UFO experiences seem best understood exactly as the public generally does—namely, as craft occupied by ETs. I say "seem" because until one of these craft is actually obtained and publicly displayed, we cannot be certain. However, judging from the Humanoid Catalog database, which contains more than 3,000 modern sightings of UFOs *with occupants*, our planet appears to be one of the major crossroads of local space for these vehicles. The case for the existence of ETs has been solidly established during the last five decades by astrobiology (the study of nonterrestrial biology, which exists quite apart from the data of ufology). Astrobiologists are pursuing SETI, the search for extraterrestrial intelligence, by using radio telescopes to listen for signals from space. And although the scientific community by and large does not accept ufology as a colleague discipline, that rejection really is due to nothing more than irrational prejudice. Dr. Michael Swords of Western Michigan University has published an excellent paper in the *Journal of UFO Studies* demonstrating irrefutably that the ET hypothesis which the SETI scientists are seeking is perfectly applicable for use in evaluating UFO reports. So the unwillingness of the scientific community to listen to ufologists is simply illogical and unscientific. But even that is changing, as astronomy continues to discover planets revolving around other stars besides our sun—and that list of planets has grown to more than 1,200. So what is the evidence astrobiologists should consider? I'll mention just three cases. The first is the world-famous case of Barney and Betty Hill, which was described in the 1965 book *The Interrupted Journey* by John Fuller. It was made into a movie for television in the late 1970s and has been shown many times since. For me, the most persuasive aspect of the case is what has become known as the Hill Star Map.

The Hill Star Map

While driving on a deserted road near Exeter, New Hampshire, in 1961, the Hills, a married couple, were both reportedly abducted and taken aboard a UFO by small, thin, gray beings with large heads. While in the craft, Betty was shown a holographic map of space, which clearly showed the route the beings had followed from their home star to Earth. The map appeared in full 3-D, as if she were looking out a porthole into space. Fast forward to 1964, when Betty and Barney underwent hypnotic therapy for symptoms which, as they later discovered, had arisen from their abduction experience. At the suggestion of their therapist, Boston psychiatrist Benjamin Simon, Betty drew a picture of the three-dimensional map she'd seen on board the craft in 1961. Her map showed our sun and other stars from the perspective of the aliens' home star. When the drawing was published in *The Interrupted Journey*, an Ohio school teacher named Marjorie Fish saw the picture and came up with the idea to use an astronomical catalog of stars to help her build a model of space by stringing beads on a wooden framework. The beads represented stars up to 40 light years away, accurately placed around the center (representing Earth) in accordance with the astronomical catalog data. It took Fish three years, working off and on, to finish her model. When it was complete, she looked at it from every single angle in an attempt to find a pattern of stars which would match Betty's map, but all her attempts at the time failed. She couldn't find a matching pattern.

Then, in 1969, a new catalog with revised astronomical data made it possible for Fish to construct a more accurate model of nearby space. The project took another three years, but when it was complete, she ultimately found a pattern of beads which was an almost perfect match for the pattern in the Hill Star Map. Based on this model, the home base of the aliens appeared to be the star Zeta Reticuli, in the constellation Reticulum, which is about 37 light years from Earth. Astronomers and ufologists debated the matter for some time before settling in favor of Fish, rather than dismissing the match as a coincidence.

Here's the reason this evidence is persuasive. The Hill Star Map was drawn in 1964 yet it contained information unknown to anyone on Earth at the time. Fish had to wait until the revised astronomical catalog was published in 1969, before human knowledge was sufficient for her to construct an accurate representation of local space. So how did Betty Hill obtain her knowledge of stars in space *eight years* before the revised catalog came out? Logic tells us that the holographic map she claimed to have seen aboard a UFO was real; therefore, it must have been of extraterrestrial origin.

Ancient Astronauts

Another case which provides strong evidence of ET contact is presented in a 1975 book titled *The Sirius Mystery* by Robert Temple, an astronomer. In it, Temple asserts that the Dogon tribe in central Africa has had accurate information about the configuration and composition of the star Sirius for thousands of years, including the fact that Sirius is a binary, or double, star. The Dogon have never had a written form of language, so their history is preserved through oral tradition. Their first contact with Europeans occurred only in the last century, when anthropologists first recorded information about them. According to Dogon mythology, ETs (which they call the *Nommo*) came to Earth many thousands of years ago and revealed information to the tribe about Sirius, which is about 8.7 light years away from Earth. The Nommo described the elliptical orbit of the companion star, called Sirius B, around the larger star, Sirius A, and its period of orbital rotation. They also said that Sirius B was very small and composed of a material heavier than all the iron on Earth. The Dogon then preserved that information in their oral tradition for thousands of years. As in the case of the Hill Star Map, these data exceed the limits of human knowledge: It wasn't until 1926 that the dark companion star, Sirius B, was discovered by astronomers to be a white dwarf star composed of ultra-heavy matter. But the Dogon's information was recorded orally many thousands of years prior. Again, these accurate data about the composition of Sirius—and indeed, the tribe's knowledge of the dark companion's very existence—strongly suggest an extraterrestrial source. The Dogon also claim there is a third star in this stellar complex. Although modern astronomy has not yet confirmed this, a search is currently under way. If this proves to be true, the Sirius mystery will be solved in favor of ET contact, in the manner of the "ancient astronauts" theory of Erich von Däniken, Zechariah Sitchin, and many other researchers who claim that primitive humanity regarded such beings as gods from outer space.

Roswell

My last case in this category is the famous Roswell Incident, in which two UFOs allegedly crashed in New Mexico in 1947 and were recovered, along with the bodies of the occupants, by the Army Air Force, who then transported the retrieved material to what is now Wright-Patterson Air Force Base in Dayton, Ohio. This case has been hotly contested among ufologists and outright denied by the Air Force. But a host of books—most notably *Crash at Corona* by Don Berliner and Stanton T. Friedman, and *Top Secret/Majic* by Stanton T. Friedman—assert that the Roswell Incident was real. *Top Secret/Majic* deals with Friedman's continuing research into a controversial set of documents known as "MJ-12" (short for "Majestic-12") and the group which was apparently behind them. The papers, which were "leaked" in 1984 by a government source, are purported to be a top secret account by President Harry S. Truman and others who describe the retrieval of a crashed UFO and four deceased aliens. Despite the vehemence of the Air Force's denials, the authenticity of the incident has been established by investigators who have documented statements by dozens of first-hand and second-hand military and civilian witnesses who attest to the reality that something extraordinary—and most probably of extraterrestrial origin—crashed near Roswell, New Mexico, and was recovered by the military.

Terrestrial Solutions

The three previous cases comprise the first part of my three-part solution to the UFO problem. Now let's look at the second of the three solutions. It would be nice if all UFO cases proved to be extraterrestrial in nature, but it's very likely that some originate from Earth itself—in other words, they are terrestrial in origin. By the way, I am not referring here to super-secret military aircraft, which were sometimes cited as the reality behind "sightings" during the first two decades of ufology. This is because many such sightings have taken place at military bases, including Air Force bases, and have caused technological problems for our own military, such as altering the codes on nuclear warheads and blocking runways so fighter planes can't take off. (This sort of activity was documented by Lawrence Fawcett and Barry Greenwood in their book *Clear Intent*.) Astronaut Gordon Cooper said that in 1957 he was filming experimental aircraft at Edwards Air Force base in Southern California when a UFO landed on the dry lake bed for about 10 minutes. His film crew got the whole thing on camera, but within hours the Pentagon had taken possession of the film. That was the last he ever heard of the whole thing. Moreover, by the 1980s, the United States had learned enough about the Soviet Union to realize that UFOs weren't secret Soviet aircraft, either—because the Soviets thought UFOs were of American origin! So it seems clear that UFOs reported in the 1950s and 60s were not super-secret military aircraft, after all.

Earthly "Alien" Craft

Ironically, however, some more recent sightings may indeed be just that. In the late 20th century, word leaked out about a secret aircraft, called the Aurora, which was being tested at Area 51, also called Groom Lake, at Nellis Air Force Base in Nevada. This supersonic vehicle flies at speeds estimated at Mach 7 (more than 4,000 miles (6,437 kilometers) per hour). But that's not all that is rumored to be hiding at Area 51: According to some ufologists, recovered alien spacecraft are also being tested and reverse-engineered so the Air Force can build its very own "UFOs." So in a curious twist, it may be that some UFO sightings are genuine in the sense that the craft are based on real alien technology—even though their occupants are human!

Aliens Under The Sea

There are even more curious possibilities for this solution to the UFO problem. Some UFOs have been sighted over large bodies of water, and involve craft which observers say burst out of the water and take off into the sky. The late biologist Ivan Sanderson wrote about this in his book *Invisible Residents*, which gives the best description of this permutation of the UFO phenomenon. Sanderson felt these sightings might be due to the presence of an undersea civilization native to Earth. He reasoned that because life began in the sea, the development of some organisms slowed when they came ashore, while the sea-living organisms continued to evolve. He cited cetaceans as an example: Although porpoises, dolphins, and whales are not technologically advanced in any sense of the word, they are highly intelligent. Some ufologists speculate that there may be advanced forms of sea life which are more intelligent than we are (and possibly even capable of UFO technology) living away from prying eyes, deep under the oceans and lakes. Of course, it may also be that ETs have established such undersea bases.

Plasma "Critters"

The next UFO experience in this category involves human contact with a lower form of animal life native to Earth's atmosphere. The discovery of these strange aerial creatures (which are akin to unicellular organisms) is told in Trevor James Constable's 1976 book *The Cosmic Pulse of Life*. He calls these airborne life-forms "critters." His text and photographs appear to reveal a class of elemental fauna unknown to science. These amoeba-like creatures, called *aeroforms*, are neither solid, nor liquid, nor gas; they exist in a fourth state of matter—plasma—and are typically invisible to us for several reasons: first, their native habitat is high in the atmosphere, far beyond the human gaze but nevertheless well within the range of the astronomer's telescope; second, they are bioenergetically propelled and move at a very high speed—thousands of miles per hour; and third, their usual condition or native state is in the infrared range of the electromagnetic spectrum, which is not visible to the naked eye. However, they have the capacity to change their density and thereby pass from one level of tangibility or visibility to another. When they appear in the visible portion of the spectrum, as they sometimes do, they are often labeled as UFOs—which, technically speaking, they are. But they are not mechanical spacecraft; they are living creatures. They grow anywhere from the size of a coin to half a mile (.8 kilometers) in diameter, perhaps even more. When they're visible, they pulsate with a reddish-orange glow. Although they can change form, they generally take on the shape of a disc or sphere. Their diaphanous structure allows for a limited view of their interior. When biologist Ivan Sanderson saw Constable's photos, he said it was like looking through a fishbowl. According to Constable's research, some "critters" have been seen up close on the ground in their full physical density. Even when they are invisible, however, they can still be detected by radar and photographed using infrared film.

In 1975, shortly after I learned of Constable's work, I got in touch with Dr. Carl Sagan and showed him some of the photographs. I was disappointed by his response. He told me the photos proved nothing and he would not even consider Constable's work unless Constable was able to produce photographs taken by synchronized stereoscopic cameras. This wasn't a bad technical suggestion, but it still demonstrated an arrogant close-mindedness about UFOs. This was in marked contrast to Allen Hynek's response when I showed him the photos. He was intrigued and eager to know more, so I put him in touch with Constable. They had some correspondence and spoke on the phone several times, which ultimately led to their meeting in person at the Los Angeles airport (Constable lived in nearby San Pedro). Their meeting led to Hynek's intention to go on a photographic "critter hunt" with Constable, but unfortunately Hynek was so busy that it never happened, and he died a few years later. But even before he had ever heard of Constable, Hynek had managed to photograph something through the window of an airplane at 35,000 feet (10,668 meters) which looked very much like a critter. Hynek said he couldn't explain the photo, and included it in his 1972 book *The UFO Experience*. Clearly, he saw potential in Constable's work. After Constable published his book, about a half a dozen other investigators followed his instructions for photographing these "critters," and have done so with positive results. I think this is an area which deserves closer study.

Earth Lights and Earthquakes

Yet another plausible terrestrial explanation for some UFO sightings may be found in the so-called earth lights. The term was coined by the English researcher Paul Devereux in his 1982 book *Earth Lights,* and further explained in his 1989 book *Earth Lights Revelations.* The books present evidence showing that geophysical activity in crystalline rock structures, especially along fault lines, produces a *piezoelectric effect.* (Piezoelectricity is electricity generated by pressure on a crystalline substance such as quartz.) The subsurface pressure generates electromagnetic fields above the fault lines, and in those fields, hot electrified balls of gas, called *ionized plasmas,* are formed. These ionized plasmas—which appear as luminous atmospheric phenomena—are the earth lights. Now, these aerial luminosities are nothing new: they've been noted throughout history around the world; however, they are usually attributed to supernatural causes and labeled variously as "will-o'-the-wisps," *ignis fatuui,* ghost lights, and so forth. Dr. Michael Persinger, a psychologist at Laurentian University in Canada, and Gyslaine Lafrenière, a research scientist there, demonstrated in their 1977 book, *Space-Time Transients and Unusual Events,* that such phenomena may have a very prosaic terrestrial origin after all. They argue that these seemingly ghostly lights are natural occurrences that are nevertheless capable of inducing hallucinations—such as seeing alien craft and creatures—in the people observing them, depending on how far away they are from the lights. The research of Devereux and his colleagues, independent of Persinger and Lafrenière's, has also enlarged upon the possibility that tectonically generated earth lights may account for some sightings of UFOs as well as mysterious ghostly figures. This line of research is known as the *tectonic strain theory.* Geophysicists have been investigating this phenomenon ever since earth lights were first reported during an earthquake. The lights weren't called UFOs, of course—just strange luminosities which sometimes appeared during a quake. In the mid-1980s, the U.S. Geological Survey, in its journal *Earthquakes and Volcanoes*, published the very first photo of one of these lights; it was snapped by someone with enough presence of mind to capture the mysterious phenomenon during an earthquake in the United States. A vaguely defined ball of light about six feet (1.8 meters) wide is clearly visible in the air.

So we have four terrestrial-based phenomena which could explain some UFO sightings. With the exception of undersea ET bases, these phenomena have absolutely nothing to do with creatures from outer space. But the list of terrestrial-based explanations needs to be enlarged by one—and a very strange one it is, indeed. It takes us past the border of physical reality and well into the metaphysical—or, more precisely, into the parapsychological. I'll call this the psycho-kinetic explanation.

Mind Over Matter?

The Swiss psychiatrist Carl Jung is known for his many contributions to the field of psychology, particularly the concept he termed the *collective unconscious*. In it, he hypothesized that we have not only a personal unconscious, which Freud demonstrated, but also a deeper "layer" of mind which is somehow shared by everyone. This aspect of consciousness includes memories of the human experience from the beginning of time. Ancient symbols, called archetypes, reside in our minds, as well. These include the Wise Old Man, the Hero, and the Evil One, and together they represent the collective experience of humanity as it finds expression in certain basic categories. We become aware of these symbols in our dreams, in altered states of consciousness, and in some paranormal situations. In his book *Flying Saucers: A Modern Myth of Things Seen in the Sky*, Jung proposed that UFOs are symbolic projections of deep human yearnings for wholeness and transformation which reside in the collective psyche of humanity. Without denying their physical nature—because there was and is plenty of empirical evidence for UFOs—Jung speculated that UFOs are either the psychic projections or hallucinations of witnesses (a *hallucination* being a visual perception without a physical referent), or real objects on which witnesses can project these mythological symbols from deep within their psyches. The oldest symbol of wholeness or totality is the circle, and so it follows that flying saucers—those round, shining objects in the sky—require a psychological interpretation as a symbol of the human yearning for certainty and completeness in an age of rapid change and uncertainty. At least, this is what Jung believed.

So some UFOs may be creations of our own minds. Sounds wild, doesn't it? But there is some research which supports this theory. In the 1970s, Dr. Gertrude Schmeidler, a parapsychologist at City College of New York, conducted research with the well-known psychic Ingo Swann. In a completely darkened laboratory, she photographed Swann as he used intention and his psychokinetic power of mind over matter to envision light streaming from his outstretched arms. Amazingly, the photos showed a visible glow around Swann's hands. Another psychic whom I know personally, Stella Lansing, used to be able to take photos of UFOs which no one else was able to see in the sky. They were beautiful 35 mm color slides of clearly delineated, apparently metallic craft. But there was one problem: in at least one instance, the image of the UFO extended from one frame across the intervening section of film and onto the succeeding frame! Now, as you know, that intervening section of film is not exposed to light from outside the camera, so there's absolutely no way anything from outside the camera could produce this kind of image. The only explanation is that the image must have been generated directly *inside* the camera by Stella's own psychokinetic power. This psychic phenomenon is called *thoughtography*, and psychiatrist Jules Eisenbud, who investigated the phenomenon in a man named Ted Serios, has since established a fairly airtight case for such "mind over matter" photography. If one person's focus and intention can produce empirically verifiable effects such as these, what might the collective intention (and unconscious psychic ability which everyone seems to have to some degree) of a large number of witnesses produce?

I'll tell you two more quick anecdotes to reinforce this point. (Actually, it's not just a point—it also *points to* something else, as I'll explain momentarily.) In 1972, my former boss, Apollo 14 astronaut Edgar Mitchell, and I got together at the upstate New York home of Dr. Andrija Puharich, along with some other scientists, to meet a young psychic from Israel named Uri Geller. Puharich had told Mitchell that Uri was a super-psychic, and because we were in the psychic research business (having just founded the Institute of Noetic Sciences), we wanted to check him out. Uri had been able to demonstrate his psychic ability in more informal settings, before the more strict testing we sponsored at the Stanford Research Institute later that year. Here's what happened that day. Uri told Mitchell to look across the room at the wall, where he said Mitchell would see an image which Uri had transmitted telepathically. Then, Uri sketched on a piece of paper the image he was going to "send" to Mitchell. Uri held the paper in his hand until he completed the mental "transmission." As Mitchell gazed at the wall he saw an image appear, seemingly made of golden light. We were all look-ing at the wall, of course, and listening to Mitchell as he described what he was seeing, but we couldn't see anything. After Mitchell finished his description, Uri showed us the paper—with the exact same image on it. We were stunned.

The second anecdote is from my own experience of the same kind of psychic phenomenon. In 1975, I met the well-known psychic Olof Jonsson at a conference in Chicago. During lunch, with several other people at the table, Jonsson demonstrated his telepathic abil-ity. He took out a deck of ordinary playing cards which he habitually carried with him. The pattern on the back of the cards consisted of small white dots against a black background. Jonsson then told me he would "mentally project" an image to me. He drew the image on a piece of paper but didn't allow anyone to see it. Then he folded it and put it aside. Next he told me to look at the back of a card lying on the table before me. As I did, it seemed to me that some of the white dots became a glowing yellow-gold. The dots which changed color formed the outline of star about one inch (25 mm) wide which stood out brilliantly against the black background. Jonsson then asked me what I had seen. "I saw a star," I told him, and described what had occurred. He then unfolded the paper and showed everyone the star he had drawn—it was a perfect match! Because no one else had seen any change in the color of the dots, it was perfectly obvious that I had experienced a visual hallucination which had been engendered by Jonsson's telepathic transmission.

This interaction between mind and matter, between the phyisical brain and the metaphysical mind, points us toward the last major category of UFO phenomena—a category which seems to come from the very frontiers of space-time itself. Let's look at what I assert is the third solution to the UFO problem: the metaterrestrial.

The Metaterrestrial Solution

The term *metaterrestrial* was coined by Dr. J. Allen Hynek, professor of astronomy at Northwestern University and founder of the Center for UFO Studies in Evanston, Illinois. It denotes something which originates outside of the ordinary three-dimensional space-time framework in which we normally function. In this sense, the word is synonymous with *metaphysical* (meaning "beyond the physical"), but it has a more scientific connotation. Some people call this realm the *extradimensional*, the *interdimensional*, the *ultraterrestrial*, or the *supraphysical*. Whatever word we use, however, it's clear we're talking about nonphysical yet very real entities which come from other dimensions or realms which exist alongside of or interpenetrate our more familiar space-time. Dr. Kenneth Ring of the University of Connecticut describes this realm as the *imaginal*, emphasizing that it does *not* mean imaginary. Some psychic and paranormal phenomena, such as materialization and dematerialization (when things appear and then disappear), seem best accounted for this way, and are still theoretically possible within our current view of reality as put forth by modern physics. As Dr. Jacques Vallée first pointed out in his 1968 book *Passport to Magonia*, many UFO incidents appear to be contemporary versions of what was recorded long ago in myths, religious texts, and spiritual traditions as encounters with the otherworldly inhabitants (for example, demons and angels) of other planes of existence. Through a process we don't yet understand, these metaterrestrial beings materialize into our space-time from their own realms or levels of reality. Those levels or realms are perforce inhabited by a wide range of beings, just as our familiar space-time is inhabited by creatures ranging from viruses to whales, and from algae to redwoods.

The case which best illustrates this metaterrestrial solution, in my estimation, is the famous so-called miracle at Fatima, which occurred in 1917 in Portugal, and is popularly known in Roman Catholic circles as "the day the sun danced" and/or "the day the sun fell." Thousands of people witnessed the event. Here's what happened: Three shepherd children—two girls named Lucia and Jacinta, and a boy named Francisco—were tending sheep in the fields near Fatima. They were all under 10 years of age. Beginning in the summer of 1915, they repeatedly saw a vague apparitional figure in an oak tree. It eventually assumed the appearance of a woman and told them it came from heaven; the children understood it to be the Virgin Mary. These Marian apparitions were typically preceded by flashes of lightning and thunderclaps; lights moving in the sky; buzzing or humming sounds; and, sometimes, sudden, violent winds and drops in temperature. The visions induced a kind of ecstasy in the children.

Word of the visions spread rapidly throughout the region. By 1917, the children were the focus of great public attention because they claimed that the woman was issuing warnings to humanity. Although no one but the children could see the manifestations, thousands of people witnessed the atmospheric phenomena accompanying them. In June, for instance, several villagers reported they saw the sun dim without any apparent cause, and the topmost branches of the oak tree bend to form a parasol, as if an invisible weight were resting upon them. After hearing a loud noise like an explosion, onlookers saw what they described as a "beautiful white cloud" rise from the tree and move eastward, while the upper branches of the tree leaned in that direction. In August, witnesses again reported that the sun dimmed and the atmosphere became suddenly hazy. A luminous globe was seen moving among the clouds; the clouds themselves turned crimson and then took on all the hues of the rainbow, which momentarily tinted the faces of the onlookers and caused the leaves on the trees to resemble flowers.

A month later, a crowd of 30,000 assembled to watch the children view the apparition. This time witnesses said the sun became so dark they could see the stars at noontime. A globe of light descended toward the children, stopped above the tree, and again changed into a mysterious white cloud. Then, out of the cloudless sky, globules of glistening light resembling shiny white flower petals began to pour from the sky. They grew smaller as they fell to the ground and dissolved into nothingness at the touch. The globe of light then rose and traveled across the valley and up into the sky.

The miracle itself occurred on October 13, 1917. By noon, an estimated 70,000 people were gathered in the field to watch the children. The crowd included clergy, college professors, politicians, military officers, non-Catholic freethinkers, and atheists alike. It was a foggy day and a cold rain was falling heavily; everyone was soaking wet. The children saw the apparitional woman coming to them from the east and went into rapture. After identifying herself as the "lady of the rosary," she issued some religious messages and prophecies and then rose again toward the sun. As the children gazed at the sky, Lucia cried out, "Look at the sun!" A spinning silver disc about 70 feet (21.3 meters) in diameter appeared, radiating multicolored lights—red, violet, blue, and yellow—which in turn saturated the clouds and the entire countryside with color.

Although it was extremely bright, witnesses were able to look at it comfortably and without harming their eyes. At that moment, the rain stopped and a circular area opened up among the clouds. The disc-shaped object, which was brightly outlined by a beveled rim, descended in the zigzag motion of a falling leaf, shining blood-red and radiating great heat, and, as some observers said, constantly "trembling" and "dancing." It paused near the ground and then rose upward into a cloud and disappeared. During this series of maneuvers, it continued to rotate rapidly and emit flashes and rays of light of various colors. One newspaper described it as changing from the grayish tint of mother-of-pearl to blue and then yellow. The entire event lasted no more than 10 minutes and was observed in detail from many miles away. When the object disappeared, everyone's clothing was dry, even though it had been soaked a few minutes earlier.

What does all of this have to do with the metaterrestrial solution? Some ufologists interpret the Fatima events as a display of advanced technology in which ETs were manipulating human belief systems via holographic projections. I acknowledge that possibility. But there is another explanation which has its roots in Eastern religions, and which offers detailed information about a class of celestial beings whose characteristics are remarkably similar to what was seen at Fatima. Some UFO contactees describe meetings with nonphysical entities which have somehow materialized into our space-time continuum from other dimensions or higher planes of existence. Names for these nonphysical entities include the *space brothers*, *extradimensionals*, and *ultraterrestrials*. Their existence is essentially incomprehensible to us and beyond our limited understanding, just as our own existence is essentially incomprehensible to insects, which in turn are similarly incomprehensible to microbes. It is from this metaterrestrial level of reality, it is said, that these higher forms of life influence and even guide human affairs.

The most common name for this sort of being is *deva*, a Sanskrit word which means "shining one," "radiant being, " or, more generally, "being of light." It is the conceptual equivalent of an angel. According to some spiritual traditions, devas belong to an entirely different kingdom of life—that is, they are neither animal, nor vegetable, nor mineral. Rather, they are a separately created, very high order of existence which has the role of supervising the lower orders. Devas exist in a nonphysical but ontologically real form which is many magnitudes of cosmological orders above that of humans. Considered in more scientific terms, devas can be described as conscious, formative principles which guide and regulate the lower forms of life. Hinduism and Tibetan Buddhism are especially rich in information about devas. Signs which traditionally announce the presence of these normally unseen entities include the sudden appearance of rainbows; the smell of perfume; multicolored flower blossoms falling from the air; sudden high winds; various celestial phenomena such as shooting stars and lights in the sky; and multicolored clouds forming themselves into unusual shapes. Sound familiar? Here is what noted spiritual teacher David Spangler told me about devas some years ago. Spangler was one of the early residents of a spiritual community at Findhorn, Scotland. The Findhorn Community became famous in the 1960s and 70s for its remarkable outdoor production of unusually large vegetables and lovely flowers in an area on the northern coast of Scotland where the soil is hardly more than sand and where the climate is quite uncongenial to such gardening. The Findhorn residents claimed they received, via psychic channeling, special assistance from the devas responsible for growing such vegetable life. Spangler was one of the clairvoyant channels for these communications. In 1974, when he was writing an essay for one of my books, I asked him about his experience of communicating with devas. He said to me, "John, if devas could be seen with unmediated vision—in other words, with the naked eye—the only thing you would see is a constantly shifting pattern of color and form." That sounds a lot like the Fatima miracle to me. It's not proof, of course. The Fatima events are too distant and too naively reported to ever be completely explained or unraveled—unless the still-secret Fatima prophecies given to the children by the Blessed Virgin Mary eventually tell us the truth about what happened there. Despite that, I find the Fatima events highly suggestive of this third answer to the question of what UFOs really are.

So the UFO phenomenon appears to be multifaceted. There is no neat, simple answer to what it's all about. This is problematic for the general public, and even many ufologists. In my judgment, they are indiscriminately lumping together all the UFO sightings and incidents into a singularly unrealistic view. They want a simple, all-purpose explanation that spans the entire spectrum of UFO reports, when none exists. As I've just shown, the evidence indicates that no single explanation can adequately cover all the experiences and events which are typically brought together under the label "the UFO phenomenon." It is a multifaceted phenomenon, and each facet—terrestrial, extraterrestrial, and metaterrestrial—is qualitatively different from the rest. Each has its own unique forms of UFOs, and each form has to be distinguished from the others of that same level.

In this sense, my analysis here can be compared to the evolution of modern physics. In ancient Greece, the atom was regarded as the ultimate unit of matter. However, science eventually discovered that the atom was not "rock-bottom reality"; it was comprised of even smaller components—protons, electrons, and neutrons. Thus, a new level of reality emerged: the subatomic. Continuing scientific research discovered a host of new particles, such as neutrinos, quarks, mesons, bosons, and other exotic forms of matter far smaller than the atom. More recently, science has discovered a still more basic or fundamental aspect of reality, the quantum level. Our present scientific understanding regards the quantum level as the one from which all the particles and the four fundamental forces—gravity, electromagnetism, and the weak and strong nuclear forces—arise. And, of course, scientists are searching for something more—something which will provide a unifying explanation for all these different forms of matter and energy existing at different levels of reality. That "something" is called the GUT (Grand Unified Theory) or TOE (Theory of Everything), and supposedly it will provide a total explanation and understanding of everything in the universe and how it all works. In a similar manner, the world is searching for a single unifying theory of UFOs because the old theories have failed in this regard. Only when we understand that the so-called UFO phenomenon is in fact multileveled and multifaceted, however, will we be able to move to a deeper understanding of this intriguing and mysterious subject and, hopefully, move toward a grand, unified theory of UFOs—the final solution to the puzzle.

Killing the Roswell Story

By Thomas J. Carey

In one of the greatest science fiction thrillers of all time, Howard Hawkes' 1951 movie *The Thing (From Another World)*, a newspaper reporter pleads with an Air Force captain to allow him to phone in a story about a crashed flying saucer near the North Pole. Only after the saucer and its alien pilot are destroyed does the Air Force allow the reporter to give his tell-all to the world. The film's director and producer were both apparently unaware that a similar scenario had actually played out in real life only four short years earlier in 1947, near the not-so-sleepy town of Roswell, New Mexico. There was one major difference, however: Instead of an arctic UFO crash involving sinister aliens versus a benevolent, truthful, and civilian-protecting U.S. Air Force, the real-life version featured apparently benevolent aliens versus a sinister U.S. Air Force determined to kill the story at any cost, even if it meant engaging in heavy-handed civil rights violations against its own civilian population—the very people it was sworn to serve and protect!

As followers of the Roswell story are aware, on July 8, 1947, the U.S. Army Air Force base near Roswell announced in a short press release that garnered big headlines the world over, that it had "captured" a downed flying saucer on a ranch not far from town. Later that same day, however, the next higher Air Force command, located in Fort Worth, Texas, retracted that story by convening a press conference to tell the world that it was all a big mistake, and that what had been found was not a flying saucer at all, but an ordinary weather balloon made of rubber, tinfoil, and balsa wood sticks. The men of the 509th Bomb Group—the only atomic strike force in the world at that time (and the one that had ended World War II by dropping atomic bombs on Hiroshima and Nagasaki)—had been fooled, and had acted precipitously with their ill-advised press release. (Just the kind of people you would want with their fingers on the atomic trigger!) End of story. Well, for the next 30 years, at least.

Ever since I teamed up with Don Schmitt in 1998 to continue a proactive investigation of the events at Roswell, we have uncovered a number of startling facts not previously known. One of these involves the killing of the original flying saucer story by the Air Force. Evidence has been steadily mounting regarding the extreme measures the Air Force undertook to institute a cover-up of the entire Roswell event—the crash and subsequent retrieval of a bona fide spacecraft from another world, along with its stranded crew— by attempting to enforce the silence of everyone, military personnel and civilians alike, who had been involved in its discovery and/or recovery, especially those who had seen the bodies. As we recounted in our best-selling 2007 book, *Witness to Roswell: Unmasking the 60-Year Cover-Up*, we now know from the posthumous release of the sealed statement of Walter Haut, the former Roswell air base PIO (Public Information Officer) in 1947 who issued the infamous flying saucer press release, that the Air Force had decided upon a cover-up strategy on the very same day that it had issued the crashed saucer story, and that the strategy as well as the initial press release had been orchestrated from Washington. This effectively ended the decades-old debate of whether the initial flying saucer press release had been the result of a local *faux pas* committed by the Roswell base commander, Colonel William Blanchard, by his intelligence officer Major Jesse Marcel, or by 1st Lieutenant Walter Haut himself. The plan's implementation was communicated to Colonel Blanchard through his boss, General Roger Ramey (commanding officer of the

"Mighty" 8th Air Force of World War II fame that had helped bomb Germany into submission), who was then headquartered at Fort Worth Army Air Field in Texas. This was also the outfit that Blanchard's 509th Bomb Group in Roswell was attached to.

It would ultimately involve the use of security personnel, not only from Roswell AAF, but from Alamogordo AAF in New Mexico, Kirtland AAF in Albuquerque, and Fort Bliss in El Paso, as well as units from White Sands (near Alamogordo) and "dark suits" from Washington, D.C. And whenever there was especially dirty business to conduct, there was a go-to guy who was up to the task already in place on the ground at the 509th in Roswell. If *his* handi-

1st Lt. Arthur Philbin of the 509th Bomb Group was used to threaten civilians to keep quiet "or else." He died a broken alcoholic years later. Photo courtesy of the Air Force.

work needed punctuating, there was yet another fellow at the ready for good measure who could be flown in at a moment's notice from Wright Field in Dayton, Ohio, to do just that.

As planned, the July 9, 1947, newspaper headlines blared out the new cover story: "Gen. Ramey Empties Roswell Saucer" and "It's Just a Weather Balloon!" Most accounts also prominently featured a photo of General Ramey or Major Marcel kneeling beside a degraded rubber weather balloon on the floor of the general's office, accompanied by a brand new, off-the-shelf tinfoil radar target that someone had attempted to tear apart. (Close-up, computer enhancements of the photos of General Ramey reveal a freshly torn left thumbnail of obvious recent origin, which suggests that Gen. Ramey either tried to tear the real stuff himself and couldn't, or helped to tear up the radar target used in the press conference.) July 10 and 11 saw public demonstrations of weather balloon launches all over the country put on by the Army Air Force and the Army Signal Corps to attempt to explain away not only the "hot" Roswell case, but all reported UFO sightings that had occurred during the previous two weeks. These launches were duly documented with photographs in most major newspapers. The captioned headline of July 10, 1947, on the front page of the *Alamogordo News* said it all: "Fantasy of the *Flying Disc* is Explained Here." As far as press interest was concerned, by the weekend of July 12, the Roswell story was as dead as the Big Band Era. But what about all the other people—military personnel and civilians alike—who *knew*? What about them?

It should be pointed out that in 1947, our government and military establishments were held in the highest regard, perhaps the highest in our nation's history, by just about all of its citizens. The United States had just vanquished the Axis powers in a terrible and costly war, and unlike the other Allied victors, it had emerged as the world's preeminent superpower with its homeland unscathed. Thus, in this victorious, pre-TV (and hence more parochial and less anxious) world of 1947, our country was much more unified in nearly every aspect of its daily life and outlook than it is today. When our government and especially our military spoke to us, we chose to believe them unquestioningly by nodding our heads in agreement. The Cold War with the communist bloc nations of Eastern Europe and Asia was just beginning, and anxious Americans looked to their government and military to protect them. Korea, Cuba, Vietnam, Iraq, and Afghanistan were just far-away places on a map, and the deep divisions that the mere mention of them would foster were still years, if not decades, in the future.

If the cover-up were to succeed, the Air Force knew it had several distinct target groups to silence, the first being the national and international press corps. As we have already seen, this was achieved with remarkable ease via General Ramey's phony, makeshift press conference of July 8, 1947, and a few balloon launches in the days that followed. The sole demurring voice was an editorial in the July 9, 1947, *Roswell Daily Record* that wondered if the Army (Air Force) was guilty of keeping secrets. Other than that, the compliant press appeared eager to close the book on both Roswell and, by extension, flying saucers—a subject it didn't understand and didn't like reporting on. The local Roswell media were another matter, however, as there were people within their ranks who knew what had really happened out in the desert, north of town. After a chance meeting in a local café with Mack Brazel (the Corona, New Mexico, rancher who first found and reported the UFO crash to authorities in Roswell), Roswell radio station KSWS reporter Johnny McBoyle somehow made it out to the crash site on his own, only to be taken into custody by the military—but not before he had seen enough to know that what had crashed was not of earthly origin. McBoyle was then taken back to the base, and while the Air Force was deciding what to do with him, he quickly tried to phone in the story to his sister-station in Albuquerque (KOAT) to get it on the Associated Press news wire. The attempt was short-circuited, however, when the teletype wire was jammed by the FBI so that nothing more could be transmitted, and McBoyle himself was supposedly prevented by the "dark suits" from doing any further reporting on the story. Apparently convinced by his captors that it was all a matter of national security, McBoyle left Roswell, never to return, and moved to a remote Idaho farm to spend the rest of his life in relative seclusion and anonymity. When Roswell researchers came calling decades later, he stonewalled them by denying that any of it took place. He passed away in 1991 within weeks of his wife's passing. In 2001, I interviewed McBoyle's son and daughter-in-law, only to learn that they were unable to ever get their father to speak about what happened at Roswell in 1947. Even while on his deathbed, he would not speak about it, not even to his wife! What could have caused a person to behave that way? Those who question that a secret such as the Roswell UFO crash could not have been kept secret for very long should look to the case of Johnny McBoyle for their answer. As an aside, the woman to whom McBoyle was speaking on the telephone in his aborted attempt to report the story, an employee at KOAT radio in Albuquerque by the name of Lydia Sleppy, became the first person to speak publicly about Roswell in 1972 (in an *Argosy* magazine article). This was six years before Jesse Marcel publicly broke his silence regarding his involvement in the recovery of something that was *not of this earth*.[1]

o°   o°   o |

Frank Joyce was an announcer for Roswell radio station KGFL in 1947. By chance, he was the first media person to interview rancher Mack Brazel soon after Brazel had come into town to report the incident. During a chance telephone interview from the Chaves County Sheriff's Office in Roswell, Brazel told Joyce of finding strange wreckage on his ranch:"Maybe it's from one of them [sic] flying saucer things people have been talking about."[2]

KGFL radio announcer Frank Joyce in 1947. He was "put on ice" for a year because he knew too much. Photo courtesy of Frank Joyce.

He also told Joyce about finding "little people" someplace else not too far from the main site. Joyce did not believe the story at first, but he nevertheless suspected that *something* may have crashed out in the desert, something that possibly involved small bodies. When the Air Force learned of this conversation during Brazel's week-long incarceration at the Roswell airbase's Guest House, Joyce became a target for silencing. But, how to do it? As everyone knows, it's only during times of extreme emergencies, such as war or marshal law, that the military has direct authority over civilians, but neither one was in force in 1947. The answer was to first cajole and then threaten a few well-placed town leaders in Roswell to do the military's dirty work for them. It worked. Faced with the threat of losing his broadcasting license if he didn't cooperate, KGFL radio station majority owner Walter Whitmore, who had been sequestering Mack Brazel at his home while obtaining Brazel's exclusive story (which Whitmore's station planned to air as a scoop), handed Brazel over to the military without a fight.

Along with the presence of a military guard, he also helped to escort Brazel around town to the major media outlets to lend an air of credibility to Brazel's new weather balloon story that the military wanted him to tell. It was during this magical mystery tour that Brazel confided off-air to announcer Frank Joyce at KGFL that "*they* [the aliens] weren't green!"[3] Earlier in the day, an officer had been trying to silence Joyce, who then promptly told the officer where he could go, so the military ordered Whitmore to take Joyce for a ride somewhere for further "enlightenment." That "somewhere" turned out to be none other than the Hines House on the Brazel/ Foster Ranch—the same ramshackle bunkhouse where Brazel, Jesse Marcel, and Counter Intelligence

Majority owner of radio station KGFL in downtown Roswell, Walter Whitmore, Sr., helped the Air Force silence Roswell civilians after being threatened with the loss of his broadcast license. Photo courtesy of Mrs. Walter Whitmore, Jr.

Corps captain Sheridan Cavitt had spent the night at a few days previously before heading to the debris field. After alighting from his car, Whitmore told a perplexed Joyce to enter the bunkhouse. Once inside, Joyce stood around wondering what was going to happen next, when the door opened and in strode none other than Mack Brazel. "I was just wondering," Brazel addressed Joyce. "You weren't planning on saying anything about what I told you the other day, were you?"

"Not if you don't want me to," replied Joyce.

"Good, because if you do, it will go hard on me—and you."

With that, Brazel started to leave but stopped at the door and turned around to face Joyce. "You know, don't you, that our lives will never be the same again."[4] With that, Brazel left, and Joyce never laid eyes on him again.

The Hines House on the old J.B. Foster Ranch still stands three miles (4.8 kilometers) from the UFO crash site. Besides providing a place for Maj. Jesse Marcel, Capt. Sheridan Cavitt, and Mack Brazel to stay on the night of July 6, 1947, it is also where KGFL announcer Frank Joyce was driven by his boss Walt Whitmore and a mysterious military man for a secret meeting with Mack Brazel to try to convince Joyce to keep quiet about the things that Brazel had told him a few days earlier.

Joyce then rejoined his boss outside and noticed that the military man who had been in the back seat of the car on the trip out to the ranch was now gone. Whitmore and Joyce drove the 75 miles (121 kilometers) back to Roswell in total silence. Apparently the military was still not satisfied that it had truly silenced Joyce to its liking, however, because Joyce revealed to us years later that he was then hauled off, against his will, to a military hospital in Texas and basically "put on ice" for a year or so without so much as a diagnosis being offered. When they finally let him out, he was told not to return to Roswell, which he didn't. Instead, he went to Albuquerque to start a new life, and ultimately became a well-known newsman and features reporter at KOB radio and television there until he retired in 1997. According to Joyce, he never spoke of Roswell for decades after the UFO crash, and it wasn't until after he had retired from KOB that he revealed the *rest of the story*[5] about Mack Brazel finding bodies in addition to strange wreckage—to Don Schmitt and me in 1998. Frank Joyce passed away in 2008 and is buried beside his wife in his native Roswell.

For obvious reasons, the military personnel involved in the UFO recovery operations—either directly or indirectly—were the easiest ones to silence. With direct authority and control over their lives through the channels of command, it was a relatively easy proposition. The Roswell airbase went in "lockdown" mode soon after authorities realized what they were dealing with, and it remained in this state for about a week. Even airmen on the base who were not involved in the UFO recovery could sense that something big was taking place. But with Roswell Army Air Field being our country's first SAC base (and whose mission it was to drop the atomic bomb on the Soviet Union during wartime), they knew not to ask too many questions or discuss their day jobs with their families at home. (Author's note: Although we have received anecdotal accounts of at least three suicides taking place on the base at the time of the incident, as well as several off-base hunting "accidents" occurring soon thereafter, so far we have been unable to verify these.) Officers were briefed separately, but the bulk of the airmen on the base—the enlisted men, including NCOs—were herded into the large hangars at the south and east end of the base, squadron by squadron, and unceremoniously read the riot act. As one squadron commander put it to his assembled troops, "Whatever you've been hearing lately, it's not true. There's no 'flying saucer.' Nothing has happened! But if you think you want to keep talking about it or trying to learn more about it, you can read all about it in Leavenworth! [a Federal prison in Kansas]."[6] For those who knew too much, we know that some— but not all—were indeed precipitously shipped out and dispersed to remote locations, such as the Arctic or the Pacific. Faced with a "Hobson's Choice" of either a stiff prison sentence at hard labor, a transfer to an undesirable duty location, a reduction in rank, or a dishonorable discharge (which in those days would forever remain a stain on one's resumé), the message got through loud and clear. This, combined with a natural sense of duty, honor, and love of country, all wrapped up in a blanket of national security, convinced most of the men and women of the 509th—members of America's "Greatest Generation"—to remain silent for the rest of their lives and take what they knew with them to their graves. Unfortunately for the recorders of history, most did exactly that.

As we've attempted to interview military personnel regarding the events that took place in Roswell in 1947, it's been interesting to see who is willing to talk and who isn't. In the hundreds of interviews we have conducted over the years, with a few notable exceptions, those least likely to talk have been the officers (as opposed to the enlisted men, such as NCOs). In general, the higher the rank, the less likely it is that the person will say anything.

Brigadier General Arthur Exon and Lieutenant Colonel Philip Corso, however, were two exceptions to this rule who have gone on the public record. Exon was the base commander at Wright-Patterson AFB in the 1960s and knew people who had worked on the

Roswell wreckage there. When Roswell researchers arrived at his door years later, he did not seem to have any problem telling them what he knew, namely, that the Roswell wreckage was extraterrestrial in origin. Corso took the additional step of actually writing a book, *The Day After Roswell*, in 1997 detailing his alleged involvement in attempting to reverse-engineer some of the wreckage.

Among the enlisted ranks, an interesting dichotomy became apparent when it came to who would talk to us and who would not, and it had nothing at all to do with rank. Those who remained in the service long enough (that is, a minimum of 20 years) to retire on a military/ government pension have, by and large, refused to talk. Even when told of Air Force Secretary

Retired Brig. General Arthur Exon was the commanding officer at Wright-Patterson AFB in Dayton, Ohio, where the Roswell wreckage and alien bodies were allegedly taken after the 1947 crash. Exon was one of the few high-ranking Air Force officers who were not afraid to tell what they knew about the crash wreckage.

Sheila Widnall's 1994 "amnesty" for Roswell veterans, most have still refused to budge. "I'm retired, and I like it that way" is a common refrain.[7] The most common response we've received from members of this group is simply, "I don't remember anything."

"Nothing?"

"That's right, nothing."[8]

One notable exception in this group was former Air Force Master Sergeant Lewis "Bill" Rickett, a key eyewitness to the physical wreckage and to the involvement of CIC captain Sheridan Cavitt and meteor expert Dr. Lincoln LaPaz in the UFO recovery. Another was then–Private First Class Elias Benjamin, who went public under a pseudonym in our 2007 book when he told of accompanying the alien bodies to the base hospital. And after telling his story for the TV cameras in an episode of the Sci Fi Channel's *Sci Fi Investigates*, his first words to me were, "Do you think I will lose my pension?"

By far the most fertile ground we have covered in our investigation has been the enlisted ranks of men and women who were stationed at Roswell at the time of the UFO incident but who did *not* choose to make military or government service a career—meaning that when we interviewed them years later, they were not retired and living on a military or government pension. It is from this group that the most numerous Roswell witnesses—too many to name— have been obtained. One name does bear mentioning, however, as he ultimately gave his life to tell the truth of his involvement in the Roswell Incident. Earl Fulford would spend a total of only eight years in the military service before getting out.

Earl Fulford [L] *with the author at the "debris field" crash site in 2008. Fulford fulfilled a life's dream by returning to Roswell after having participated in the famous incident.*

In 1947, he was an NCO stationed at Roswell Army Air Field servicing B-29 "Superfortress" bomber engines when he was commandeered and driven with 20 other enlisted men and non-coms out to the boondocks of the desert. As described in our book *Witness to Roswell*, Fulford and the others were told to "vacuum" the desert floor of "anything that wasn't natural" and to place the collected material in burlap bags, which they did. When I called him in 2006, Fulford told me that he had never told of his Roswell involvement to anyone up to that point, but he had recently suffered another heart attack. "It's time," he told me, "to get this off my chest once and for all. I've never told anyone but my wife, but now it's time." We brought him to Roswell in 2008 and took him out to the location of the debris field on the old ranch, where he had picked up the strange pieces of wreckage so many years before, thus fulfilling for him a life's dream, according to his wife. After returning home to Florida, almost immediately he flew out to California to appear on a nationally televised TV show to tell his story. At age 82 and with a history of heart attacks, the strain was apparently too much: Within mere days of his return to Florida, his heart gave out for the last time. He died in the hospital a free man, watching his favorite pastime—NASCAR.

To underscore the point being made here about service careerists vs. non-careerists and the influence that status exerts on a potential witness's decision to talk, I would point out that two of the most important witnesses to Roswell were officers: former Major Jesse Marcel, the RAAF base intelligence officer who broke his silence about Roswell in 1978, thereby kick-starting the civilian investigation of the 1947 events; and former 1st Lieutenant Walter Haut, the Roswell base PIO who issued the infamous press release and who later told all posthumously in a sealed statement that was featured in our book (first released in 2007). Yes, both men were officers, but neither one was a retired career officer living on a government pension.

By far the biggest challenge for the military authorities was how to silence the civilians who had direct knowledge of the UFO crash, especially those who had seen or knew about the bodies. When airplane crashes occur in an uninhabited locale, it is civilians—in this case, the outlying ranchers and their extended family members—who usually reach the crash sites first. It was Mack Brazel, the foreman of the J.B. Foster Ranch near the town of Corona in Lincoln County, along with a neighbor boy, 7-year-old Timothy "Dee" Proctor, who were the first to visit the debris field on the morning of July 4, 1947. It would be two days before Brazel would make the long, dusty drive to Roswell in his ancient pick-up truck to report it. In the meantime, as word of the crash got around to the other ranchers (Brazel had visited at least three other ranches to get someone else to take a look at the wreckage), many of them hopped in their pick-ups to see for themselves and perhaps grab a souvenir or two, as well. Although Brazel had come into town on Sunday, July 6, to report his find to the local sheriff, George Wilcox, nothing was generally known in Roswell about a crash involving a flying saucer until the following day, when a second crash site was discovered—with strange little bodies—just north of town. According to a local Roswell book store owner, Patricia Rice, "Word of the crash traveled around town in about 20 minutes!"[9] Like the first site, the "debris field site," the second site—the so-called impact site—had also been discovered by civilians, this time by a group of archaeologists looking for ancient "kill sites" left by paleo-Indians. Both discoveries preceded the military's knowledge of them and their arrival at the second crash site. Brazel, Marcel, and Cavitt were still at the first "debris field" site scratching their heads when the second site was discovered. After alerting the authorities in Roswell of the crash, and prior to the arrival of the military "in force" (that is, in numbers sufficient enough to take charge of and secure the site), quite a few civilians were able to see everything first-hand, up close and personal. Without direct authority over them, how could these local civilians have possibly been silenced by those sworn to protect them from foreign enemies?

We do know that the Chaves County Sheriff, George Wilcox, never ran for public office again. According to his surviving family members, "Roswell [the UFO incident] *destroyed* him"[10] [emphasis mine]. As we discuss in our 2009 book *Witness to Roswell: Unmasking the Government's Biggest Cover-Up,* we now know why. The Air Force co-opted and used Sheriff Wilcox as its "silencer" of Roswell civilians who knew too much, especially those who knew about the bodies.

Chaves County Sheriff George Wilcox was used by the Air Force to silence Roswell civilians who knew too much about the UFO crash. He never ran for sheriff again, and his family said that the Roswell Incident "destroyed" him. Photo courtesy of Phyllis McGuire.

In this role, Wilcox became a true "messenger of death" by threatening those witnesses and their families, including children, with death if they ever talked.[11] Not a good platform on which to run for re-election! In those cases where Wilcox knew a targeted witness too well (for example, Roswell fireman Dan Dwyer and his family) and perhaps refused to "make the delivery," the Air Force called upon one of its own security personnel in the 509th at Roswell, 1st Lieutenant Arthur "The Hammer" Philbin, to do the deed. Philbin, a tough guy from Brooklyn, had been a New York police officer in a former life. His threatening of Dan Dwyer's wife and daughter, Frankie Rowe, with a billy club is well-known to followers of this case. He allegedly died a broken, drunken recluse. Philbin's activities also included visits to the ranchers outside of town. We have firsthand accounts of the military basically ransacking ranches in its desperate search to uncover souvenirs from the crash. Floor boards were ripped up, bags of cattle feed were slashed open, and water tanks were drained in the madness. And of course, lives were threatened into silence. Just to make sure, a few days, weeks, or months later (we are not really sure when), the Air Force unleashed perhaps its top thug, a worthy by the name of Hunter Penn, and sent him to Roswell to "interview" the outlying ranchers in order to "encourage" their continued silence. Penn's daughter related to UFO researcher Anthony Bragalia that her stepfather (whom she called a "brutal person") "had a fascination with ice picks," and thinks he might have used one at Roswell.[12] In 2008, my co-author Don Schmitt interviewed a fellow by the name of Bert Schulz during a speaking engagement at a conference in Nevada. Schultz had been a B-29 electrician assigned to the 393rd Bomb Squadron at the Roswell airbase just a few months after the UFO incident. Aside from the occasional scuttlebutt regarding the incident a few months previous to his assignment, Schulz told Schmitt about a much more disturbing fact, something that was enough to sour him on the military as a potential career: "There was still a lot of talk about the MPs harassing civilians over the affair. The MPs got pretty rough with some of the ranchers out there, *and they were bragging about it!*"[13]

Arthur Farnsworth ran the original Ford dealership in Roswell, the Roswell Auto Company, in 1947. He was the head of a family-owned business that dated back to the early part of the 20th century and to Henry Ford himself. A pillar of the Roswell community, he was a well-known and well-respected businessman throughout the area. Arthur and Vera Farnsworth had three daughters, two teenagers, as well as the youngest, Sue, who was age 7 at the time. In addition to a home in Roswell, the family also owned a ranch a few miles northwest of town. Besides running the Ford dealership, Arthur was known to visit the ranch several times a week to check on things. Soon after the publication of our first book in 2007, I received an e-mail from a gentleman living in Roswell who said that at a recent Roswell High School class reunion, he ran into a former classmate who told him that her father had been threatened by the military at the time of the Roswell incident. That's all the information he had, so I asked him for the contact number of the former classmate and if she would talk to me. A few days later, I found myself talking to 67-year-old Sue Farnsworth Bennett, now a successful business-woman in her own right. She related to me the following account.

Even though she was the youngest of the three Farnsworth daughters, she was "best buddies" with her father because both of her older sisters had had bouts of polio and were incapacitated to some extent. Therefore, it was Sue who helped her father out with the chores at home and out at the ranch. She also shared those spe-cial father-daughter moments with him when she needed his coun-sel. As Sue recalled it, "At one point in the summer of 1947, I noticed a real somber look cross my father's face, and it didn't go away. In fact, it changed more and more into a look of fear after a day or two." Unable to contain her concern for her father any longer, Sue asked him what was wrong one day when they were at the ranch. Without saying a word, he motioned to her to follow him on horse-back, and they rode out to a remote and secluded part of the ranch, whereupon he dismounted, as did she. "Whenever we wanted to discuss something without anyone else hearing, we would go to this spot." Like so many times before, Sue and her father sat down on their favorite rock and stared out at the peaceful, desert landscape before them. Like many of her friends, Sue had overheard talk of the flying saucer crash from adults talking about it in town, but she was not prepared for what her father was about to confide to her now. "Your father was threatened by the military a few days ago," Arthur Farnsworth told his daughter. Looking around carefully, even though they were way out in the middle of nowhere, he contin-ued in a low voice, "What I tell you now you must promise never to tell anyone. A few days ago, a flying saucer crashed on a ranch not far from here, and the military told us that if we ever said anything to anyone about it, they would kill all of us—and our families too!"

Sue Farnsworth Bennett never saw her father so scared as in 1947, after the military told him that he and his family would be killed if he ever talked about the crash.

He then told his daughter that he had gone out with other neighboring ranchers when word of the crash got around. "We saw some things we weren't supposed to see," he said. He did not go into any detail about what he had witnessed with his young daughter and ended the discussion with, "Remember, not a word to anyone—ever!" That was all he would ever reveal to her. The two of them then saddled up and rode back to the ranch house, never to speak of it again. Speaking to me 60 years later, Sue Farnsworth exclaimed, "He was a strong man who wasn't afraid of anything, but, in my entire life, *I never saw my father so scared!*"[14] Arthur Farnsworth's near-death experience sounds to us like the handiwork of Arthur Philbin or Hunter Penn doing what they did best, scaring people to death. And all this over a balloon? Think about it.

Many readers are probably unaware that just prior to and during the week that the Roswell Incident was making headlines, there were three additional "crashes" of weather balloons of the identical type seen in the July 8, 1947 press conference photos. One occurred in California, one in Ohio, and another in upstate New York. All were retrieved by civilians, and in no case did a "Roswell scenario" of secrecy, intimidation, death threats, or special press conferences take place. Each was quickly identified locally as a prosaic, rubber weather balloon with its attached, tinfoil radar target. In at least one case the civilian who retrieved it was given the choice of either keeping it or turning it in. *It was no big deal.* How was it, then, that it was *only* at Roswell that the behaviors I describe in this essay actually took place? How could it have been that civilians a thousand miles (1,600 kilometers) from Roswell who were not at all familiar with the balloon/radar target devices falling on their heads could identify them with little or no difficulty, whereas the elites of our military forces located at Roswell, who *were* familiar with them, could not? Moreover, such balloons were launched on a daily basis from the town of Roswell itself and from the airbase 7 miles (11.3 kilometers) south of Roswell. Everyone was familiar wvith them. The RAAF was also aware of the high-altitude "Project Mogul" balloon arrays, which consisted of multiple rubber weather balloons and tinfoil radar targets that were then periodically released from Alamogordo, New Mexico, in order to monitor the Soviet Union's first detonation of a nuclear device. Certainly this was nothing that would have dumbfounded even a 6-year-old, let alone the men of the 509th. As the saying goes, it doesn't add up. One must conclude, then, either that the men of the 509th were complete dopes, or that the balloon explanation for the Roswell incident simply doesn't work. Applying a healthy dose of Occam's Law of Parsimony here can yield only one reasonable conclusion—namely, that the balloon explanation cannot prevail. The men of the 509th represented the elite of the United States military forces in 1947. When the unique and reprehensible conduct employed by the Air Force, as described herein, to "kill" the Roswell story is combined with the testimonies of scores of first-hand eyewitnesses, both military and civilian, who have gone on the record describing an extraterrestrial encounter, the *simplest* explanation that *best fits the known facts* of the Roswell Incident must prevail: A UFO crashed in the high desert of eastern New Mexico for reasons unknown, and was recovered and subsequently covered up by elements of the U.S. military, with acquiescence of the U.S. political establishment.

Unfortunately, the U.S. Air Force today, despite a mountain of evidence to the contrary, still clings to a variation of its initial weather balloon fiction to explain away the Roswell wreckage. To try to refute the reports about small bodies, as told by eyewitnesses, the Air Force has twisted itself into a knot that has caused Occam's Razor to hemorrhage and register "Tilt!" Likewise, its time compression theory, which seems to make only pro-Roswell witnesses forgetful, coupled with the theory of "dummies from the sky" (high-altitude parachute drops using anthropomorphic, dime-store mannequins) caused howls of derisive laughter from the normally sympathetic anti-UFO press corps when these theories were presented to them in 1997. It was the Air Force's *fourth* explanation for the Roswell incident. Would anyone reasonably be able to believe a fifth, if the Air Force offered it up? To quote the late Don Adams' TV character Maxwell Smart, after he is caught in yet another lie, "Would you believe...?"

Notes

1. Berlitz, Charles, and William L. Moore. *The Roswell Incident*. New York: Grosset & Dunlap, 1980. Major Marcel was famous for stating that what crashed at Roswell "fell to the earth, but was not of this earth."

2. Frank Joyce, personal interview, 1998.

3. Ibid.

4. Ibid.

5. The late radio commentator Paul Harvey always featured a "Rest of the Story" segment in each of his daily broadcasts whereby he would add interesting new or inside-information, that listeners most likely did not know previously, to well-known stories, old and new. And Harvey would always end these segments in his most sonorous voice with, "And now you know...the rest of the story!"

6. Harry Girard, telephone interview, 2005.

7. Wyly, Percey, telephone interview with William Moore, 1981. From "Crashed Saucers: Evidence in Search of Proof" by William L. Moore, in MUFON 1985 UFO Symposium Proceedings: the Burden of Proof. Seguin, Texas: Mutual UFO Network, Inc., 1985.

8. George Houck, telephone interview, 2010.

9. Patricia Rice, telephone interview, 2000; and quoted from her "Letter to the Editor" in the *Dallas Morning News*, July 6, 1997.

10. Barbara Dugger, personal interview, 1991; Phyllis McGuire and Elizabeth Tulk, personal interviews, 2000.

11. Ruben Anaya, personal interview, 1994; Pete Anaya and Mary Anaya, personal interviews, 2002; Barbara Dugger, personal interview, 1991.

12. Michelle Penn, telephone interview with Anthony Bragalia, 2008.

13. Bert Schultz, personal interview, 2008.

14. Sue Farnsworth Bennett, personal interview, 2008.

Identity Crisis:
When Is a UFO Not a UFO?

By Marie D. Jones and Larry Flaxman

Imagine that your spouse has just run into the room, shouting at the top of his or her lungs, "I just saw a UFO!" Farfetched? Perhaps. But, let's suppose for a second that this very scenario just occurred. More than likely the next thing you would hear would be a harried, breathless description of a flying object that was behaving unlike anything typically seen in the skies. Days, weeks, and maybe months later—perhaps long after you have forgotten about the incident—you glance at the day's newspaper and see a short paragraph (not even a full article) in which a perfectly reasonable explanation is given for the erstwhile UFO that your spouse was initially so excited about. You find that it was something as simple as a plane, a satellite, or a comet. For those UFO sightings that remain enigmas, however, other explanations beg for our attention. From the traditional "nuts and bolts" idea of a spacecraft from another planet to the unlikely possibility of interdimensional time travelers coming to warn us about the future, the world of ufology has expanded beyond the limitations and explanations of the early days, when most UFOs were either Russian spy prototypes, weather balloons, or swamp gas.

Times, and UFOs, have changed.

The Early Days

Unidentified flying objects have been reported throughout history, but we will focus first on the time period from 1947 onward. That enigmatic year is often referred to by ufologists as the beginning of the modern history of UFOs, because this was when the UFO became household headline news, and would henceforth be forever ingrained in our minds. Two amazing events occurred that year, bringing the possibility of alien visitation into mainstream discussion. The first occurred on June 24, 1947, when a private pilot named Kenneth Arnold spotted several objects in the sky while he was flying his small plane near Mt. Rainer in Washington. He later described these mysterious objects to the press as "saucers skipping across water," and a savvy reporter then coined the term "flying saucers" as a result. The second event occurred in the early part of July, when something crashed in the remote New Mexico desert near the town of Roswell, setting off a firestorm of controversy that continues even to this day. Witnesses claimed it was an extraterrestrial craft that crashed to Earth, and that dead alien bodies had been recovered and subsequently transported by the government and hidden in some secret location. Regarding the Roswell incident, the U.S. government has maintained its position that it was simply a weather balloon that had crashed—nothing more, nothing less.

These two events served to cement and solidify the UFO enigma in the public imagination. During World War II, fighter pilots reported seeing strange luminous balls (dubbed *foo fighters*) zipping about the skies, yet because of the events of the time, many believed they were a secret spy technology courtesy of our enemy, the Germans. The earliest explanations for UFOs tended to be fairly simplistic: They were either man-made objects or naturally occurring ones, and were often easily explained with further study.

UFOs and IFOs

The immediate official government reaction to such sightings in the early days of the modern era of UFOs was always the same: witnesses were actually seeing any number of things, from stars to planets to prototypes to gliders. Most of the time officials were correct about this. In this sense, the most common type of UFO is really just an IFO, or Identifiable Flying Object. Again, the list of possible man-made candidates is long: satellites, space stations, and even the Space Shuttle have all been initially identified as UFOs. Many sightings of UFOs have eventually been attributed to natural phenomena, as well, including stars and planets (especially Venus), bizarre cloud shapes, comets, meteors, and, according to one Colin Price, head of the Geophysics and Planetary Sciences Department at Tel Aviv University, something he calls "sprites." In February of 2009, *ScienceDaily* reported on the work of Price, who proposed that the cause of many UFO sightings was nothing more than a natural phenomenon caused by thunderstorms. Price contended that these "sprites" were in fact flashes of electrical energy high up in the atmosphere, between 35 and 80 miles (56 and 128 kilometers) above the earth, produced by the excitation of the electric field from lightning. Sprites can be huge (one was reported as being 30 miles (48 kilometers) high and 30 miles (48 kilometers) wide), but from a distance they are unidentifiable to the less knowledgeable viewer. These bizarre flashes of light can even appear to purposefully "dance" in the sky, thus giving the impression that there is some sort of intelligence behind them.

As we learn more about what goes on up in the skies, we often find very simple explanations for what seemed unnatural previously. Among the most widely reported IFOs are:

- Planes and airships (blimps, gliders)
- Birds flying in formation
- Kites
- Searchlights

- ♂ Weather balloons
- ♂ Spacecraft (Shuttle, satellites, space station)
- ♂ Swamp gas (ball lightning)
- ♂ Military craft, missiles, and prototypes (spy planes, the Stealth bomber, drones)

And in his book *The NASA Conspiracies*, author Nick Redfern lists the many theories that have surfaced to explain the Roswell case alone, including:

- ♂ Weather balloon
- ♂ Top-secret "Mogul" balloon (meant for clandestine monitoring of Soviet A-bomb tests)
- ♂ Crash of a Nazi V-2 rocket with monkeys on board
- ♂ An atomic mishap
- ♂ An accident involving an early "Flying Wing" aircraft secretly built by German scientists, and whose blueprints were brought to the United States after WWII
- ♂ An actual extraterrestrial spacecraft

So many explanations, so little truth—especially from the military, once they hastily retracted a front-page statement about a UFO crash in the *Roswell Daily Record*!

In 2001, UFO investigators from MUFON, the Mutual UFO Network, told ABCNews.com in an article titled "Earthly Explanations for UFO Reports" that about 90 percent of the up to 400 monthly reports they investigate are easily explainable. Keep in mind that this was back in 2001, when we didn't have the knowledge and technology of today, such as cell phones with cameras, at our disposal. Yet even today, millions of people the world over continue to think they've seen something they cannot identify in the skies, and, with Facebook, Twitter, and YouTube, find an immediate global audience for their experiences.

During the early history of UFOs, paranoia regarding the outcome of the war fed into conspiracy theories of UFOs as spy planes, which continued to fuel the public's "us vs. them" mentality. Throughout the Korean and Vietnam wars, and the Cold War tension that carried us into the earliest part of 1991, people often ascribed the darkest of political origins to UFO reports. Did the Soviets, the Nazis, or the South Koreans (or whomever we feared at the moment) have bigger, faster, better technology than we did? And, were we being watched, possibly even by our own government and military bodies? Conspiracy theories took center stage for those who could not believe that everything in the sky was purely natural in origin. This paranoia continues even to this day, when our fears come more from other universes than from other countries, as we are now relatively secure in our technological superiority.

Few people have the scientific acumen needed to be able to readily identify an atmospheric anomaly such as a lenticular cloud (a stationary, lens-shaped cloud which often takes on the classic form of a UFO), and even fewer are savvy enough to be able to identify every cutting-edge military prototype currently being tested. This was seen firsthand during the initial tests of the Stealth bomber, which caused a wave of UFO reports in the U.K. and the United States during the late 1980s and '90s. Objects in the sky will continue to be misidentified, especially those that are seen from a distance. But what about those closer encounters that seem to defy natural explanation of any kind?

The Extraterrestrial Hypothesis

By far the most fun and common "otherworldly" explanation for UFOs has always been the extraterrestrial hypothesis, which states that some UFOs are actual spacecraft piloted by extraterrestrial entities from other planets. This hypothesis has its origins in the UFO history from the 1940s through the 1960s, and was first referred to by French ufologist Jacques Vallée in his 1966 book *Challenge to Science: The UFO Enigma*, and later, by the physicist Edward Condon in 1969. (Condon is also credited with first using the more popular shortened term, ETH.) The term took off in popularity amongst the serious UFO research crowd. In the past, most people believed that UFOs were from other planets, galaxies, and star systems. Sure, science fiction novels and movies, and even TV shows such as *Star Trek* or *Sliders*, spoke of alternate universes, but scientists were not yet ready to consider that as a viable theory. We earthbound humans were content to imagine that aliens were coming to us from Vega, the Pleiades, or the Andromeda Galaxy. Thanks to advances in technology such as the Hubble telescope, our view of the universe has substantially expanded, and we now know that it is much bigger and even more densely populated with stars, planets, and galaxies than we had ever thought previously. Thus, the list of possible candidates for alien "home bases" has grown exponentially. For all we know, aliens could be coming from places on the outer reaches of the universe that we have yet to identify.

According to some abductees (who claim to have been taken against their wills aboard UFOs and subjected to various tests), these home bases are well within our reach—it's just that the aliens figured out a way to get here first. The most notable of these claims came from the classic and well-documented Betty and Barney Hill abduction case, which occurred in September of 1961. In this fascinating case, the Hills claimed they were both abducted and taken aboard a craft, subjected to medical testing, and even shown a map that pointed toward the location of the aliens' home base (according to the map, somewhere near the Zeta Reticuli double star system).

Today, we have cutting-edge theories on how intelligent life could make the long and arduous trip here, from the use of infinite and self-regenerating zero point energy to anti-gravity and propulsion systems that were once tested in top-secret laboratories here and abroad. The possibility that we've been reverse-engineering UFO craft is one of the many conspiracy theories surrounding the mysterious military facility known as Area 51 in the Nevada desert. Some researchers claim that one of the craft currently being examined is none other than the one that crashed in Roswell. Those who have heard of Operation Paperclip, the program that brought Nazi scientists to America after World War II, will be familiar with the flying saucer prototypes of Viktor Schauberger, an Austrian inventor who met with Hitler in 1934, and who has since been linked to a number of conspiracy theories, some stating that he developed everything from an impulsion-based hovering craft to a turbine-based UFO.

In any event, UFOs are generally thought to be genuine alien craft, able to travel vast distances in the blink of an eye via some yet-to-be-discovered mechanism. They may very well be coming from the darkest reaches of our expanding universe, for it seems that every month we are made privy to new and exciting discoveries of planets, suns, and star systems in the so-called *Goldilocks zone*. A term made famous by physicist Paul Davies, the Goldilocks zone is that "just right" location in the cosmos that allows life to exist. What kind of life we're talking about remains to be seen, of course, but will no doubt be as vastly diverse as life is here on our little, not-so-lonely-anymore planet.

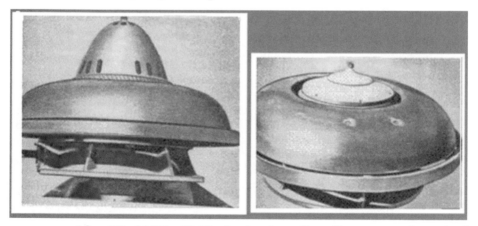

After World War II, Nazi scientists allegedly came to the United States to share their technological acumen with American scientists. This is a prototype of one of Viktor Schauberger's "UFO" craft.

The Alternate Universe Theory

Blame it on Max Tegmark, Michio Kaku, or Brian Greene, or just blame quantum and theoretical physics, but the concept of parallel universes is no longer the domain of science fiction. It may soon become scientific fact. A *parallel universe* is a hypothetical self-contained, separate universe with laws of nature all its own, and which exists right alongside our universe. According to quantum mechanics, parallel universes are separated from each other by a single event that occurs on a quantum level. A specific group of parallel universes is called a *multiverse*, a theory made famous by physicist Hugh Everett in his "many worlds" interpretation of quantum mechanics. Another theory is that of *bubble universes*, which suggests that universes with physical constants different from our own might be "stacked" above and below ours—imagine bubbles on top of other bubbles, each connected to the other via *wormholes* (shortcuts through time and space).

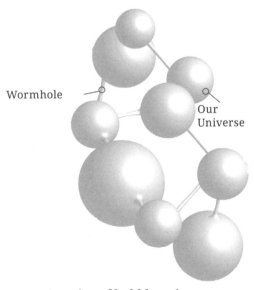

Wormhole

Our
Universe

A series of bubble universes connected via wormholes.

Thanks to science fiction/fantasy books, movies, and TV shows, most of us are familiar with the concept of wormholes. This is not necessarily just science fiction, however: many physicists believe that they are either temporal (connecting two points in time) or spatial (connecting two points in space), thus allowing for something or someone traversing through the universe to make a much shorter trip than might otherwise be required (or possible). Bending or warping the time-space continuum to allow for both inter-universal and intra-universal travel may be right around the corner, should we master the physics on either end.

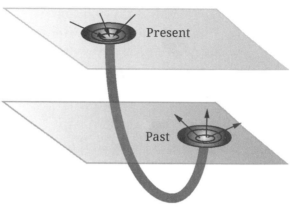

If there are indeed other universes out there, might we assume they contain some kind

One type of wormhole connects two different points along the landscape of time.

of life, and that some of that life would be intelligent enough to figure out how to get here from there? Again, "they" may have already figured out how to use wormholes or the infinite zero-point energy that many physicists suggest fills empty space, allowing for quick and easy travel from all points universal and beyond. Or, if "their" laws of physics permit on their end, they may have already found ways to bend space and time and access any number of other universes that we cannot even conceive of yet. Perhaps they have mastered time travel, as well, depending on their level of knowledge, skill, and technological advancement. In fact, one of the most brilliant minds of today, the Japanese-American theoretical physicist Dr. Michio Kaku, wrote about this in his book, *Parallel Worlds: A Journey Through Creation, Higher Dimensions and the Future of the Cosmos*. In it, he posited that alien civilizations trillions of years ahead of us may find, or may have already found, ways to travel to our much younger universe. He even suggests an actual framework for the existence of alien civilizations as being of three types. A Type 1 civilization is truly a planetary society that has mastered all forms of terrestrial energy. The energy output of a civilization such as this is perforce much greater than our own. It would take at least 3,200 years for us humans to reach Type 2. A Type 2 civilization has an energy output of a small star, and is advanced enough to build a sphere around their planet to maximize their energy output.

And finally, a Type 3 civilization is so advanced that they have begun colonizing other star systems. Their energy output is massive compared to ours, and they have mastered the science of bending time and space. A Type 3 is capable of interdimensional travel and possibly even time travel.

Kaku and others dedicated to hard science may not necessarily believe in UFOs and alien visitation, but can at least point to the *possibility* for future contact based upon our known laws of nature and physics. But remember, we still don't know what their laws of nature and physics are. Again, we are still talking about craft that have mass, shape, and form, and travel from one location to another; that leave marks or other physical evidence on the ground; that can be touched and photographed; and that can appear to many witnesses at one time. In other words, *quantifiable things*. However, many UFO reports describe something not quite physical at all.

The Interdimensional Hypothesis

Why do so many UFO reports speak of objects that flicker in and out of view, or appear and then disappear in a blink of an eye, as if they were materializing and dematerializing out of thin air? In order to answer this question, noted ufologist Jacques Vallée advanced the IDH, or interdimensional hypothesis. He posited that aliens were coming from other realities or dimensions that are co-existing alongside our own, and that this type of sighting might explain more of the supernatural, spiritual, and even mythological connotations often ascribed to UFOs in the past. Vallée wrote extensively about the interdimensionality of UFOs, and, along with Dr. J. Allen Hynek, the noted astronomer and ufologist who consulted on the famous Project Blue Book, laid out the hypothesis in detail in the 1975 book *The Edge of Reality: A Progress Report on Unidentified Flying Objects*. He expanded on this idea in his 1979 book *Messengers of Deception: UFO Contacts and Cults*, which presented mounting evidence pointing away from the more traditional ETH (extraterrestrial hypothesis).

The idea that UFOs could be coming from other dimensions paved the way for researchers to link them to supernatural phenomena such as angels, ghosts, demons, cryptids, and even psychic abilities. To Vallée, religious and spiritual beliefs had more in common with the interdimensional theory than with the idea that aliens were popping over to Earth from Vega or Venus. Many eyewitnesses report the seeming shape-shifting ability of craft and creatures, as well as their holographic appearance. These details seem to fly in the face of the extraterrestrial hypothesis. Although Vallée was initially a proponent of the ETH, he later felt that it was too narrow in that it could not account for the many reports that ventured outside of the extraterrestrial box, so to speak. So he cited the following arguments to defend a multidimensional visitation hypothesis:

1. Unexplained close encounters are far more numerous than a mere physical survey of the earth by aliens would necessitate.
2. The humanoid body structure of alien entities doesn't appear to have originated on any other planet and is not adapted for space travel.
3. The reported behavior of alien entities in thousands of abduction cases is inconsistent with or contradictory to the hypothesis of genetic/scientific experimentation on humans by advanced aliens.
4. UFOs are not a contemporary phenomenon.
5. UFOs seem to be able to manipulate space and time, which itself suggests a radically different alternative explanation.

Vallée, who served as the model for the Claude Lacombe character (played by François Truffaut) in the movie *Close Encounters of the Third Kind*, also suggested that the UFO phenomenon involves a non-human consciousness or intelligence that seems to masquerade or shape-shift according to the culture it comes into contact with.

In other words, whoever or whatever is behind the UFO enigma socially manipulates contactees according to their individual beliefs and the greater cultural context.

Another reason that the interdimensional hypothesis may make sense is that many witnesses attest to the distinct "holographic" nature of UFOs and alien entities, as if they were images being projected onto our three-dimensional world from a different (read: higher) source. Witnesses often state that the craft or entities resembled projections, as though they were movies on a screen (the "screen" in this case often being the night sky itself). In the 1990s, physicists Leonard Susskind and Gerard Hooft suggested that we might even be living in a "holographic universe," in which our everyday experiences of reality are holographic projections of physical processes originating on a distant, multidimensional surface. The human brain would be the mechanism that turns this holographic input into a three-dimensional representation of reality.

Other researchers in the fields of ufology and the paranormal have taken up the interdimensional cause, also suggesting that the IDH might also apply to demonic entities, angels, and cryptozoological creatures (cryptids), as many of them also resemble projections or holographs. Noted author and researcher Brad Steiger wrote in the 1977 *Blue Book Files Released in Canadian UFO Report* that "we are dealing with a multidimensional paraphysical phenomenon that is largely indigenous to the planet Earth," a belief that is mirrored by many in the field of paranormal studies to this day. Ufologist and journalist John Keel was another who abandoned the ETH in favor of something more bizarre. In Keel's case, his studies of UFOs and other Fortean mysteries led him to link UFOs to ghosts, demons, and even monsters, which he documented in his book *UFOs: Operation Trojan Horse*. In 1971, he coined the term *ultraterrestrials* to describe aliens as shape-changing, non-human entities clearly not of this earth.

Modern ufologists and paranormal researchers write about the interdimensional aspects of sightings and reports, too, including Nick Redfern in his book *Three Men Seeking Monsters*, which documents his travels seeking every manner of cryptid, from ghostly devil dogs to giant black cats to ape-men and lake monsters. Many eyewitness reports describe entities that resemble holographic images or projections, or appear and disappear out of and into thin air—again, an important detail that seems to contradict a more, well, terrestrial explanation. In their stunning book *The Vengeful Djinn: Unveiling the Hidden Agendas of Genies*, paranormal researchers Rosemary Ellen Guiley and Philip J. Imbrogno examine the links between interdimensional beings called *djinn*, or genies, and the reports of UFO entities, ghosts, demons, angels, and cryptids, finding even more commonalities amongst the behaviors and manifestations of these various entities. In fact, the authors suggest that many people who thought they were encountering aliens from another planet may have instead been interacting with these ancient djinn.

An even stranger aspect of the interdimensional hypothesis comes from those who believe that these alien craft and their occupants are time travelers. An acclaimed naval scientist named George W. Hoover, Sr., who had been made privy to the Roswell wreckage in the 1950s, stated that he believed we were dealing with something far stranger than anyone could imagine. Hoover Sr. allegedly told his son, George W. Hoover, Jr., and later a researcher named William J. Birnes, that the visitors were clearly from the future, and that they may have even been "us" from a future Earth! As a naval intelligence officer with top-secret clearance, Hoover admitted he was himself involved in secret attempts at reverse-engineering the crash materials, and that the visitors used the power of consciousness to manipulate reality. He described these amazing time-traveling entities as *extratemporal*. Hoover died in 1998, and the Roswell controversy continues to rage on.

Perhaps the most disquieting aspect of this interdimensional hypothesis involves claims that alien entities have communicated some kind of sinister ulterior motive to the witnesses, sometimes through ESP. So not only do we have to concern ourselves with aliens watching us, but also with interdimensional beings with an agenda that might involve some kind of major cross-dimensional conspiracy or plot to take over our world—or our souls! Clearly, it's much better to believe that a UFO is simply a craft from a distant star system with two drivers in search of a decent interstellar stop-over.

Collective Visions and Altered States

Perhaps UFOs don't come from outer space at all; perhaps they come from within, as constructs of the human mind. Perhaps the entire UFO enigma is more about a collective archetype than actual craft from other planets. Truly this would make such sightings and reports a sociological phenomenon common to all human beings—which, of course, it is. As the Claude Lacombe character in *Close Encounters of the Third Kind* said, "It is an event sociological." It makes sense that we've always looked outside of ourselves for answers to what UFOs are, but interesting research into the human brain and certain hallucinogenic plants and drugs suggests that there may be something that resides within the collective unconscious that shapes not only what we see, but how we interpret what we see. Skeptical scientists and psychologists have long shouted that UFO sightings are nothing more than figments of the imagination or even mass hallucinations. Although this explanation doesn't take into account actual physical evidence such as videos and photographs, it might not be entirely off-base. The human mind is indeed capable of some pretty strange things: just think of cults, mass hysteria, religious fervor, the mob mentality, and even shared visions, especially those of a religious or spiritual nature. Add to the already impressionable human brain a plant-based hallucinogen such as salvia or ayahuasca, and often the reported images and impressions are remarkably similar from culture to culture. In his book *Ayahuasca Visions: The Religious Iconography of a Peruvian Shaman,*

Pablo Amaringo states that images drawn during vision quests often include iconography that closely resembles the classic spaceships and alien entities described by UFO witnesses. French anthropologist Francoise Barbira-Freedman extensively researched the Lamista of San Martin, shamans who used the ayahuasca brew and reported similar visions; some even reported that they interacted with beings that came out of spacecraft. Some might argue that the iconography of UFOs and aliens is so widespread and common that anyone could see this sort of thing while they are in an altered state. However, many indigenous peoples do not have the same kind of access to the media, Internet, books, and so on, and thus would not have been exposed to this kind of imagery. Of course, not everyone who sees UFO is on hallucinogens, which points to the intriguing theory that these drugs are actually triggering a chemical that already exists in the brain. The chemical lies dormant until an environmental or physiological trigger (a hallucinogen, for example) is pulled, so to speak. And yes, the human brain contains just such a chemical.

N-Dimethyltryptamine (DMT) is a naturally occurring psychedelic compound of the tryptamine family. DMT is found in several plants and in trace amounts in humans and other mammals, and is often ingested as a psychedelic drug, in either extracted or synthesized forms. Depending on the dose, effects can range from short-lived milder psychedelic states to powerful immersive experiences and a loss of connection to reality. As it pertains to the ayahuasca experience, DMT has been dubbed the "spirit molecule" due to the often mystical and spiritual nature of the experiences and visions. One of the noted pioneers of DMT research is Dr. Rick Strassman, who began his groundbreaking research into this curious substance in the 1990s using human volunteers at the University of New Mexico's school of medicine. His findings showed distinct links between DMT and everything from déjà vu and mystical experiences to alien abduction scenarios—all occurring *within the brain* under the influence of this powerful psychedelic. Under Strassman's controlled studies, he found that the DMT was possibly the link or mechanism that allowed the spiritual nature to manifest. It was, he stated, "the brain's own psychedelic." If we were able to find a mechanism by which the naturally occurring DMT in our brains was individually or collectively triggered, could this substance also account for UFO and alien entity sightings?

Due to the discovery of primitive cave drawings, it's probably safe to assume that UFO imagery has been around since the beginnings of human existence on earth. Our religious texts and myths speak of fiery craft in the heavens and entities from above. Popular folklore and fiction are filled with such images and visions, as well. It would seem that we simply refuse to believe we are alone, even as the rational, intellectual, scientific side of us demands empirical proof—preferably a craft landing on the White House lawn with a family of entities disembarking and high-fiving the President.

In early March of 2011, Dr. Richard B. Hoover, an astrobiologist at NASA'S Marshall Space Flight Center, shocked the world by claiming that he had found conclusive evidence of alien life, in the form of fossils of bacteria found in a rare class of meteorite called CI1 carbonaceous chondrites. Hoover's findings were published in the peer reviewed *Journal of Cosmology*, and additionally claimed that these microorganisms were similar to many found right here on Earth. A few days later, NASA came out with a statement indicating the findings were not valid and that there was no scientific evidence of such a discovery. Somewhat ironically, NASA was allegedly embroiled in many of it's own UFO cover-ups and conspiracies, and later formally distanced itself from Hoover's work. Those on both sides of the UFO fence—believer and skeptic—claimed that Hoover's work and findings were sketchy and possibly even invalid, but this was less important than the public's reaction. True or not, many people reacted as if they had just seen an actual alien disembarking from a craft. Yet for those who claim to have seen something they truly cannot explain, this finding was trivial at most.

The only way we will ever fully understand just what UFOs are in all their various permutations, where they come from, and why they are here, is if we have full disclosure of all global government documents along with full disclosure *from the aliens themselves*. We all know that governments lie (to protect national security, of course!), but the fact is that they may not know as much as we think they do. Perhaps our government knows something, but not the entire big picture. In the end, just having our government and others around the world admit to what they know is rather meaningless until we find out the truth from the horse's mouth. Unfortunately, chances are slim to none that will happen anytime soon.

And so, the conspiracies, misidentifications, and questions without answers rage on, even as we continue to watch the skies for more clues to the UFO enigma. Those who seek evidence for one theory will find it, just as those who buy into another theory will find data to back up that particular pet hypothesis. Like a multiple-choice question, we have several potential answers about the origin and nature of UFOs. As UFO sightings continue to be reported to and in the media, logged into UFO databases, and pored over by field research organizations all over the world, perhaps the best answer to the question is simply to choose the box that reads "all of the above."

Hybrids: Memories of the Future

By Erich von Däniken

In 2008, the British House of Commons decided that scientists in the United Kingdom would be allowed to cultivate hybrids or chimeras from embryos containing both human and animal genetic material. Politicians complained that the British were "increasingly going down the wrong track" in bioethics,[1] while, in the view of scientists such as John Burn, professor at Newcastle University, there was nothing wrong with the new embryology act: "A cell cannot have a soul."

What are these geneticists trying to do? Are they playing God in their dodgy laboratories?

The breeding of plant cultivars is nothing new. Take, for example, the breeding of fruit trees: certain characteristics of one tree are transferred to another through a process called *grafting*. In this process, the genetic characteristics of one tree "migrate" to another with minimal human interference. Such breeding of trees, flowers, and cereal grains is an everyday occurrence, and no one gets excited about it. In cloning, however, a cell is artificially stripped of its nucleus, which is then implanted into the enucleated cell from another living thing. This is precisely how Dolly the sheep was created in 1997; she was an exact copy of the donor animal. In this case cells from the same animal species were used. (Dolly has meanwhile had healthy young of her own.) With hybrids, however, *different* species are involved—for example, human and bovine. A cell from both the human and the cow is enucleated; then the human cell nucleus is injected into the empty cell of the cow. A brief electrical shock stimulates the cell to start dividing, and the bovine cell multiplies with the human genetic information. You may think this is madness, but Nature has actually been doing the same thing for millennia—again, without human intervention. A retrovirus such as the AIDS virus, for example, tunnels into a cell and copies its own genetic information into the genetic material of the host cell. The latter then multiplies and propagates the virus. Again, no geneticist is involved.

But why do researchers now want to combine humans and animals? Have they gone insane? All basic research pursues long-term goals; in genetics, the hope is that sometime in the near future, genetic information will be able to be replaced in such a way that diseases such as Alzheimer's or MS will be eradicated. This is called *therapeutic cloning* and it is still in its infancy. But here's the rub: because geneticists require cells for their research, they used human egg cells. This inevitably set off a firestorm of political and religious controversy because the "practice material" was, after all, human. The egg cells of cattle, in contrast, are available in their billions from slaughter houses. Despite public fears, however, scientists are not looking to emulate Frankenstein and create a mooing biped. This is because cells multiply into ever larger cell clusters. Once they turn into a living thing, the cluster must be implanted into a womb, but this is strictly prohibited by law. And even if it were to happen in secret, British law demands that human/bovine hybrid embryos be destroyed within 14 days. Furthermore, the probability that such cell clusters would survive is extremely slight. But not impossible. That depends on the biotechnological facilities of the laboratory concerned.

Much worse things have long been happening outside of Britain. Australian geneticists working with the biologist Andrew Pask (Melbourne University) transplanted the genetic material from a Tasmanian tiger into a mouse embryo and succeeded in making the cells multiply. The most chilling thing about this is that the Tasmanian tiger had long been extinct—the cell material used had been preserved for a good 100 years in an alcohol solution. Professor Andrew Pask promptly announced that the same technique could be used to bring animals such as dinosaurs "back to life" if enough of their DNA (deoxyribonucleic acid) could be found. Even the "resurrection" of a Neanderthal was not ruled out.[2] Similar experiments are being conducted around the world in several laboratories; an "animal bank" containing embryos and the basic genetic material from animals of all kinds has existed for years in London. Clearly, genetics is catching up with *Jurassic Park*.

Strangely enough, I reported about these seemingly new events more than 40 years ago in my book *Memories of the Future*. And I quote:

W here does that first, audacious thought come from, that the cells of the body should be preserved so that the corpse, held in a location with hundredfold security, can be reawakened to new life millennia later? [...] Did an alien intelligence already know the methods for treating bodies so that they could be brought to life again x-thousand years later?[3]

What is being attempted today—and will one day succeed— already existed millennia ago. Witnesses from antiquity testify to this historical fact. Manetho is the name of one such person. He was a scribe in the holy temples of Egypt. The Greek historian Plutarch mentions Manetho as a contemporary of the first Ptolemaic king (304–282 BC).[4] Manetho wrote his seminal three-volume work in Sebennytos, a town in the Nile delta. The second witness, Eusebius (d. 339 AD), was also a historian. He entered church history as the bishop of Caesarea and quotes from many ancient sources, as he expressly notes in his *Chronography*. Manetho and Eusebius supplement one another in their descriptions of ancient records. Manetho starts his history by listing the gods and demigods, whereby he specifies periods of rule that would make modern archeologists shudder. According to Manetho, the gods ruled over Egypt for 13,900 years, and the following demigods for another 11,000 years.[5] The gods created various beings, Manetho says—monsters and hybrid creatures of all kinds. This is confirmed by the Church father Eusebius. The following quotation, which was in turn informed by other, even more ancient sources, is reminiscent of the current debate about these hybrid beings:

Τhe Gods also begat human beings, with two wings, and then others with four wings and two faces and one body and two heads, women and men, and two natures, namely female and male; furthermore, human beings with goat's legs and horns on their heads; and still others with horses' hooves, and others in the shape of a horse at the rear and a human shape at the front...they also made bulls with human heads and dogs with four bodies whose tails came out of their rear ends like fish tails; also horses with dogs' heads... as well as other monsters still, with horses heads and human bodies and with the tails of fish; furthermore, all kinds of dragon-like monstrous beings...and a lot of wondrous beings of many kinds and shapes different from one another, whose images they kept in the Temple of Belus depicted one next to the other.[6]

Strong stuff, this, what Eusebius digs up from his ancient sources. "Human beings with two wings"? Nonsense, you may assert. But why, then, do their images stare out at us from steles and reliefs and sculptures in all the major museums? In archeology these enigmatic creatures are called *winged genii*. Human beings "with goats' legs and horns on their heads"—more high-octane rubbish? How about taking a look at Sumerian and Babylonian cylinder seals? There are hundreds of depictions of such chimeras. Beings with "in the shape of a horse at the rear and a human shape at the front"? Enter the Centaur! The gods produced "bulls with human heads"? The Cretan Minotaur!

The past is overrunning the future. Hitherto we have explained these chimeras from antiquity in psychological terms: all of them are wishful thinking, fantasy, or mythology. What is a sphinx? A hybrid.

Everyone thinks of the giant lion shape with a human head at the foot of the great pyramid of Giza. But sphinges (the plural of sphinx) can be found in every variation: a lion's body with a ram's head; a dog's or goat's body with a human head; a ram's body with a bird's head; a human's body with a bird's head; and so on. Whole avenues of the greatest variety of sphinges have been wrested from the desert sands. Anyone who has ever wandered through a large museum or leafed through an illustrated book about Sumer, Assur, and Egypt, even just once, can intone the song of songs of these "wondrous beings" (Eusebius).

On the black obelisks of Salmanasar II, which reside today in the British Museum, stocky men can be seen leading two strange creatures with human heads and animal bodies on a short leash. They are definitively not apes, as some have tried to suggest. Two other hybrids are held on a loose chain. One of the chimeras is sucking its thumb, while the other is thumbing its nose. The pictures speak for themselves: these monsters were clearly alive—why else would the men have needed the short leash and chain? The accompanying cuneiform writing refers to "captured human animals" which are being led away as tribute.

Likewise, the underground caverns in Ecuador contain not just a metallic library,[7] but also hybrids, as the eyewitness Petronio Jaramillo Abarca reported:

> Imagine my surprise when I came across figures in a third cave chamber which were half human and half animal, as if all the myths had combined in a show of gold and gems.... There were bodies with the heads of hawks, with horses' hooves, wings; birds with human arms and legs; [and] donkeys with the faces of men. Many different combinations of human beings and animals....[8]

If these monsters were real living things produced by the gods, it begs the question: what on earth were they for? What would be the advantage for these dubious gods? This is not the place to explain that the gods of mythology, the involuntary founders of the great religions, were, in reality, extraterrestrial visitors from distant solar systems. My 30 books do just that. But I will say this: A space travelling species would likely be familiar with many planets besides Earth—other worlds that are hotter or colder, or which have different gravity, depending on their size. Let's suppose for a moment that these alien ETs traveled to Earth and observed a scaly monster dozing by the Nile that appeared oblivious to the heat—a crocodile. Or, perhaps they observed a lion bringing down a gazelle. *What would happen*, the aliens asked themselves, *if we combined the scaly armor of the crocodile with the skeleton and musculature of the lion and created a new life form? One that could be used on a planet with far different conditions than those on Earth?* This is precisely how the creation of the chimeras began. The gods proudly observed their experiments. Then the time came for their return to the mother spacecraft. They did not need to transport any of the chimeras; the intact genetic material of the hybrids—the genetic information—was sufficient. The new species of animals then adapted to their respective environments on various planets.

How, you may ask, can such a hypothesis be substantiated?

To begin with, we need to find indicators, and there are plenty of those. Historians of antiquity such as Manetho, Plutarch, Strabo, Plato, Tacitus, Diodorus, Herodotus, and later, the Church father Eusebius, wrote about it. Manetho reports that the artists and stone masons had painted these creatures and sculpted them in stone. This is true—there are still many of these works extant today. We also know about the worship habits of ancient peoples. Their gods descended to earth on "skiffs" and "winged sun disks" (Egypt); on "heavenly pearls" (Tibet); on "flying shells' (eastern Polynesia); on "vimanas" (India); or, in the Old Testament, on the throne chariot of the Lord. As I have documented many times over, these cannot have been natural phenomena, because the gods instructed humans and passed on information. Extraterrestrials, worshipped and feared by stone-age people as gods, mastered the high art of genetics and used it here on earth. Their motive? To create beings for use on other planets.

A long time ago, a holy monster lived in Egypt called the Apis. The Egyptians considered the Apis to be a descendant of the cosmos, a work of the god Ptah. This earliest veneration is documented by depictions of star-studded bulls' heads which were found at Abydos. The Greek historian Plutarch (c. 50 AD) writes that the divine bull had not entered into life by natural means, but through a ray of light from the heavens.[9] Herodotus, too, records that the Apis was conceived by "a ray of light from the heavens."[10] And August Mariette found a small stele dedicated to the Apis in the so-called Serapeum under the Saqqara desert. Inscribed on it is the following: "You do not have a father; you have been created by the heavens."[11] Furthermore, the Apis bull possessed particular characteristics which were absent from other bulls. Again from Herodotus: "The so-called Apis has the following marks: it is black; on its forehead it has a square white mark, and on its back the image of an eagle; it has double the number of hairs in its tail, and below the tongue one can see the image of a beetle." Various other bulls existed alongside the Apis, but they were not seen as equal with the Apis. So where are the mummies of this sacred creature?

On September 5, 1852, the energetic Frenchman August Mariette—later to establish the Egyptian Museum—stood in a subterranean passage at Saqqara. In the dust covering the ground he noticed the footprints which priests had left behind millennia ago. In front of him stood two mighty sarcophagi. The 40-ton covers of the sarcophagi were lifted with difficulty using crowbars and a block and tackle. As Mariette commented:

In this way I could be certain that an Apis mummy was lying before me.... My greatest concern was for the head of the bull, but I did not find one. In the sarcophagus there was a bitumous mass of very smelly matter which crumbled at the slightest touch...in the midst of this disorder small bones and, as if by accident, fifteen small figurines....[12]

Mariette observed the same thing when he opened the second sarcophagus: "No bull's head, no larger bones, on the contrary, an even greater profusion of bone fragments."[13] Sir Robert Mond, who undertook excavations in the so-called Bucheum (a site in the rock below the temple ruins of Hermonthis), also made the same disappointing observation. The sarcophagi either contained nothing at all or stinking bitumen (asphalt) with bone fragments. Instead of the expected bull mummy, a sarcophagus with a mixture of jackal and dog bones was found.[14]

The Briton Sir Robert Mond, together with two Frenchmen, discovered more sarcophagi in the subterranean site at Abusir. They were certain that they would at last find the mummies of bulls because the mighty granite vats contained bulls' heads with horns. The French specialists Monsieur Lortet and Monsieur Gaillard carefully cut the thousands-of-years-old bindings and removed the linen layer by layer. They could not believe their eyes. Inside lay the bones of various animals in no particular order, some of which could not even be assigned to a specific species. The second sarcophagus, 2.7 yards (2.5 meters) long and 1.09 yards (1 meter) wide, contained a mixture of at least seven different animals. Here, too, there were two bones that could not be assigned to a particular species. The ancient Egyptians mummified all living things. Dogs, cats, crocodiles, birds, fish—everything. They did so (and this is not in dispute among Egyptologists) because they believed in reincarnation. It was essential for the body to be preserved if it was to be reborn. Anything else would have been sacrilege, blasphemy. As Sir Robert Mond wrote, "The burial of a mummy in any other form than the whole body was inconceivable in ancient Egypt."[15] So why the broken bones?

The colossal sarcophagi in the Serapeum under Saqqara are made of Aswan granite. Aswan lies 620 miles (1,000 kilometers) distant from Saqqara. Imagine the labor that went into transporting the materials, let alone hewing the passages and side niches out of the rock under Saqqara. Thousands of miles away in Aswan, specialists blasted away the hardest granite in Egypt right out of the rock. Then these enormous, heavy parcels were transported 620 miles (1,000 kilometers) down the Nile, with three rapids to overcome. (Today they have locks for shipping.) Once in Saqqara, the gigantic rocks were cut and polished in an incredible way. The pictures document it. Each sarcophagus weighs between 60 and 100 tons (54 and 91 metric tons)! Strong arms along with levers and rollers maneuvered the blocks, hewn from a single piece, into the tunnels and niches prepared for them. They cannot have been lowered from above with ropes because the ceiling is solid rock. And all this mighty effort for what? To throw chopped up bones into them, pour on greasy asphalt, and heave a 40-ton cover on top? There must have been a motive other than the belief in reincarnation, because if that had been the case, the body would *not* have been allowed to be destroyed.

Was it the frenzied activity of grave robbers? Did monks smash the contents of the sarcophagi into fragments of bone? The theory of grave robbers does not explain how bones from *different* animals were found in one sarcophagus. In that respect God-fearing monks might be capable of a lot more; they might have smashed the content with iron bars. But this explanation is not sufficient, either. There would have been visible traces of such religious destructive frenzy: torn bandages, statuettes of gods smashed or melted down. What was it that Auguste Mariette wrote after he had opened the sarcophagi? "In the stinking mass there lay a number of small bones, clearly *already fragmented in the period when they were buried*" [emphasis mine]. Why did the archeologist Sir Robert Mond discover bones in bull sarcophagi which he assumed were "those of a jackal or dog"? I would not blame any anthropologist for not investigating these bones further under such circumstances. Why, indeed, should such an absurd idea as "dogs with four bodies whose tails came out of their rear ends like fish tails" (Eusebius) even arise?

Dr. Ange-Pierre Leca is a physician and specialist in Egyptian mummies. In his book he writes about a sarcophagus with "wonderfully bandaged bulls" which were discovered in the chambers of Abusir: "[A]gain it appeared to be a single bull but the bones of seven animals were once more found...including those of a giant old bull. A third one must have had two heads."[16] *Two heads?* Look it up in good old Eusebius: "Wondrous beings, of many different kinds and different from one another...*and one body with two heads*" [emphasis mine]. What appears to be so absurd and nonsensical to the Egyptologists becomes comprehensible with the logic of today. The gods had left, but some of their chimeras were still alive. Would they spread fear and horror among people of the future if they were reincarnated? This serious thought weighed on the priests. Finally they found a solution to their dilemma. As long as the monsters were alive, they were pampered, worshipped, and deified. Once they died, however, the bones of these disturbing creatures were to be smashed and mixed with asphalt. Heavy sarcophagi were to be hewn out of the hardest granite, so massive and strong that no reincarnated monster could ever break out of its tomb. These mighty sarcophagi were not intended for reincarnation; on the contrary, they were meant as prisons for eternity.

How can this be proven?

Only a few bones with intact DNA are needed for our clever geneticists to be able to determine whether it is a result of natural evolution or artificial manipulation. Any interference with the genome, even thousands of years ago, can be confirmed today. Perhaps such an analysis has already been done, but has been prohibited from being published. This would be understandable, as people would hardly be able to cope with the shock regarding their "gods." Evidence of even a single chimera existing in ancient times would prove without a shadow of doubt the intervention of extraterrestrials. Why? *Because our ancestors millennia ago had not yet mastered genetics.* Because the histories and depictions of antiquity speak about it. And because the ETs had a compelling motive for it: the creation of life forms adapted to the conditions on other planets.

Memories of the future—that's what I call it.

Notes

1. Schweitzer, Sandra. "Dubiose Mischung." *Die Welt.* May 25, 2008.

2. Kulke, Ulli. "Auferstehung der Toten." *Die Welt.* May 23, 2008.

3. Von Däniken, Erich. *Erinnerungen an die Zukunft.* Düsseldorf: Econ-Verlag, 1968, pp. 140 ff.

4. Unger, Georg, F. *Chronologie des Manetho.* Berlin: Weidmannsche Buchhandlung, 1867.

5. Wadell, W.G. *Manetho.* Cambridge, n.d.

6. Karst, Josef. *Eusebius Werke, Volume 5, "Die Chronik."* Leipzig: 1911.

7. Von Däniken, Erich. *History Is Wrong.* Pompton Plains, NJ: 2009, Chapter 2.

8. Hall, Stan. *Tayos Gold.* Rottenburg: Kopp, 2008, p. 243.

9. Eberhard, Otto. *Beiträge zur Geschichte des Stierkultes in Ägypten.* Leipzig: Hinrichs, 1938.

10. Herodotus. *Historien.* Greek–German, Volume II. Trans. Josef Feix. Munich: E. Heimeran, 1963.

11. Mariette, Auguste. Le *Séraphéum de Memphis.* Paris: Gaston Maspero, 1882.

12. Ibid.

13. Ibid.

14. Mond, Robert, and Oilver H. Myers. *The Bucheum, Vol. I.* London: Egypt Exploration Society, 1934.

15. Ibid.

16. Leca, Ange-Pierre. *Die Mumien.* Düsseldorf: Econ-Verlag, 1982.

Glossary

abduction The taking of a person by force or trickery.

alien A life form from another planet.

anecdotal An unofficial account of something conveyed by story or conversation.

centaur A mythological creature with the body of a human and the head of a horse.

cloning The process of creating an exact replica of a living being.

cognoscenti A group of people considered to be well informed or educated on a particular topic.

crop circle Mysterious patterns created in crop fields that are often attributed to aliens.

decontamination chamber A sealed-off enclosure that is used to rid a person or thing of harmful or deadly material.

extraterrestrial A life form that is not from Earth.

hypnagogic Relating to the state that occurs immediately before sleep.

hypnopompic Relating to the state that occurs just before waking up.

interdimensional Occurring in between dimensions.

meteorology The study of weather and climate.

minotaur A mythological creature that is half man and half bull.

multiverse A state of being in which the universe is considered just one component.

obfuscate To make unclear or obscure.

parallel universe A universe theorized to exist in tandem with our own.

phenomenon An occurrence or event of significance.

polygraph A machine that measures biological markers that indicate that the person may be lying.

Roswell A southeastern New Mexico town where a secretive 1947 crash led to speculation of a UFO.

sarcophagus An elaborate stone coffin.

surreptitious Something kept secret.

terrestrial Of or relating to the ground or Earth.

ufology The study of UFOs and aliens.

For More Information

Center for the Study of Extraterrestrial Intelligence

PO Box 265

Crozet, VA, 22932-0265

E-mail: info@cseti.org

Web site: www.cseti.org

The Center for the Study of Extraterrestrial Intelligence (CSETI) is a nonprofit organization designed to enhance the understanding of extraterrestrial intelligence.

Center for UFO Studies

Box 31335

Chicago, IL 60631

(773) 271-3611

Web site: www.cufos.org

The Center for UFO Studies (CUFOS) is an international group of experts dedicated to the study of UFOs and extraterrestrials.

NASA

Public Communications Office

NASA Headquarters

Suite 5K39

Washington, DC 20546-000

(202) 358-0000

Web site: www.nasa.gov

NASA's vision is "to reach for new heights and reveal the unknown so that what we do and learn will benefit all humankind."

National UFO Reporting Center

P. O. Box 700

Davenport, WA 99122

webmaster@ufocenter.com

Web site: www.ufocenter.com

Founded in 1974 by Robert J. Gribble, the National UFO Reporting Center serves to document possible UFO-related events.

Web Sites

Due to the changing nature of Internet links, Rosen Publishing has developed an online list of Web sites related to the subject of this book. This site is updated regularly. Please use this link to access the list:

http://www.rosenlinks.com/MUSD/UFOs

For Further Reading

Alexander, John B. UFOs: *Myths, Conspiracies, and Realities.*
New York, NY: Thomas Dunne Books, 2012.

Carey, Thomas J., Donald R. Schmitt, Edgar D. Mitchell,
and George Noory. *Witness to Roswell: Unmasking the
Government's Biggest Cover-up.* Franklin Lakes, NJ: New
Page Books, 2009.

Coppens, Philip, and Daniken Erich. Von. *The Ancient Alien
Question: A New Inquiry into the Existence, Evidence, and
Influence of Ancient Visitors.* Pompton Plains, NJ: New Page
Books, 2011.

Davies, P. C. W. *The Eerie Silence: Renewing Our Search for
Alien Intelligence.* Boston, MA: Mariner Books, 2011.

Däniken, Erich Von. *Twilight of the Gods: The Mayan Calendar and
the Return of the Extraterrestrials.* Pompton Plains, NJ: New Page
Books, 2010.

Dolan, Richard M., and Bryce Zabel. *A.D., after Disclosure: When
the Government Finally Reveals the Truth about Alien Contact.*
Pompton Plains, NJ: New Page Books, 2012.

Greene, Brian. *The Hidden Reality: Parallel Universes and the
Deep Laws of the Cosmos.* New York, NY: Vintage, 2011.

Jayawardhana, Ray. *Strange New Worlds: The Search for Alien
Planets and Life beyond Our Solar System.* Princeton, NJ:
Princeton University Press, 2011.

Kaku, Michio. *Parallel Worlds: A Journey Through Creation, Higher Dimensions, and the Future of the Cosmos.* New York, NY: Anchor Books, 2006.

Kaufman, Marc. *First Contact: Scientific Breakthroughs in the Hunt for Life beyond Earth.* New York, NY: Simon & Schuster, 2011.

Kean, Leslie. *UFOs: Generals, Pilots, and Government Officials Go on the Record.* New York, NY: Three Rivers, 2010.

Kitei, Lynne D. *The Phoenix Lights: A Skeptic's Discovery That We Are Not Alone.* Charlottesville, VA: Hampton Roads Publishing, 2010.

Maloney, Mack. *UFOs in Wartime: What They Didn't Want You to Know.* New York, NY: Berkley, 2011.

Randle, Kevin D. *Crash: When UFOs Fall from the Sky: A History of Famous Incidents, Conspiracies, and Cover-ups.* Franklin Lakes, NJ: New Page Books, 2010.

Romanek, Stan, and J. Allan Danelek. *Messages: The World's Most Documented Extraterrestrial Contact Story.* Woodbury, MN: Llewellyn Publications, 2009.

Sasselov, Dimitar D. *The Life of Super-Earths: How the Hunt for Alien Worlds and Artificial Cells Will Revolutionize Life on Our Planet.* New York, NY: Basic Books, 2012.

Schulze-Makuch, Dirk, and David J. Darling. *We Are Not Alone: Why We Have Already Found Extraterrestrial Life.* Oxford, England: Oneworld, 2011.

Von, Ward Paul. *We've Never Been Alone a History of Extraterrestrial Intervention.* Charlottesville, VA: Hampton Roads Publishing, 2011.

Index

About the Contributors

Thomas J. Carey

A native Philadelphian, Tom holds degrees from Temple University and California State University–Sacramento, and attended the University of Toronto's PhD program in anthropology. An Air Force veteran who held a Top Secret/Crypto clearance, Tom was also a Mutual UFO Network (MUFON) State Section Director for Southeastern Pennsylvania from 1986 to 2002, a Special Investigator for the J. Allen Hynek Center for UFO Studies from 1991 to 2001, and a member of the CUFOS board of directors from 1997 to 2001. He began investigating aspects of the Roswell incident in 1991 for the Roswell investigative team of Kevin Randle and Don Schmitt, and since 1998, has teamed exclusively with Don Schmitt to continue a proactive investigation of the case. He has authored or coauthored more than 30 published articles about the incident, and has contributed to a number of other books on the subject, as well. He has appeared as a guest on numerous radio and TV shows throughout the country, including *Coast to Coast AM, Jeff Rense, Mancow, Fox and Friends, CN8 Friends Saturday*, and *Larry King Live!*, and has contributed to a number of Roswell-related documentaries, both on-screen and behind the scenes. Tom was a consultant and interviewee (with Don Schmitt) on the highly acclaimed and rated SciFi Channel documentary, *The Roswell Crash: Startling New Evidence*, the Learning

Channel's *Conspiracy Theory*, the Travel Channel's *Weird Travels*, the SciFi Channel's *SciFi Investigates*, and the History Channel's *The UFO Hunters*. His 2007 book (with Don Schmitt) *Witness to Roswell: Unmasking the 60-Year Cover-Up*, was the number-one best-selling UFO book in the world in both 2007 and 2008, and the revised, expanded, and updated sequel, published in 2009, continues to be a best-seller. Tom and his wife, Doreen, have two grown children and reside in Huntingdon Valley, Pennsylvania.

Gordon Chism

Gordon Chism was born and raised in Reno, Nevada. Throughout the years, he has earned his way as a shop owner, light manufacturer, building designer, tennis teacher, sculptor, and now, a writer. Gordon has written and self-published three books, most recently *As I Remember: A 1940s Childhood*. His second book, *The Thinking Person's UFO Book*, was awarded a 2009 IPPY Bronze medal in the science category and was a finalist in the 2009 Next Generation Indie Book Awards in the social change category. Gordon has three bright and beautiful daughters and three wonderful grandchildren. Edward O. Wilson and Woody Allen are his heroes.

Stanton T. Friedman

Nuclear physicist–author-lecturer Stanton T. Friedman first became interested in UFOs in 1958. Since 1968, he has lectured on the subject at more than 600 colleges and 100 professional groups in 50 U.S. states, nine Canadian provinces, and 18 other countries. He has published more than 90 UFO papers and has appeared on hundreds of radio and TV programs, including *Larry King Live!*, and in countless documentaries. He is the original civilian investigator of the Roswell incident, and the coauthor *Crash at Corona: The Definitive Study of the Roswell Incident*. His book *Flying Saucers and Science* (New Page Books) is currently in its fourth printing. He is also the coauthor of *Captured! The Betty and Barney Hill UFO Experience* with Kathleen Marden, Betty Hill's niece. On July 2, 2010, he was inducted into the

UFO Hall of Fame in Roswell for his long-term investigative efforts into that important case. He is a dual citizen of the United States and Canada, and currently resides in New Brunswick, Canada.

Micah Hanks

Micah Hanks is a full-time journalist, radio personality, author, and investigator of the unexplained. He has been featured as a guest on many television and radio programs, including the History Channel's *Guts and Bolts*, the Travel Channel's *Weird Travels*, CNN Radio, and the *Jeff Rense Program*. He is also a regular contributor to *UFO Magazine*, which features his column, "Mirror Images," in each issue.

Marie D. Jones and Larry Flaxman

Marie D. Jones is the best-selling author of *2013: End of Days or a New Beginning? Envisioning the World After the Events of 2012* and *11:11: The Time Prompt Phenomenon: The Meaning Behind Mysterious Signs, Sequences and Synchronicities* (with Larry Flaxman). She is also the co-author of *The Resonance Key: Exploring the Links Between Vibration, Consciousness and the Zero Point Grid*; *The Déjà vu Enigma: A Journey Through the Anomalies of Mind, Memory, and Time*; and *The Trinity Secret: The Power of Three and the Code of Creation*—also with Larry Flaxman, her partner in ParaExplorers.com, an organization devoted to exploring unknown mysteries.

Marie has been interviewed on more than 100 radio talk shows, including *Coast to Coast AM*, *NPR*, *KPBS Radio*, *Dreamland* (which she co-hosts), *X-Zone*, the *Kevin Smith Show, Paranormal Podcast, Cut to the Chase, Feet 2 the Fire, World of the Unexplained*, and the *Shirley MacLaine Show*, and has been featured in dozens of newspapers, magazines, and online publications all over the world. She is a staff writer for *Intrepid Magazine*, and her essays and articles have appeared in *TAPS ParaMagazine, New Dawn, Whole Life Times, Light Connection, Vision, Beyond Reality*, and several popular anthologies such as the *Chicken Soup* series. She has lectured at major paranormal, new science, and self-empowerment events, and is a popular public speaker. She worked as a field investigator for MUFON (Mutual UFO Network) in Los Angeles and San Diego in the 1980s and '90s, and co-founded MUFON North County. She currently serves as a consultant and director of special projects for ARPAST, the Arkansas Paranormal and Anomalous Studies Team. Marie is also a licensed New Thought/metaphysics minister.

Larry Flaxman has been actively involved in paranormal research and hands-on field investigation for more than 13 years. He melds his technical, scientific, and investigative backgrounds together in pursuit of no-nonsense, scientifically objective explanations for anomalous phenomena. He is the president and senior researcher of ARPAST, the Arkansas Paranormal and Anomalous Studies Team, which he founded in February of 2007. Under his leadership, ARPAST has become one of the nation's largest and most active paranormal research organizations, with more than 150 members worldwide. ARPAST is also a proud member of the TAPS family (The Atlantic Paranormal Society). Widely respected for his expertise on the proper use of equipment and techniques for conducting solid investigations, Larry also serves as technical advisor to several paranormal research groups throughout the country.

Larry has appeared on the Discovery Channel's *Ghost Lab*, and has been interviewed for *The Anomalist*, the *Times Herald News*, the *Jacksonville Patriot*, *ParaWeb*, the *Current Affairs Herald*, and *Unexplained* magazine. He has appeared on hundreds of radio programs, including *Coast to Coast AM*, *TAPS Family Radio*, *Encounters Radio*, *Higher Dimensions*, *X-Zone*, *Ghostly Talk*, *Eerie Radio*, *Crossroads Paranormal*, *World of the Unexplained*, and *Haunted Voices*. Larry is a staff writer for *Intrepid* magazine, and his work has appeared regularly in *TAPS ParaMagazine*, *New Dawn*, and *Phenomena*. He is also a screenwriter and popular public speaker, lecturing widely at paranormal and metaphysical conferences and events all over the country.

Kathleen Marden

Kathleen Marden earned her BA in social work at the University of New Hampshire in 1971. After graduate studies in education at the University of Cincinnati, and later, at the University of New Hampshire, she began her professional career as a social worker and eventually entered the field of education as a teacher. Later, she was promoted to a supervisory position, coordinating education programs and supervising education staff. She eventually left her job in 1990 to pursue a career as a UFO investigator, researcher, and writer. As the niece of Betty and Barney Hill, Kathy had the opportunity to observe and learn from many of the great abduction researchers.

Kathy has appeared on dozens of television and radio programs in the United States, Canada, and Europe, including the History and Discovery channels, NH Chronicle, FOX News, and *Coast to Coast AM*. Kathy is currently a full-time writer and lecturer, speaking at numerous major UFO conferences throughout the United States. She is also the author of two books with Stanton T. Friedman: *Captured! The Betty and Barney Hill UFO Experience;* and *Science Was Wrong,* both published by New Page Books. Kathy resides in Groveland, Florida.

Jim Moroney

Jim Moroney has a fresh and unique insight into the alien agenda. A stunning personal encounter experience in 1987 provided the basis for his understanding of the UFO phenomenon and instilled a sense of direction for his future research. Jim acquired a diploma from Lambton College and a degree from the University of Waterloo. He married, raised two children, and established a respectable career in health and safety while acquiring two professional designations (one in Canada and another in the United States). He went on to instruct courses at universities and colleges in Canada, and is currently the director of the Alberta Municipal Health and Safety Association. For many years, Jim kept his exper-iences from the public and chose to remain anonymous. In late 2009, however, things began to change, as Jim knew they would, and the public's desire for a greater understanding also grew. Frustrated with a lack of quality information on the subject, and filled with concern for the well-being of all those who have had or will have similar experiences, he wrote *The Extraterrestrial Answer Book*. Jim has become a powerful and recognized speaker at UFO Conferences and has appeared on local and national television shows and documentaries.

Nick Pope

Author, journalist, and TV personality Nick Pope used to run the British government's UFO project at the Ministry of Defense. Initially skeptical, his research and investigation into the UFO phenomenon and access to classified government files on the subject soon convinced him that the phenomenon raised important defense and national security issues, especially when the witnesses were military pilots, or when UFOs were tracked on radar. While working on the MoD's UFO project, Nick also looked into alien abductions, crop circles, animal mutilations, remote viewing, and ghosts. He is now recognized as a leading authority on UFOs, the unexplained, and conspiracy theories. He does extensive media work, lectures all around the world, and has acted as presenter, consultant, and contributor on numerous TV and radio shows.

Nick Redfern

Nick Redfern works full time as an author, lecturer, ghostwriter, and freelance journalist. He has written about a wide range of unsolved mysteries, including Bigfoot, UFOs, the Loch Ness monster, alien encounters, werewolves, psychic phenomena, chupacabras, ghosts, the Men in Black (MIB), and government conspiracies. He has written for Britain's *Daily Express* and *People* newspapers and *Penthouse* magazine, and writes regularly for the newsstand publications *UFO Magazine, Fate, TAPS ParaMagazine,* and *Fortean Times*. His many previous books include *The NASA Conspiracies,*

Contactees, Memoirs of a Monster Hunter, There's Something in the Woods, and *Strange Secrets.* Nick Redfern's latest book, *The Real Men in Black,* will be published by New Page Books in the summer of 2011. Nick has appeared on numerous television shows, including VH1's *Legend Hunters*; the BBC's *Out of This World*; the History Channel's *Monster Quest* and *UFO Hunters*; the National Geographic Channel's *Paranatural*; and the SyFy Channel's *Proof Positive.* Redfern is the co-host, with Raven Meindel, of the popular weekly radio show *Exploring All Realms.* Originally from England, Nick Redfern lives in Arlington, Texas, with his wife, Dana. He can be contacted at his Website, Nickredfern.com.

Donald R. Schmitt

Donald R. Schmitt is the former co-director of the J. Allen Hynek Center for UFO Studies (CUFOS) in Chicago, where he served as a special investigator. For 10 years he was also on the board of directors and held the position of director of special investigations. Previously, he was a state director for the Mutual UFO Network (MUFON) for Wisconsin and a field investigator for the Aerial Phenomena Research Organization (APRO). Schmitt is the coauthor of three best-selling books, including *UFO Crash at Roswell, The Truth About the UFO Crash at Roswell,* and *Witness to Roswell.* The Golden Globe–nominated movie *Roswell* was based on his first book. *Witness to Roswell,* written with coauthor Thomas J. Carey, was the number-one UFO book in the world for 2007–2008. A professional college lecturer, Schmitt has given presentations all over the world, and has been a guest on shows such as *Oprah,* CBS *48 Hours, Larry King Live!, Good Morning America, CNN Reports,* and hundreds of other programs. He has been interviewed by *Time, Forbes, Air and Space,* and *Popular Science* magazines. He has also consulted on more than 30 documentaries and has supervised three archaeological expeditions to the famous Roswell crash site. As of this writing, his last book has been optioned for motion picture production rights by

Stellar Productions. Schmitt is a *cum laude* graduate of Concordia College.

Erich von Däniken

Erich von Däniken was born on April 14, 1935, in Zofingen, Switzerland, and attended the St. Michel Jesuit school in Fribourg. He published his first book, *Chariots of the Gods,* in 1968. It was a world-wide best-seller that has been followed by 31 subsequent books. He is the most widely read and most copied nonfiction author in the world. His works have been translated into 28 different languages and have sold more than 63 million copies. Several of his books have also been turned into films, and Erich's ideas have been the inspiration for a whole range of different TV series. His most recent books include *History Is Wrong, Twilight of the Gods,* and *Odyssey of the Gods,* all published by New Page Books.

John White

John White is an author and educator in the fields of consciousness research and higher human development. He holds a BA degree from Dartmouth College (1961) and a MA in teaching from Yale University (1969). A Vietnam veteran, he attended college on a ROTC scholarship and then served four years as a naval officer, primarily in antisubmarine warfare and nuclear weapons. He has been director of education for the Institute of Noetic Sciences, a research organization founded by Apollo 14 astronaut Edgar Mitchell to study human potential for personal and planetary transformation, and president of Alpha Logics, a school for self-directed growth in body, mind, and spirit. He has personally investigated the UFO phenomenon and written about it in books and magazines for decades. As a lecturer and seminar leader, Mr. White has appeared at colleges, universities, and spiritual centers throughout the United States and Canada, and before public and professional organizations. He has also made radio and TV appearances throughout the United States and Canada.

Mr. White is author of *The Meeting of Science and Spirit* and *A Practical Guide to Death and Dying*; and of the forthcoming books *Enlightenment 101: A Guide to God-Realization and Higher Human Culture* and *The Pledge of Allegiance and The Star-Spangled Banner: A Patriot's Primer on the American Spirit*. He has also edited anthologies, including *The Highest State of Consciousness*; *Psychic Exploration*; *Kundalini*; *Evolution and Enlightenment*; and *What Is Enlightenment?* His writing has also appeared in *Reader's Digest*, the *New York Times, Esquire, Omni, Woman's Day,* and many other national publications, and his books have been translated into 10 languages.

He is now retired from the corporate world and spends his time communicating "information for transformation." He and his wife, Barbara, have four children and five grandchildren, and live in Cheshire, Connecticut.